DUBLIN

A New Illustrated History

A lock on the Grand Canal, 1961.
(Courtesy of Dublin City Library and Archive,
Fáilte Ireland Tourism Photographic Collection)

DUBLIN

A New Illustrated History

JOHN GIBNEY

The Collins Press

First published in 2017 by
The Collins Press
West Link Park
Doughcloyne
Wilton
Cork
T12 N5EF
Ireland

A CIP record for this book is available from the British Library.

Hardback ISBN: 978-1-84889-330-6

Design and typesetting by Anú Design
Typeset in Garamond
Printed in Poland by Białostockie Zakłady Graficzne SA

Supported by Dublin City Council

Comhairle Cathrach
Bhaile Átha Cliath
Dublin City Council

To my parents

Sauvegrain a barber, Jean chamard a wea...
joyner, Ettiene ferret a joyner, Jean Corneille Sarget waver, Raimond fabre
...pothicary, françois morgue Shoomaker, were forced to leave the
Kingdom of france, by reason of the severe persecution agrinst the
Protestants there, and are all very fitt objects to receive the benefit of th
above generous Act, of this honourable City, in favour of the said
french persecuted Protestants. Dublin aprill the 19 169...
Bartholomew Bal...

The Point Theatre Dublin
SUNDAY 21st JUNE 1992 Doors 7pm
DCG & MCD presents
NIRVANA
Teenage Fan Club
The Breeders

NO ALCOHOL. NO REFUNDS; NO RE-ADMISSION;
NO CAMERAS OR RECORDERS.
TICKET HOLDER ASSUMES ALL THE RISK OF
INJURY AND ALL RESPONSIBILITY FOR PROPERTY
LOSS, DESTRUCTION OR THEFT AND RELEASE
THE PROMOTERS FROM ALL LIABILITY.

£14.25
inc.
Booking fee

TICKET NO.
06383

GROUND FLOOR
STANDING
RIGHT OF ADMISSION RESERVED
(THIS PORTION TO BE RETAINED)

ORMOND
STREET
CHARLES STREET
ARRAN
MARKET
ESSEX BRIDGE
UPPER ORMOND QUAY

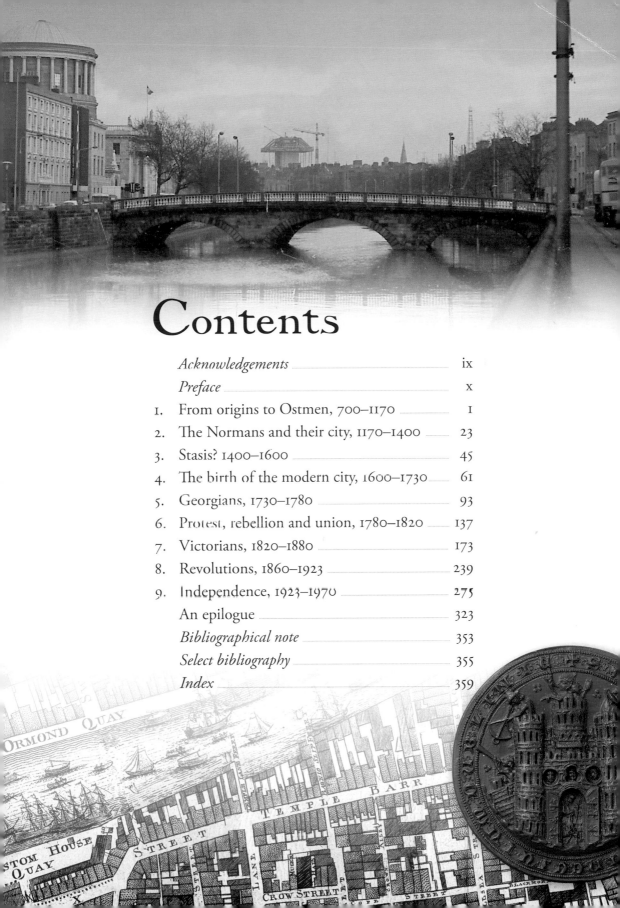

Contents

Winetavern St and Christ Church Cathedral, 1968. (Courtesy of Dublin City Library and Archive, Fáilte Ireland Tourism Photographic Collection)

Acknowledgements

This book has its origins in a wide range of history- and heritage-related activities – walking tours, teaching, research – that I have been involved in in Dublin over the past fifteen years. A number of people have helped play a role in its creation, even if they might be surprised to hear that they had anything to do with it. In no particular order, and with apologies in advance to anyone I may have forgotten, my thanks to Ruth Andrews, Julie Burke, Tony Canavan, Lorcan Collins, the late Brendan Costello (who hopefully would have enjoyed this book), David Dickson, Tara Doyle, Seán Duffy, Donal Fallon, Tony Finn, Tommy Graham, Brian Hanley, Edward Madigan, Conor McNamara, Brian Ó Conchubair, Maria O'Shea, Rhonda Wynne, and the students at both Trinity College Dublin and University College Dublin who sat through various courses on Dublin history. I would like to single out Grace O'Keeffe, Lisa-Marie Griffith and Ciaran Wallace for reading earlier drafts at short notice and helping me to avoid various pitfalls; all mistakes that remain are my own. In particular, I would like to thank Mary Clarke and Máire Kennedy of Dublin City Library and Archive for their extremely generous support and assistance. For permission to reproduce material in their possession, my thanks to Dublin City Library and Archive, Marsh's Library, Glasnevin Trust, and the Royal Irish Academy. My apologies to any individuals or institutions I have forgotten. Finally, I would like to thank friends and family for their support over the years, especially my parents, Joan and Charlie, and above all Liza Costello and Martha Costello Gibney.

Author's note: spelling in quotations has generally been modernised, except where the original spelling dictated a phonetic purpose; uncertain words and interpolations have been included in square brackets.

Preface

One obvious vantage point from which to get a sense of the size of Dublin in the twenty-first century would be a boat in Dublin Bay; or, failing that, Bull Island, or the North or South Bull Walls that jut into the bay and frame the mouth of the River Liffey. Much of the topography – the hill of Howth, the Dublin and Wicklow Mountains – is essentially the same as it was over a thousand years ago, and can perhaps give a sense of what an early traveller, or sailor, or raider, might have seen as they arrived in the bay and prepared to make landfall. What has changed dramatically is the impact of human settlement; the lights of the city at night, as seen from the bay,

Dublin Bay, looking south from Bull Island at low tide. The remains of a boat are visible in the foreground. (*Image by author*)

or Howth, or the Dublin Mountains, reveal the scale of that settlement in spectacular fashion. What this book is concerned with is to explain how the city of Dublin grew from its origins, with the aid of an array of images and a selection of observations and commentaries on the city made down through the centuries. Its focus is, for the most part, the traditional city located between the Grand and Royal Canals. It cannot detail every specific incident, individual, building or event in Dublin's history, but it is not intended to do that; rather, it offers the broad brushstrokes that will give an overview of the development of the Irish capital from its origins to the present day.

From origins
to Ostmen

❧

700-1170

I

Dublin was the first urban settlement on the island of Ireland, and for most of its history it was the largest. Yet who lived there first? It is very hard to know who the first Dubliners were. There have, it seems, been people living there for thousands of years. What we now call Dublin began life as a cluster of settlements near the mouth of the River Liffey and around a number of smaller rivers, most of which were driven underground over time. We know very little about the original inhabitants. There was probably only one large set of man-made structures along the river prior to the eighth century, namely the monastery of Cell Maignean, in the vicinity of modern Kilmainham (to which it lends an anglicised version of its name) near the River Camac. Nevertheless, the identity of these early inhabitants remains obscure. The

> 'Who were the original inhabitants of Dublin, is a matter both as uncertain and obscure as the time in which it was built: at best, we are under the disagreeable necessity of founding our reasonings on conjecture.' – John Warburton, James Whitelaw & Robert Walsh, *History of the City of Dublin: From the Earliest Accounts to the Present Time* (London, 1818) vol. i, p. 47.

limelight of Dublin's early origins tends to be hogged by the Scandinavians known as Vikings who settled in the region from the ninth century onwards, but there were Irish people living in the vicinity of what became Dublin long before the Vikings arrived, and they seem to have lived in two places. The names of the city are drawn from both of these other places, but if the arrival of the Vikings can be taken as a seminal moment in the origins of Dublin – and, in terms of its history as a significant urban settlement, it makes sense to do so – it is worth trying to imagine what Dublin looked like before the Vikings arrived.

Dublin is the oldest and largest urban area on the island of Ireland, a reality shaped by geography. It lies in a bay that sits on an extended break in the chains of low-lying mountains that surround the Irish coast and, crucially, faces eastwards, towards Britain and towards the continent, regions to and from which people might migrate, trade and travel. The topography of Dublin is quite straightforward: boulder clay resting on limestone (which was pressed into service as a ubiquitous building material in later centuries). Dublin Bay began east of modern Capel Street, and tidal flats akin to those of modern Sandymount lay east of Jervis Street and Parnell Square, and the same could have been said of the east of College Green and Nassau Street. The familiar term 'rath' used in the Greater Dublin area reflects the etymology of many abandoned ring forts and this area, as it was settled by the Vikings over time, would also become dotted with their burial mounds. A defining geographical feature was and is the principal river that drained into the bay: the Liffey, or An Ruirthech as it was originally called, which made Dublin an attractive proposition to seafaring peoples, though Dublin Bay itself was characterised by vast and often treacherous shallows. South of the Liffey was a ridge running east–west. Its contours have eroded over the centuries, but for the past millennium it has been crowned with a religious landmark: Christ Church Cathedral.

However, to invoke the cathedral at this stage is to put the cart before the horse. The original settlements that became Dublin emerged at the western end of the ridge, at the lowest crossing points of what was then a much wider and wilder river (in 770, for example, an army was apparently drowned while trying to cross it). But the Liffey served as a junction for a number of ancient routeways, so the Vikings who get the credit or the blame for establishing Dublin were by no means impinging on virgin territory when they got here.

Most cities and towns in the world are located beside rivers, and Dublin has lots of rivers. Today, most of them are underground within the city centre, apart from the Liffey itself. Downstream from Heuston Station, many small streams can be seen at low tide emerging from small openings on the quay walls. Moving away from the city centre along James Street, one eventually comes across the River Camac, which flows through Inchicore and Kilmainham. Moving back into the city centre, on the south quay wall between the modern Millennium Bridge and Grattan Bridge is a large culvert covered with a large metal grille. This is the outlet for the River Poddle, one of the two rivers that shaped Dublin, and which still flows under Dublin Castle, St Patrick's Cathedral and the Coombe, just as it has for centuries.

In the eighth century, the Poddle would have been tidal up to a point near the modern location of St Patrick's Cathedral; the River Liffey, on the other hand, would have been tidal as far as modern Chapelizod, and would have been much, much wider than it is today. It may well have been between 300 metres and two kilometres wide at high tide, depending on where one stood. There were a number of islands in the river (the name of Usher's Island beside the modern Guinness Brewery is a reminder of this), and a settlement called Áth Cliath (usually translated as 'hurdle ford') grew up around the lowest crossing point in the river, probably in the vicinity of the modern Four Courts at the bottom of Church Street. The crossing itself was probably a basket weave of wood or saplings woven together and laid over the exposed mudflats, crossing the end of an island and the river. Áth Cliath was to be found here, and there are indications of some kind of enclosed settlement measuring perhaps 335 metres north–south and 260 metres east–west. Traces survive in the modern streetscape, which in these older central areas of the city is usually underlaid with some kind of medieval pattern.

'The overthrow of the Uí Téig by the Ciannacht at Áth Cliath. There was a great slaughter of the Laigin. A number of the Ciannacht were drowned in the full tide as they returned.' – An Irish army falls foul of the Liffey in 770, from Seán Mac Airt and Gearóid Mac Niocaill (eds), *The Annals of Ulster (to A.D. 1131)* (Dublin, 1983), p. 225.

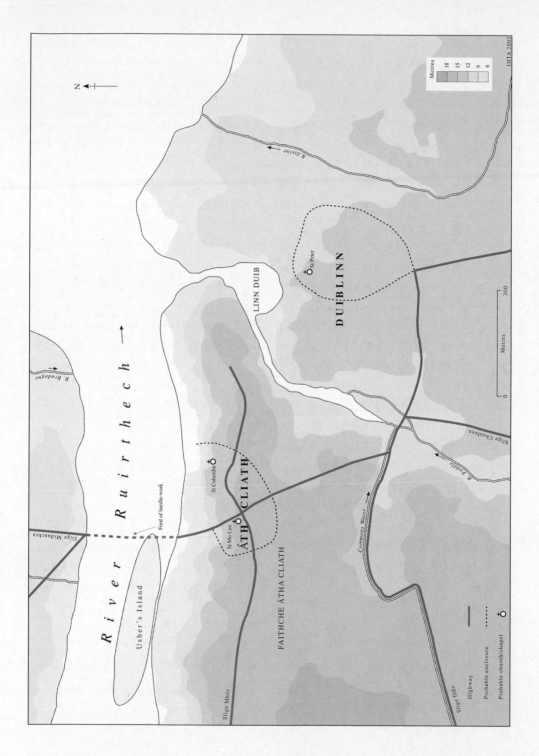

Dublin *circa* 840, indicating the major routeways and the two settlements of Áth Cliath and Duiblinn. The topography is very different from that of the modern era, with the Liffey (or Ruirthech) and its estuary being much wider than in subsequent centuries. (Royal Irish Academy, *Irish Historic Towns Atlas*)

Here was a natural intersection. At this time, pathways and roadways traversed the entire island of Ireland. These are known to have existed from at least AD 700 and the most important of them met in the vicinity of the ridge south of the Liffey. The four principal routeways and their modern corresponding streets were the Slige Dála, which ran roughly along Cork Street and Ardee Street; the Slige Chualann, which ran down along Francis Street; the Slige Midhluachra, along St Augustine Street and Bow Street; and, last but not least, the Slige Mhór, presumably the most significant or substantial one, which ran along what is now James's Street and Thomas Street. These all met in and around the area of Cornmarket and the medieval church of St Audoen's. It makes sense that Áth Cliath was in this area at the junction of these north–south and east–west routeways. The modern route of Stoneybatter and Manor Street may well be a fragment of one of them, as are many of the other streets that survive.

Yet the names of the city provide inadvertent links to a number of layers of Dublin's past. Technically, there are two names for Dublin (a fact noted as far back as the sixteenth century by the chronicler Richard Stanihurst). The Irish name, Baile Átha Cliath, refers to one ancient settlement. Dublin, however, refers to another, the monastic settlement known as Duiblinn, the perimeter of which is often assumed to survive in a circular street pattern near Whitefriar Street, south of Dublin Castle, in the south inner city. This may well be a trace of an ancient ecclesiastical settlement that existed around the same time as Áth Cliath, though again it remains obscure. Claims that a shadowy abbot called Bearaidh, who supposedly presided over a monastery in this area until his death in 650, have more to do with the errors and conjectures of later chroniclers than with facts that can be established. We can say, however, that Duiblinn took its name from another geographical feature, a murky tidal pool marking the junction where the River Poddle met the River Liffey, which was probably located in the vicinity of Dublin Castle. The name Dublin is an anglicised version arising from the Irish terms 'linn duib' or 'dubh linn', referring to a dark or black (presumably muddy) pool. It is assumed to correspond to the castle garden that exists today, though definitive proof remains elusive.

Certainly there was a body of water hemmed in around this area – traces survive in the curved angle of the streetscape, and a hint of it can be seen in the oldest surviving map of Dublin, that of John Speed, dating from 1610. This was almost certainly used by the Vikings upon their arrival as the pool would have been fed by the Poddle and the Liffey; it may well have been used before their permanent settlement was established in 841.

Having flagged the existence of the Vikings, it makes sense to explain precisely who they were.

Dublin's location on the east coast of Ireland, facing Britain and nestled in a wide bay, was naturally attractive to a seafaring people such the Vikings; the location of the bay was also within range of Scandinavia itself (most of the Vikings who would settle in Dublin came from Denmark and the Atlantic coast of Norway, or at the very least were descended from people from these regions). They had begun to attack the Irish coastline from the end of the eighth century and initially they were little more than hit-and-run raiders. They were striking at locations in the Dublin region from the 830s onwards, with monastic settlements being particular targets; these were the nearest things to urban settlements on the island at this time, and consequently were natural concentrations of wealth, supplies and people who might be taken captive. Being followers of a different set of religious beliefs, Vikings were hardly likely to respect the sanctity of Christian settlements. Monasteries were by no means immune from attacks by Irish lords, though the bond of Christianity may have stayed their hand somewhat; the Vikings showed no such restraint, a fact that was bound to outrage the monks who recorded details of their raiding activities. Yet, hyperbole aside, Viking brutality was no myth; theirs was a warrior culture, and the ferocity of their attacks was a weapon in itself, instilling fear and panic in those who might yet fall prey to them.

But there were physical limitations to their reach. They could strike inland to some degree, and could use the major rivers to navigate the Irish interior, but more sustained raiding would require more substantial and, indeed, permanent bases along the Irish coastland, where they could spend the winter and from which they could raid further inland. A Viking fleet of sixty ships was recorded near the Liffey in 837, and by the 840s they had established a base, or longphort, in Dublin. Over time, they adapted one of the settlement names of Dublin to Dyflinn. Their base was probably located in the vicinity of the pool created by the junction of the Liffey and the Poddle, which would have served as a natural harbour. The Danes emerged as the dominant grouping among the Vikings of Dublin, with the arrival of Olaf the White as king of Dublin

'The first taking of Ath-Cliath by the foreigners.' – A curt description of events in Dublin in 837, in the midst of widespread reports of contemporary Viking raids and clashes with the Irish, from John O'Donovan (ed.), *Annals of the Kingdom of Ireland, by the Four Masters* (Dublin, 1845–56), vol. i, p. 457.

marking the advent of a period when the Vikings of Dublin became a significant factor in Irish affairs. It should be said that many of the Viking warriors who flooded into Ireland during this period were themselves colonists, having come from Viking settlements in Britain as well as from Scandinavia itself. There were Vikings settling in Temple Bar West by the late ninth century; there is evidence of ironworking in places such as Essex Street, of property plots and even a stone routeway.

The Vikings may also have seized the island later known as Usher's Island, which was eventually assimilated into the southern bank of the River Liffey, which would have been strategically more valuable and easier to defend. This may also explain why Viking burials were found so far inland along the Liffey, in the vicinity of Kilmainham. When Kingsbridge (now Heuston) Station was constructed in the 1840s, a number of Viking graves were found in the area of Kilmainham, relatively close to the River Liffey. They were found by engineers creating new railway works for the Great Southern and Western Railway, and two burial sites were located, one probably near the old monastery and another perhaps 800 metres west at Islandbridge. These Viking graves may well have utilised earlier native Christian burial sites and were located on a gravel ridge, since eroded, beginning at the junction of the Liffey and the Camac. The major finds came between 1836 and 1848, beginning with a skeleton found with weapons near the Royal Hospital Kilmainham. The railway construction of the 1840s uncovered more artefacts, weapons, tools, jewels and human remains; and more finds would follow in the 1860s, the latter of which were described in minute detail by William Wilde, the father of Oscar Wilde.

Yet more finds would emerge in the 1930s during the construction of the National War Memorial Gardens at Islandbridge. Of the burials themselves, some seem to have been monastic settlers, while others appear to have been warriors. But these were most likely outliers, the main longphort was almost certainly the site adjacent to the modern Dublin Castle, and may have been initially about 20 by 400 metres in size. The grave of one Viking warrior, excavated near South Great George's Street in 2005, revealed a young man who had been buried with great ceremony, perhaps having fallen in battle in Dublin or elsewhere. His upper body was very well developed, as one might expect from a man who carried and brandished weapons, or did the rowing that would have been required to put such weapons into service. The initial role of the Vikings in Irish life was as raiders, but over time, to cut a long and complex story short, the Dublin Vikings, despite not coming from an urbanised culture themselves, morphed into traders and also into mercenaries, renting themselves out to the fragmented world of the Irish lords in their own inter-dynastic squabbles.

'Sir William Wilde, Vice-President, brought under the notice of the Academy an account of the antiquities of Scandinavian origin, lately found in the fields sloping down from the ridge of Inchicore to the Liffey, and to the south-west of the village of Islandbridge, outside the municipal boundary of the city of Dublin, where, there was reason to believe, some of the so-called Danish engagements with the native Irish took place. These antiquities consisted of swords of great length, spearheads, and bosses of shields, all of iron; also iron knives, smiths' and metal smelters' tongs, hammer heads, and pin brooches, & c. Of bronze there were four very beautiful tortoise-shaped or mammillary brooches found, likewise some decorative mantle pins and helmet crests of findruin, or white metal; beams and scales of the same material, and leaden weights, decorated and enamelled on top, and in some cases ornamented with minerals.' – W.A. Wilde, 'On Scandinavian antiquities discovered near Islandbridge, County Dublin', *Proceedings of the Royal Irish Academy*, 10 (1866–69), 13.

Viking or Norse Dublin was originally a base for major raids in both Ireland and the Irish Sea; sixty ships were recorded in Dublin Bay in 837, but 200 ships were recorded in 871, and the Vikings of Dublin were sufficiently powerful to capture the old Roman city of York in 867. The Vikings' world stretched from Dublin on the western edge of Europe to the Baltic and even as far as Russia. It is often suggested that the Vikings were briefly expelled from Dublin from 902 to 917, though there seems to have been continuity in terms of settlement, so any such expulsion was most likely confined to a handful of families within the ruling elite of the town. Whatever expulsion did happen was due to an alliance of Irish kings at the start of the tenth century, but the Vikings soon returned, and this time they survived.

In 919 an attack by the Uí Néill was repulsed near Islandbridge, and having seen off this renewed challenge from the Irish, the second wave of Vikings to settle in Dublin proved more powerful and ambitious than their predecessors. They lost control of York, and were unable to establish a permanent foothold in Ulster, but by the second half of the tenth century, under the leadership of kings such as Olaf Cuarán and his son Sitric Silkenbeard, they had firmly re-established themselves. They were not, however, invulnerable: the Dublin Norse fought twenty-five engagements in Ireland between 917 and 1014, and were defeated in fifteen of them.

By the end of the tenth century, the Dublin Vikings seemed to have abandoned any

The re-emergence of Viking Dublin: excavations at Wood Quay, October 1978. (*Courtesy of Dublin City Library and Archive, Dublin City Council Photographic Collection*)

An early Dubliner: a human skeleton revealed at the Wood Quay site, October 1978. (*Courtesy of Dublin City Library and Archive, Dublin City Council Photographic Collection*)

'The destruction of Ath-Cliath by the Irish, ie, by Conghalach, son of Maelmithigh, heir apparent to the sovereignty of Ireland; Braen, son of Maelmordha, King of Leinster; Ceallach, son of Faelan, heir of Leinster. The destruction brought upon it was this, ie, its houses, divisions, ships, and all other structures, were burned; its women, boys and plebeians were carried into bondage. It was totally destroyed, from four to one man, by killing and drowning, burning and capturing, excepting a small number who fled in a few ships.' – A brief account of the sack of Dublin in 942, from John O'Donovan (ed.), *Annals of the Kingdom of Ireland, by the Four Masters* (Dublin, 1845–56), vol. i, pp. 651–3.

attempts to capture large tracts of territory. In this they were unlike later settlers and colonists and were happy, or at the very least content, to remain within their coastal enclaves. Dublin was attacked at regular intervals by Irish chieftains and kings. The reason why the Vikings remained in their coastal enclaves was precisely the reason why Viking towns became attractive targets – they had become wealthy trading centres. We know a great deal about life in Viking Dublin thanks to the extensive excavations that took place in the city from the 1960s onwards, especially those that took place at Wood Quay in the 1970s. As Dublin Corporation, now Dublin City Council, built its new headquarters on the ridge beside Christ Church, layers of the modern city were stripped away until the Viking foundations were quite literally revealed, and along with the street planning and dwellings, the leftovers of material life have been found in abundance.

The Norse of Dublin were more concerned with the Viking trading empire that stretched across Europe than with Ireland beyond their town's hinterland. They traded with the Irish, acted as mercenaries in Irish dynastic struggles and often had to contend with the ambitions of Irish kings who still looked at Dublin with envy. At some point after 917, the Vikings erected earthen fortifications, and these were built for good reason: Dublin itself was attacked by the Irish on at least thirteen occasions between 936 and 1013. The Leinster king Máel Sechnaill mac Domhnaill defeated a Viking army at the ancient royal site at Tara in 980 before besieging Dublin in 981 and again in 989, after which he successfully extracted an annual tribute in gold from the Dubliners. As early as the mid-tenth century, defences had been in place along the Liffey along with flood defences, and Dublin began to be known as a 'dún', indicating its evolution into a recognisable town and trading centre. At the turn of the eleventh century, Dublin would have been fortified with an earthen embankment topped by wooden fences, and it may well be that the area in and around Christ Church and other central areas that lay within the original defences reflect the street plan of the Viking city. Máel Sechnaill's great rival Brian Boru then besieged Dublin in 1100. It fell after five days, a defeat that was followed by an orgy of killing, rape and plunder, as captives were taken and sold into slavery.

III

While the year 1000 was, no doubt, a terrible date for the inhabitants, it offers a vantage point from which to survey the embryonic city and its hinterland. Dublin had perhaps 2,000 inhabitants at this time and possibly 400 houses. It was enclosed and fortified, but it had begun to expand along what is now High Street. Its focal point would have been the area around Castle Street, Fishamble Street, Werburgh Street and Christchurch Place. Houses were simple rectangular structures with curved corners and a small hole in the roof to permit the release of smoke. The interior would have been spartan, with the roof being held up by posts, and raised platforms for sleeping. Woodchips and sawdust would have been used on the floors. The expansion of the city and also the accumulation of debris began to cause the ground to rise, and later in the Middle Ages, the accumulation of rubbish would be used to reclaim land from the River Liffey itself. Most of these houses, because they were made of wood, might have survived for only twenty to twenty-five years. The lifespan of those living there was short: perhaps only 10 per cent of the population would have lived beyond sixty and possibly 50 per cent of women were dead by the age of thirty-five. Within Dublin's hinterland, there were some outlying hamlets in areas such as Swords, Finglas, Clondalkin, Tallaght and Dalkey.

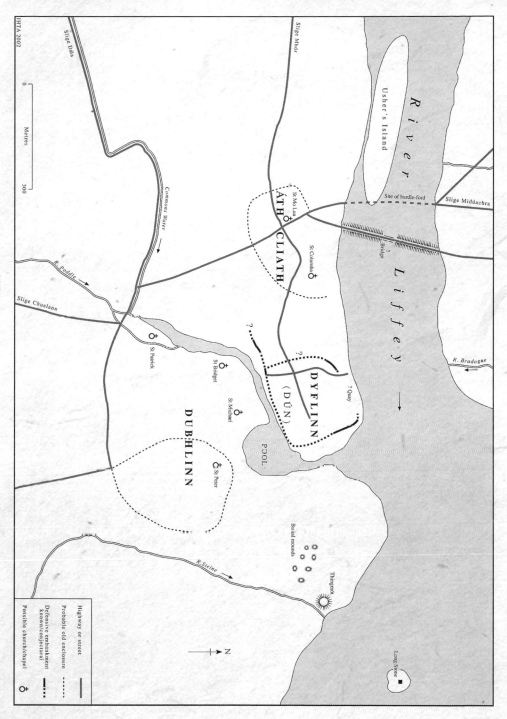

Dublin *circa* 1000. A defensive structure of some kind is visible around the location of the main settlement. (*Royal Irish Academy, Irish Historic Towns Atlas*)

The remains of Viking-era buildings excavated at Wood Quay, October 1978. The wooden remnants are clearly visible, having been preserved in the damp ground, and they give a sense of the cramped scale of the Viking habitations. (*Courtesy of Dublin City Library and Archive, Dublin City Council Photographic Collection*)

Dublin's hinterland did not just provide wood for ships. It provided the berries, oats, nuts, meat and fish that may have been the staple diet of the locals, not to mention the cereals used to make bread, porridge and ale. People would have eaten fruits, nuts, meat, fish (including herrings), dairy products; some species of berries and herbs were used as seasonings and for adding to beer. The damp ground around the settlement was a natural preservative for organic material. The average temperature may well have been slightly warmer than it is today, and the Viking settlement was surrounded by much arable land. Perhaps 20,000 acres would have been required to feed the city, growing wheat, barley, oats and beans (bread, beer and porridge would have been staple foodstuffs for the population). There would have been woodlands in nearby river valleys such as those of the Liffey, the Camac, the Coombe, the Poddle and the Steine, and trees such as alder, birch, willow, ash and holly were all to be found here. (Deer and wolves were to be found in the woodlands as well.) Hazel could be used to make houses, and the oak forests of Wicklow provided plenty of raw material for the city's fleets, which not only traded across the Viking world but were regularly hired out as mercenary vessels in disputes. To some extent, Dublin was seen as foreign by the native Irish themselves, but it was still seen as valuable and, over time, this ensured that the Irish and the Norse would intermingle and intermarry, as well as come into conflict with one another. The full extent of Scandinavian settlement is unclear. It is also unclear whether the locals simply accepted it and carried on. There were large numbers of craftsmen in Dublin, who served the everyday needs of the population, but they also worked with metals such as copper, gold and lead, which were found in Leinster, especially in Wicklow.

The Vikings would raid within a radius of perhaps 75 kilometres from Dublin; and some of these attacks would have been slave raids. Dublin's slave trade was linked to the Viking role in Irish politics, and it peaked in the tenth and eleventh centuries. Taking captives had been a feature of early Viking hit-and-run raids, albeit on a limited scale. But the growing demand for labour in the North Atlantic world saw slave raids become a feature of Viking warfare from the tenth century onwards. The Irish seemed to respond in kind as direct retaliation, and slave trading became a means of turning a profit as Dublin's power may have declined. Some slaves were captured by the Dublin Vikings themselves, while others would have been received or taken as payment for their mercenary activities as their naval power was hired out around Britain and the Irish Sea.

Viking Dublin was no longer a town for raiding from; it became a trading port. Shallow-draught ships could navigate the Liffey, and links began to be established or strengthened with towns such as Chester and York, and with Scandinavia itself. The extent of the Viking trade network is evidenced by some of the artefacts that have been found in the city: silk from the Silk Road, and coins from as far away as Samarkand and Baghdad. Dublin's trade seems to have increased from the tenth century onwards. It was now a major trading centre, both nationally and internationally. Over time, the Vikings began to detach themselves and stand aside from the dynastic disputes that characterised the politics of pre-Norman and pre-conquest Ireland. Kings such as Sitric Silkenbeard, for example, became aligned with one king or another; in his case, against Brian Boru, who would die in 1014 in the Battle of Clontarf outside Dublin, on the northern edge of the bay. Having been defeated by Brian Boru in 999, Sitric had resented the imposition of Brian's authority in his quest for pre-eminence, and readily aligned himself with Máel Sechnaill (though this did not prevent the latter capturing and burning the city and suburbs yet again the following year).

When the city was rebuilt, the boundaries of the settlement began to expand westwards and by the eleventh century Dublin, having lost much of its military and political, if not commercial, influence, could be classed as a 'Hiberno-Norse' town. Certainly, the shift from raiding to trading was well under way by the mid-tenth century. Dublin in the eleventh century had perhaps 4,500 inhabitants, and the Norse of Dublin were culturally distinct from the Irish in two ways: the language they spoke; and the pagan religion they practised. Yet these distinctions weakened over time. Peoples and languages from around Ireland and Britain would have been seen and heard on Dublin's streets, and a new faith would also have been evident. Máel Sechnaill had taken the so-called 'Ring of Thor' from Dublin in 995, but when he expelled Olaf in 981 the old king took refuge in the Christian monastery of Iona, a hint that Christianity was making headway among the Norse of Dublin, and coexisting with the traditional Norse faiths. To some degree, the spread of Christianity may have been helped by intermarriage with the Irish, though the missionary activities of Columban monks may also have helped to win converts. Olaf's son Sitric, like his father before him, had gone to great lengths to ensure Dublin's pre-eminence; among

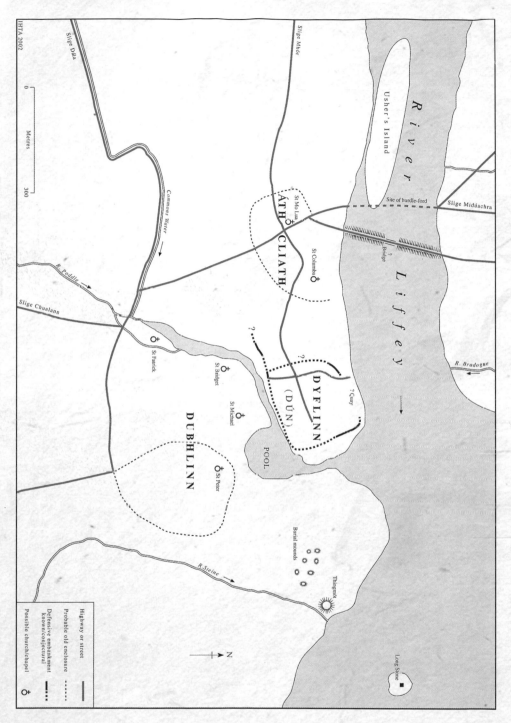

Legend:
- Highway or street
- Probable old enclosure
- Defensive embankment known/conjectural
- Possible church/chapel

Map labels:

IHTA 2002

Metres
0   300

Slige Dála

Slige Mhór

Usher's Island

R i v e r

St Mo Lua

ÁTH
CLIATH

St Columba

Site of hurdle-ford

Slige Midúachra

? Bridge

L i f f e y

Commons Water

R. Poddle

Slige Chualann

St Patrick

St Bridget

St Michael

DYFLINN
(DÚN)

? Quay

R. Bradogue

DUBHLINN

St Peter

POOL

Burial mounds

R. Steine

Thingmót

Long Stone

→ Z

Dublin *circa* 1000. A defensive structure of some kind is visible around the location of the main settlement. (*Royal Irish Academy, Irish Historic Towns Atlas*)

The remains of Viking-era buildings excavated at Wood Quay, October 1978. The wooden remnants are clearly visible, having been preserved in the damp ground, and they give a sense of the cramped scale of the Viking habitations. (*Courtesy of Dublin City Library and Archive, Dublin City Council Photographic Collection*)

Christ Church Cathedral, overlooking the Wood Quay site. The cathedral lay at the eastern end of a ridge, on the site of the church originally built by Sitric. The origins of the current structure date back to the 1170s, and throughout the Middle Ages it was the main cathedral of the English colony in Ireland. It was built on the site of an earlier cathedral and was originally associated with an Augustinian monastery, but became a cathedral of the Church of Ireland in the sixteenth century, after the Reformation. Christ Church overlooked the medieval core of the city, and while its location has changed beyond all recognition it remains one of the last visible remnants of the medieval city. Its medieval character is more obvious in the interior: the exterior was heavily renovated in the late nineteenth century thanks to the generosity of the distiller Henry Roe. (*Courtesy of Dublin City Library and Archive, Dublin City Council Photographic Collection*)

A sizeable section of the old city wall being excavated at Wood Quay in 1973. (*Courtesy of Dublin City Library and Archive, Dublin City Council Photographic Collection*)

Cook Street in the 1970s, showing the largest remnant of the wall above ground, with a car and passers-by for scale. Behind the wall is the medieval spire of St Audoen's; the church itself was built *circa* 1200. (*Courtesy of Dublin City Library and Archive, Dublin City Council Photographic Collection*)

Ce sont les loys e les usages de la cite de
... les queux chescun cytein deit bien ga
... fyauntement ... Blaunch ... e ...
establiz par auncien temps.

Ce sont les loys e les usages de
la cite de Wynchestre est ... partie ...
et un cytein fiert un forcin ... pur
quant il est mort avant bataille, po
... sourdre. le cytein ly purveye ...
... homes pur ... le ... de ... selonc ...
... e est ... entour ... le ...
bataille ... ... Du ... q ... ...
... ... de anys ... si ... sont ... ...
... la ... ... Chescun ... ...
deinz la cyte deit tenir ... pie ... l ...
... ... Chescun ... ...
... ... pur choisir que le gard ...

The Normans
and their city

❧

1170-1400

Around 1170, Dublin was fortified and densely urbanised with a distinct ethnic make-up. It had strong links across the Irish Sea and far beyond, with a loose autonomy and, presumably, a sense of its own distinctive nature. Dublin was important as a source of fighting men and had become increasingly important in terms of Irish dynastic struggles in the century prior to 1170; the date which roughly marks a dividing line between the Hiberno-Norse town and the Anglo-Norman period.

Throughout the Middle Ages a number of languages were spoken in the city: Irish, Old English, Norse and Latin, though the latter was used only in religious contexts. In 1170, there were at least seven churches in the city, some of which had international connections: St Werburgh's, for example, had links to Chester, while St Olaf's was traditionally Scandinavian, and the presence of the church of St Nicholas, the patron

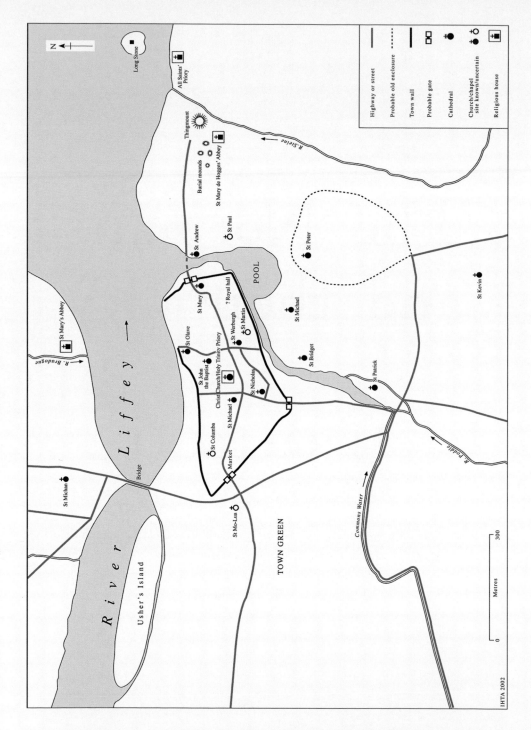

Dublin *circa* 1170. The city and surrounding locality would have changed radically since 840. The walls of the city are clearly demarcated, with a range of other man-made features within and without their boundaries; note the elevated assembly place known as the 'Thingmót', or 'Thingmount'. The latter is the anglicised version. (Royal Irish Academy, *Irish Historic Towns Atlas*)

saint of merchants and sailors, is also suggestive of the city's activities at this time. There were also numerous churches outside the city walls. One thread that acted as a formal link to a wider power was that the Christian diocese of Dublin, uniquely in Ireland, recognised the primacy of the English see of Canterbury rather than that of Armagh, but this external link was perhaps the exception rather than the rule. Yet it seems that Dublin frequently traded with the Norman world even before the Normans arrived; the foundation of St Mary's Abbey, north of the Liffey, hints at the increasing influence of the Normans even before 1170.

I

All of this begs the same question that was applied to the Vikings: why did the Normans come here? The arrival of the Normans in Ireland famously arose from the machinations of Irish dynastic politics, in which Dublin had long been embroiled. The Norse of Dublin were, at this juncture, aligned with the Leinster king Diarmait Mac Murchadha against the putative high king, Ruaidrí Ua Conchobair of Connacht. Mac Murchadha's eventual expulsion from Ireland saw him solicit the aid of a loose coalition of Norman aristocrats, led by Richard Fitzgilbert de Clare, the Earl of Pembroke – better known as Strongbow – to regain his lost patrimony, and his new allies invaded Wexford in 1169 intent on obtaining a suitable reward for the assistance they were providing. The military power of the Norman elite ensured that they cut a swathe through south Leinster and in September 1170 they captured Dublin swiftly and with considerable bloodshed.

Ascall Mac Torcaill, the Hiberno-Norse king of the city, unsuccessfully sought to recapture it via a naval attack in 1171 (and was eventually beheaded for his trouble), while Ua Conchobair himself attempted to recapture the city later in the same year.

'A miracle was wrought against the foreigners [Danes] of Ath-Cliath on this occasion, for Mac Murchadha and the Saxons acted treacherously towards them, and made a slaughter of them in the middle of their own fortress, and carried off their cattle and their goods, in consequence of their violation of their word to the men of Ireland.' – The Norman capture of Dublin in 1170, from John O'Donovan (ed.), *Annals of the Kingdom of Ireland, by the Four Masters* (Dublin, 1845–56), vol. ii, p. 1177.

But the city's wall withstood a two-month siege and his attempt to starve Dublin into submission was broken by a Norman counter-attack that robbed the besiegers of much of their supplies. Negotiations took place thereafter, with the archbishop of Dublin, the ascetic reformist Lorcán Ua Tuathail, being nominated by the citizenry to represent them to the besiegers. His background presumably helped; he was the brother-in-law of Mac Murchadha and the uncle of Strongbow's new bride, Aoife. He subsequently enjoyed good relations with the English and with Strongbow personally, but proved to be the last Irish archbishop of Dublin in the Middle Ages.

The ultimate consequence of Dublin falling under the sway of the Normans was that it soon came under the jurisdiction of the English king. The older Ostman elite was expelled, which led to an enduring piece of folklore: that they had settled on the northern side of the Liffey, giving their name to a region called Ostmantown, a tradition that survives in the modern name Oxmantown. The establishment of the new church of St Michan's suggests that there is a grain of truth in this, but based on the surviving records of the Guild Merchant, Scandinavian merchants (or at least their descendants) remained active in the city. In any case, the Normans were Dublin's new rulers; the issue then arose of whether or not they were the right Normans. Henry II, who had granted Mac Murchadha the right to recruit figures such as Strongbow, remained wary of their ambitions and sought to rein them in. He arrived in Dublin for a brief visit in October 1171, and aimed to impress in grandiose style.

Henry dealt with a range of issues that had arisen in the previous two years. Most significantly, he reserved the town as a possession of the English monarchy. Having received the submission of a number of Irish kings who viewed Henry as a potential

'Henry King of the English, Duke of Normandy and Aquitaine, and Count of Anjou to the archbishops, bishops, abbots, earls, barons, justices, sheriffs, ministers and all other his faithful, French and English and Irish of all his land, greeting. Know that I have given and granted and by this present charter confirmed to my men of Bristol my city of Dublin to be inhabited. Wherefore I wish and firmly command that they inhabit it and hold it of me and my heirs, well and in peace, freely and quietly and honourably, with all liberties and free customs which the men of Bristol have at Bristol, and throughout all my land.' – The text of Henry II's 1172 charter, cited in James Lydon, 'Dublin in Transition: from Ostman town to medieval borough' in Sean Duffy, *Medieval Dublin II* (Dublin, 2001), p. 129.

The tomb of Strongbow in Christ Church, as depicted in a nineteenth-century lantern slide. It had long been an attraction for curious visitors, but the current version is a reconstruction; the original was badly damaged when the roof collapsed in 1562. (*Trevor Ferris*)

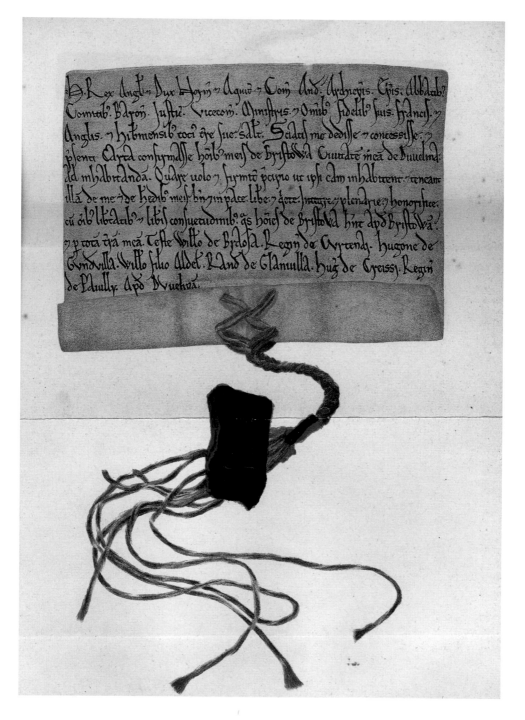

The 1172 charter granted to Dublin by Henry II. (*Courtesy of Dublin City Library and Archive*)

bulwark against the depredations of figure such as Strongbow (and thus the lesser of two evils), in 1172 Henry issued Dublin's first charter, granting Dublin to the 'men of Bristol', and according them the same rights. While there were extensive links between Dublin and Bristol even prior to this, from Henry's point of view it was a convenient means of rapidly rewarding loyal subjects in Bristol and opening the door to new, and dependable, settlers in what was, for him and them, a new town. A second charter followed in 1174, and in 1192 Henry's son, John, having succeeded his father as king, issued another, even more extensive charter to this relatively new royal possession.

II

Dublin was the capital of the new lordship of Ireland, created by Henry II in 1177 (his son, John, assumed the title 'Lord of Ireland'). Urban dwellers in medieval Europe were stratified. The Normans came from a more urbanised culture than their Norse predecessors. The term 'burgess', for example, taken from the Latin word *burgus*, meaning 'town', referred to urban dwellers with the greatest rights of citizenship, as suggested by the royal charters. The 1172 charter granted a form of legal autonomy while also placing major restrictions on the activities of foreign traders and merchants; the 1192 charter also created a system of guilds that would regulate crafts and trade, and which would play a crucial role in the governance and civic life of Dublin for centuries.

There was, perhaps, more continuity than upheaval. Dublin must have had some kind of centralised authority prior to the arrival of the Normans; after all, who was responsible for building its fortifications? The lack of written records leaves this obscure, though hints can be gleaned from various external sources. Many of the place names mentioned in the 1192 charter to demarcate the city boundaries were of Irish origin. But the importance of the charters is that collectively they created a new framework for the government of Dublin and defined the various rights that the inhabitants were to possess. They defined the boundaries of the city, which were staked out in relation to various religious institutions that had existed prior to 1170, such as St Mary's Abbey to the north, and the recent Anglo-Norman foundation of the hospital of St John of Jerusalem near Kilmainham to the west. They also established new layers of administration and bureaucracy – sheriffs, bailiffs, up to the justiciar (the king's representative) – and these were often based on the establishment of new forms of property rights.

This new administration was very much a man's world. While women were excluded from political life and office, however, they did enjoy some legal and economic rights,

The two sides of the seal of Dublin, dating from 1230. The seal represented the authority of the city, as confirmed in the various charters. In this case, the obverse depicts a fortification that may foreshadow the image of three castles that eventually became the Dublin coat of arms. The archers hint at the necessity for the city to be defended, while the niches above the gate seem to show severed heads. Dublin's maritime heritage is highlighted by the depiction of a merchant vessel on the reverse. (*Courtesy of Dublin City Library and Archive*)

and they could become citizens and own property. They were often appointed as co-executors of their husband's will, which was a concrete indication of status and respect. Both Gaelic and colonial Ireland were patriarchal societies, in which women were very often obliged to focus on the domestic sphere, whether as homemakers or servants. Yet women were not simply confined to hearth and home. They could join at least some of the guilds, though not as full members, and other occupations were open to them: brewing, tavern-keeping, baking, even labouring (though women labourers were poorly paid relative to their male counterparts).

Yet political and mercantile activity was generally a male preserve. The guilds themselves were a very good example of this. They were to all intents and purposes specialised institutions, offering support to their members, regulating prizes and administering punishments and discipline if need be. They also fulfilled charitable functions and, at certain times such as feast days, guilds were very prominent in the street life of the city. The Guild Merchant, the oldest and most important of the guilds, arose from the immigration of English merchants and craftsmen to Dublin from the West Midlands and the South of England after 1170. There were perhaps thirty guilds by 1500, regulating virtually all aspects of trade and commerce; the guilds were the progenitors of the city council, eventually based in the Tholsel near Christ Church.

The city council in the Middle Ages consisted of twenty-four individuals generally drawn from the city's mercantile elites, an oligarchy that would persist well into the early modern period. What they concerned themselves with could be broken down

'There is in Dublin in the church of Holy Trinity, a cross of most wonderful power. It has the form of a crucifix. Not many years before the coming of the English, and during the time of the Ostmen, it opened its hallowed mouth and uttered some words. Many people heard it. It had happened that a certain citizen had invoked it, and it alone, as the witness and surety of a certain contract. As time went on the other contracting party denied the agreement and completely and steadfastly refused to return the money which the other had given him according to the terms of the contract. The citizens, more in irony than for any serious reason, declared that they should go in a body to the aforesaid church and hear what the cross would say. The cross being adjured and called to witness, gave testimony to the truth.' – *The First Version of the Topography of Ireland* by Giraldus Cambrensis, trans. John J. O'Meara (Dundalk, 1951), pp. 68–9.

into a number of categories. The most obvious related to the administration of the city, for example the regulation of public hygiene, food quality and public safety, the regulation of crime and punishment and the administration of law and order. The old city walls of Dublin were dotted with a number of prisons throughout the Middle Ages, some of which survived into the early modern period. Medieval Dublin had its own secular bureaucracy, and from 1229 the freemen could elect a mayor; a right that had only been conceded to London in 1214, and which was seen as a mark of status. Dublin had a city council and courts, and alongside the traditional sources of authority there were also the ecclesiastical liberties that lay outside the boundaries of the city walls: St Patrick's, St Sepulchre, St Thomas, St Mary's and Christ Church. There was an inevitable tension between the jurisdictions of the Crown and the Church in relation to the exercise of authority, but certain major crimes such as murder were reserved to the royal courts. The ecclesiastical liberties ultimately gave their name to the area known as the 'Liberties' in the south-west of the city, though the five liberties themselves covered both sides of the River Liffey over time.

Dublin, like many other medieval towns and villages, was a focal point for trade and, indeed, depended on trade for its own supplies. Its natural hinterland formed much of what is modern County Dublin. Trade was both internal and external. The city was a major mercantile centre, and was integrated into the wider Norman world as the Middle Ages wore on. Grain, fish, furs and cloth were exported, while wine, spices and clothes were imported. Fairs, usually related to religious festivals, began to be established from the mid-thirteenth century. These would be taxed by the authorities and they would prove to be major events in the city's public calendar. Medieval fairs were not just focal points for trade. They engendered a carnival atmosphere, with entertainment and food on offer.

'Rates for fines: For insulting the Mayor, forty shillings; for insulting any of the twenty-four jurats, twenty shillings; for insulting any of the other citizens, who are of good repute, ten shillings; for reviling disorderly persons, two shillings, with remission of half; reviling a foreigner, twenty pence, with remission of half; for maltreating a sergeant of the town, forty pence to be paid, if accepted; if blood be shed, half a marc; if blood of a foreigner be shed, the fine shall not exceed forty pence.' – J.T. Gilbert and Rosa Mulholland Gilbert, *Calendar of Ancient Records of Dublin* (1889–1922), vol. i, pp. 225–6.

Dublin was notoriously inaccessible as a port. There was major land reclamation at Wood Quay, culminating in the construction of a stone quay wall there by 1260, which was intended to provide deeper berths for ships, and Dublin benefited from a more general expansion of trade across twelfth- and thirteenth-century Europe with imports of wine, coal, cloth, salt and timber. Dalkey was used as an outer port due to the silting of the river and the fact that the Liffey remained inaccessible to many ships. But the fairs could still be frequented by merchants from across continental Europe. Dublin's key exports proved to be wood, hides, grain and furs; wine was a particularly common import in the Middle Ages. In fact, wine was one of the largest imports into Dublin in the period.

The everyday realities of life in medieval Dublin should not be ignored. There was a clock on the Tholsel in 1466 and church bells also gave an indication of time. The use of candles made chandlers an important guild; they were closely linked to the butchers, as tallow was the usual material for making candles. There was also a place for entertainment. Carvings on Christ Church depicted minstrels as early as 1200, and harpers, horn players and other musicians were common too. Some were itinerant players; others were settled residents. Acrobats and contortionists were known in Gaelic Ireland, and jugglers performed with blades and spears. Many such processions were organised by the guilds, with Corpus Christi processions, in which each of the guilds was accorded a part, being particularly prominent. Theatrical performances could take place with the sanction of the religious authorities. Inevitably, performers were sometimes viewed with suspicion by the secular authorities, not least because those travelling through the city could be spies. Legislation would be passed to restrict their activities. Maypoles were often viewed as focal points of mischief and a recurring source of complaint was the moral turpitude of apprentices and servants, who as late as 1620 were the victims of restrictions against transporting bears and bulls through the city for baiting.

The city authorities were also responsible for dealing with the supply of water. The Poddle and the Dodder were crucial water sources throughout the Middle Ages, and there was a large cistern near St James's Gate. This cistern, which was apparently created by the monks of St Thomas' Abbey, ran via an aqueduct down towards the city itself (though the wealthy could obtain a private water supply). The disposal of waste, both animal and human, was a vital part of life in the city itself. Cesspits for human waste were sited at the back of houses. Animal waste, on the other hand, was valuable and could be harvested. Public dung heaps could be found on Hangman's Lane, now Hammond Lane, and can be seen on maps of the city well into the modern

Ces sunt les leys e les usages de la cité de Diue
liuer les queux chescun cytein deit bien garder
e franchement sannz bleincure kar il sunt
establiz par aunciien temps.

C es sunt les leys e les usages de
la cité de Dublin ceo est a saver ke
er un cytein fiert un forein par
auint il est mort aduint bataille po
er sourdre le cytein ly puysea od ...
... bornes ... ouint le bastun de chescun forein
borne er est ... entrouutre cytein ... iames
a bataille ... ¶ Dautre part ...
... ¶ Dautre part chescun buyage
... la cité deit ... ¶ Dautre part chescune ...
... ¶ Dautre part e

A page from the 'chain book' of 1317, containing the various laws and regulations that applied in
Dublin throughout the Middle Ages. It was so called because it was originally attached by a chain in the

'Fines on bakers for faulty bread: for the first offence, fifteen pence; for the second, thirty pence; for the third offence, they shall stand in the pillory and swear to leave the city for a year and a day. If they seek afterwards to return, they must renounce their trade, if they have not sanction from the mayor and commonalty. Under penalty of half a mark, bakers must put their stamps and names on their bread. For the misdeeds of his servants every master-baker shall answer by life and limb, if he have not property.' – J.T. Gilbert and Rosa Mulholland Gilbert, *Calendar of Ancient Records of Dublin* (1889–1922), vol. i, p. 224.

era. Animals, especially pigs and dogs, would have been a common sight in the city, while butchers, fishmongers and indeed many ordinary home owners were obliged to maintain a certain level of public hygiene, both in their businesses and around their homes. The houses themselves would have been crammed tightly on irregular plots. Space was maximised by building two or three storeys high. Shops opened directly onto the street via a wooden counter, with certain streets offering specific services. All in all, medieval Dublin was a cramped, dark, raucous environment, but one that was tightly regulated in order to ensure that it operated smoothly. How such regulation actually operated in practice, however, is another story entirely.

III

Dublin had been overspilling its walls before 1170. The area within the walls was only 44 acres. Yet there was a city outside the walls as well – Dublin had a number of suburbs. Dublin had 11,000 inhabitants by *circa* 1300, but many, if not most, resided outside the walls. The existence of the Liberties was an obvious example of this spillover, but suburbs had grown from the twelfth century and in the later Middle Ages, four could be discerned. The northern suburb, Oxmantown, lay west of St Mary's Abbey. Some of its streets, such as Pill and Hangman's Lanes, were evident from the Middle Ages, while Church Street was adjacent to St Michan's Church. This may well have been a de facto town in its own right, with markets and the like. The eastern suburb was focused on Hoggen Green (later College Green), and contained many traces of Viking life and death in the form of burial mounds, the Steine and the Thingmount, while All Saints Priory and the nunnery of St Mary de Hogges were both originally founded by Diarmait Mac Murchada.

The street furthest to the west was St James's Hospital, a transit point for the Camino de Santiago pilgrimage. Moving south, the name of Kevin Street hints at a link to the monastic founder of Glendalough; it is linked to St Kevin's, which was the most southerly church in the city. This was a much more cluttered area, with St Patrick's Cathedral and the Archbishop's Palace and many other churches and religious foundations, especially Mary's Priory within the circular roadway, which may denote one of the original settlements. Also in this area was a leper house and the remnants of the black pool, while the dam over the Poddle gave Dame Street its name.

The western suburb was slightly elevated, which permitted a watercourse that led directly into the old medieval centre. That made it a natural focal point for markets and for fairs, and eventually the Fairgreen would be located under the city walls at what is now Francis Street. (St John the Baptist Hospital for the poor and sick was also in this area.) Like so much else, the monastic wealth of this region was later wiped out in the Reformation.

This was medieval Dublin beyond the city walls. While the walls themselves had successfully withstood a siege in 1171, they began to be rebuilt soon after the invasion, and Henry II and his successors implemented a series of taxes intended to pay for their upkeep. The most obvious change was the construction of a series of substantial defensive towers around the circuit of the walls. Little enough remains of the medieval city as most of it was made of perishable material. In terms of what remains above ground, old street names give an indication of the older purposes of the city. Fishamble Street was the fish market. Ship Street was derived from Sheep Street, indicating a livestock market, and Cook Street outside the city walls was a traditional venue for cooking, located outside the walls to avoid the risk of fires. It is hardly unrealistic to envision a medieval Dubliner buying a pie on Cook Street before retiring for ale in Winetavern Street. Ironically, the walls are perhaps one of the last archaeological remnants of the Anglo-Norman and, later, English city. The emphasis on the archaeological record means that knowledge about medieval Dublin and Viking Dublin has really only come to light since the 1960s. The waterlogged ground on which the city developed ensured the preservation of a great deal of material, but the construction of cellars in the eighteenth and nineteenth centuries destroyed much of the post-1300 archaeology.

To that extent, the archaeological record is restricted to the Vikings and the early phases of the Norman era. Yet some impressive fragments survive – churches, the two cathedrals and the remains of the wall, rendered in a most dramatic style on Lamb Alley and Cook Street. It is possible to walk the route of the old walls and an obvious

The archiepiscopal palace of St Sepulchre, located on modern Kevin Street and depicted here by Gabriel Berangar in 1765. Originally built as the residence of John Cumin, archbishop of Dublin from 1181 to 1212, it has been heavily rebuilt over the centuries and since 1836 has been a police station. (*National Library of Ireland*)

Further excavations of the city wall, from 1991. Note the red-brick foundations on the left, resting on the earlier structure. The construction of cellars in later centuries destroyed a great deal of Dublin's archaeological heritage from the later Middle Ages: what has survived are the older, deeper layers. (*Courtesy of Dublin City Library and Archive, Dublin City Council Photographic Collection*)

starting point is Isolde's Tower in Exchange Street, which roughly follows the line inside the old medieval walls. The tower would have been the major fortification of the north-eastern corner of the medieval city and the first fortification that visitors coming upriver by boat would have encountered. The estuary of the River Poddle flowed through what is now Parliament Street and the tower itself would have overlooked the junction of the Liffey and the Poddle. Moving westward from this point, however, brings one into the area of the old medieval city and into the circuit of its walls, helpfully indicated today by a succession of metal plaques located on plinths throughout this area. King John defined the territorial limits of the city in his 1192 charter, and the Normans engaged in extensive land reclamation. A new wall north of Cook Street to encompass the reclaimed area had been built by the 1240s. Isolde's Tower was simply one of a number of extensive new towers, resting on four-metre-thick walls, that acted as the first line of defence against marauders coming up the river, and also served as a venue from which to display the heads of those executed, as a salutary warning to those who might follow suit.

By the late thirteenth century, the construction of the city's defences was slackening. The towers were used for both defensive and commercial purposes, and this is indicated most strongly in the story of Geoffrey Morton, a Dublin merchant who may well have originally been from London and who by the late 1290s was well connected within Dublin's mercantile community and the royal administration. He was involved in procuring supplies for military campaigns in Gascony and in Scotland, and in 1303 he was appointed mayor of Dublin, despite having had no administrative experience with any municipal authorities. He became embroiled in a long-running and acrimonious feud with the treasurer, Richard de Beresford, arising from suspicions that merchants such as Morton were landing wine at Dalkey to avoid paying tax to the Crown. Morton became embroiled in a dubious case in which he claimed that Isolde's Tower, of which he was a tenant, needed repairs that were to be paid from his purse. He subsequently claimed and was granted the right to demand tolls by way of recompense as the tower was adjacent to the only bridge in the city. In 1311 it was alleged that the tower had in fact been intact and any damage had been caused by Morton extending his own house to the walls. The authorities concluded that Morton and his wife were indeed the tenants and were bound to pay for its upkeep anyway, that he was charging excessive and illegal tolls that were discouraging merchants, and that he had built up to the wall, removing battlements and impeding access. He continued to fight the case up to his death, but the story shows the importance given to the medieval walls well into the Middle Ages. The

The base of Isolde's Tower. Its traditional name was apparently taken from the daughter of a legendary king, though it was later known as Newman's Tower after it was leased to a property speculator, Jacob Newman, in 1604. Newman soon began to fill in the Poddle estuary and reclaim much of the surrounding area. In the event of an attack on the city, Newman would have had to return the tower to the authorities. Even as late as the seventeenth century, it was still seen as vital to Dublin's defences, though by the end of the eighteenth century, it seems to have been in ruins. (*Courtesy of Dublin City Library and Archive, Dublin City Council Photographic Collection*)

walls were seen as necessary to defend Dublin against any invaders or enemies who might attempt to enter the city.

The construction of what became Dublin Castle began in 1204, and was largely completed by 1230 under the authority of the archbishop of Dublin, Henry Blund. Some kind of fortification seems to have existed prior to 1170, but a new one was required and it was inextricably linked to the defence and the structure of the city. It reflected a feudal obligation to provide for the protection of the city itself. It did not have a keep, consisting instead of a substantial enclosure on the south-eastern corner of the walls, with a moat on its northern and western side. The old wall can be traced in relation to Dublin's existing street plan. These were massive excavations and the earth would most likely have been recycled into embankments. There was a certain degree of complacency about maintaining the city defences in the Middle Ages. Dublin remained vulnerable to attacks from Wicklow – indeed, the massacre of perhaps 300 inhabitants at Cullenswood on Easter Monday 1209 by the Irish of Wicklow was commemorated up to the late seventeenth century – and its expansion in the thirteenth century took place within the cocoon of the colonised region around Dublin that would later be known as the English Pale.

The symbolic value of Dublin Castle was not automatically reflected by reality; like much else, it became a victim of complacency during a time of peace, and was seen to be in need of serious repair in 1315. The suburbs were burned deliberately, on the orders of the mayor, Robert de Nottingham, in 1317 when the city was besieged by a Scottish army under Edward Bruce, who had invaded Ireland in 1315 and who, two years later, encamped an army of perhaps 6,000 troops in the vicinity of modern Castleknock. Given that the city walls were deemed to be in poor condition and the reputation of the Scots had preceded them, the western suburbs were burned; there were also ad hoc attempts to strengthen the walls with stones cannibalised from the

'AD 1327 : Adam Duff O'Toole was convicted of blasphemy in Dublin, viz. for denying the incarnation of Christ, the trinity in union, for affirming that the blessed virgin was a harlot, that there was no resurrection, that the scriptures were a mere fable, and that the apostolical see was an imposture and a usurpation, and the next year, pursuant to his sentence, was burned on Hoggen-green near Dublin.' – Walter Harris, *The History and Antiquities of the City of Dublin, from the Earliest Accounts* (Dublin, 1766), p. 264.

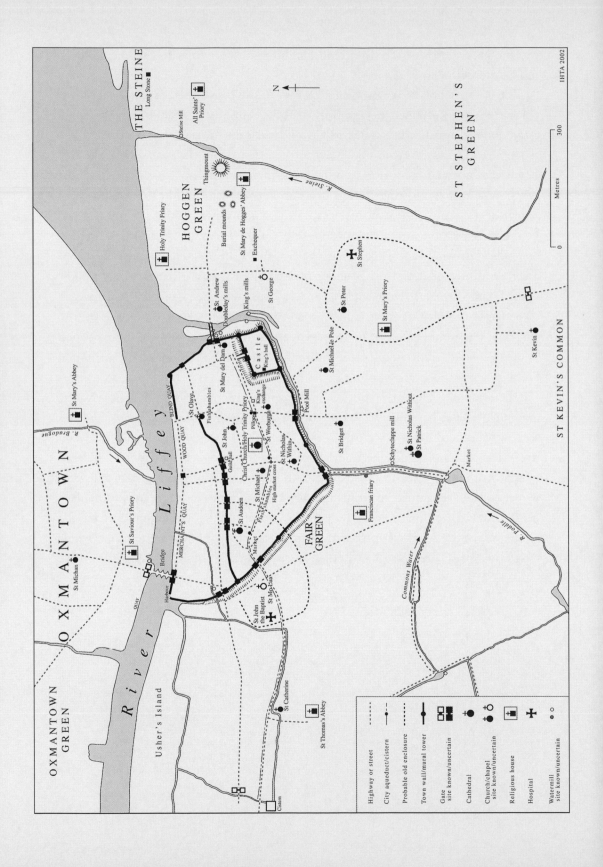

IHTA 2002

Dominican Friary of St Saviour's, which had been demolished for the purpose. The further expansion of the city was almost certainly hampered by the Black Death in 1348 as the arrival of bubonic plague devastated Ireland and Dublin. The population of Ireland as a whole may have declined by as much as half between then and 1400, though by a grim arithmetic that depopulation may have allowed an improvement in the living standards of those lucky enough to survive.

'It first broke out near Dublin, at Howth and Dalkey; it almost destroyed and laid waste the cities of Dublin and Drogheda; insomuch, that in Dublin along from the beginnings of August to Christmas, 14000 souls perished.' – John Clyn, a Franciscan in Kilkenny, records the outbreak of the plague, to which he himself seems to have succumbed. Walter Harris, *The History and Antiquities of the City of Dublin, from the Earliest Accounts* (Dublin, 1766), pp. 167–8.

Opposite page: Dublin *circa* 1300. By this time the topography of the locality had changed dramatically. Land extended out to the old Viking 'Long Stone', a monument that may have commemorated their occupation of what became Dublin, and silt had reduced the old black pool to little more than an inlet. (Royal Irish Academy, *Irish Historic Towns Atlas*)

Stasis?

❧

1400-1600

Dublin seems to have declined throughout the late fourteenth and fifteenth centuries. The surviving records are filled with hints of depopulation in the generations after the Black Death, of empty and derelict plots of land, and of signs of general decrepitude. The bridge collapsed in 1385 and would not be replaced for forty-three years. Virtually all the gates of the city needed repairs in the late fifteenth and early sixteenth centuries. The castle was deemed to be in ruins as early as 1462 and there would be intermittent attempts to repair its walls in the late fifteenth and early sixteenth centuries.

By the mid-fifteenth century, English control in Ireland was essentially restricted to the four medieval counties around the administrative capital of Dublin – Dublin itself, Meath, Louth and Kildare constituted what later generations would refer to as the English Pale. The late medieval Gaelic revival and the parallel decline of the

English colony in Ireland in the fifteenth century left the Pale as the only region in which the authority of the English monarchy remained valid. Reasserting control over the island of Ireland as a whole would remain a preoccupation of English governments until the end of the sixteenth century, though the manner in which this was to be done remained open to question.

I

The most obvious way of securing Ireland for the kings of England, however, was simply to depend upon the colonists, and pre-eminent amongst those colonists at the end of the fifteenth and the beginning of the sixteenth century were the FitzGerald Earls of Kildare. When the eighth Earl, Gearóid Mór, succeeded his father in 1478, he exerted his influence by physically preventing the new lord deputy, Lord Grey, from taking office by demolishing the drawbridge to Dublin Castle. Yet instead of being punished by Henry VII, Kildare himself was promoted, and the supremacy of the Earls of Kildare is best illustrated by their involvement in a number of Yorkist plots arising from the English Wars of the Roses. Kildare supported the pretender Lambert Simnel, who was crowned as Edward VI in Christ Church in 1487, and Kildare even governed for a brief period in his name. Simnel's supporters claimed him to be Edward, Earl of Warwick, the son of the Duke of Clarence, the nephew of Richard III, who had been detained in the Tower of London and supposedly escaped. He was rumoured to have absconded to Ireland, though the circumstances of Simnel's arrival and time in Ireland is unclear. However, in May 1497, 1,500 German mercenaries, paid for by the former King Richard III's sister, the Duchess of Burgundy, arrived in Ireland. This seemed to tip the balance, and Kildare had Simnel proclaimed as Edward VI in May or June 1497 (the precise date is unclear, but it was possibly 27 May). A crown for the ceremony was taken from a statue of the Virgin Mary in St Mary's Church, and in the procession Simnel was supposedly carried aloft by the allegedly enormous Sir William Darcy

Lambert Simnel held aloft on the streets of Dublin, presumably on the shoulders of Sir William Darcy of Platten and with Christ Church in the background, as depicted in one of the murals within the rotunda of Dublin City Hall. The murals were originally painted under the direction of James Ward of the Dublin Metropolitan School of Art and unveiled in 1919; arguably they contain a subtly nationalistic undertone, in this case by depicting a challenge to the authority of the English monarchy in Ireland. (*Courtesy of Dublin City Library and Archive*)

Three of the 'mummies' of St Michan's. The eleventh-century church of St Michan's was, for much of the Middle Ages, the only parish church north of the Liffey, in the emerging suburb of Oxmantown. Given the medieval origins of this church, it is sometimes claimed that these wizened characters are equally old; one was traditionally dubbed the 'Crusader'. The vault in which they are interred was not used before 1685, alas, and probably formed part of the seventeenth-century renovation of the church. Their precise age remains uncertain. (*Courtesy of Dublin City Library and Archive, Fáilte Ireland Tourism Photographic Collection*)

of Platten. Simnel subsequently travelled to England with the German mercenaries and an Irish force. His rebellion was defeated and he ended up working in the royal household, but it took some time for his supporters in Dublin to disavow him. Many were willing to do so but were afraid to brook Kildare, and the issue dragged on until July 1488, when an English army of 500 landed in Dublin and negotiated with Kildare to return to the king's favour.

II

From the early sixteenth century, the English were attempting to exert control over their dominions – one of which was Ireland. This took on greater importance against the backdrop of the break with Rome, as England was left isolated as a Protestant power in Catholic Western Europe and was thus vulnerable to possible attack by Catholic powers. This was one of the contexts in which internal threats were dealt with more severely, most especially the Earls of Kildare themselves. Kildare was officially reprimanded in the 1530s, but in June 1534, his son Thomas, Lord Offaly, better known to posterity as Silken Thomas, embarked on a rebellion, beginning by marching into the Chapter House of St Mary's Abbey to a council meeting, placing the Sword of State on the table and openly rejecting royal authority. The Kildare Rebellion was simply an attempt by this house to remind the king of their authority in Ireland and how indispensable they had been to the government of the Lordship of Ireland. They had done this in the past, but now they lived in different times, given the break with Rome and attempts to consolidate royal authority in the north of England, Ireland and Wales. There was a gap between Offaly's original gesture on 11 June and the events of 25 July that prompted the citizens to secure Dublin against attack. The archbishop of Dublin, John Alen, was leaving Dublin when his boat ran aground at Clontarf and he was forced to spend the night in Artane, where he was dragged from his bed and brutally killed by Offaly's supporters. Offaly then began attacks in Fingal and north County Dublin before deciding to besiege Dublin itself.

The king's sergeant at arms, John Whyte, oversaw the defence of the castle. Much of the ordnance in the castle had been taken by Kildare, but some weapons remained and supplies (and possibly more weapons) were obtained from the citizens, along with a new chain for the castle drawbridge. An initial attack on the castle failed due to the inadequate artillery used by Offaly, which made little impact on the fortifications. A subsequent attack on Ship Street was repelled after the houses were burned by the defenders using 'wildfire', a type of incendiary weapon. Another attack on Newgate failed after Offaly's men were attacked by a force that came out from the city after an attempt was made to burn the gate.

The English government responded in a brutal and unprecedentedly hostile manner. Kildare himself was imprisoned in the Tower of London, where he died in September 1534. In October 1534, Henry VIII sent Sir William Skeffington to Ireland with 2,300 troops to crush the rebellion. The Reformation soon followed. Legislation passed by a parliament that sat in Dublin in 1536 and 1537, and that briefly followed the new lord deputy, Lord Grey, on a campaign around the country, created the Irish Reformation and the Church of Ireland. It had a practical outworking in Dublin with the destruction of relics at the behest of George Browne, the archbishop of Dublin, most obviously the 'Bachal Isu' (the 'Staff of Jesus', supposedly given to St Patrick by an angel). This was the most famous of a number of relics kept in Christ Church Cathedral, and it had been venerated by pilgrims throughout the Middle Ages.

III

In 1537, following an Act of Parliament the previous year, Dublin's religious houses began to be shut down, beginning with the dissolution of the nunnery of St Mary de Hogges. All its buildings were destroyed. The Reformation proceeded apace as institutions were dissolved in Dublin even though they had intended to lease out and sell their lands beforehand. In 1541 came the Act for the Kingly Title in which Ireland was formally transformed into a kingdom under Henry VIII and his successors, as opposed to a lordship technically held by the kings of England by grant of the papacy. In this new dispensation, the various factions in Ireland could be brought under one single jurisdiction, as loyal subjects of a Crown to which they would pledge their allegiance. This symbolism was exemplified in its pronouncement at a service in St Patrick's Cathedral in Irish for the benefit of Gaelic chieftains who were present.

The dissolution of religious institutions created an unexpected market for land in Dublin and elsewhere. Monastic lands were desirable, and indeed some religious institutions, seeing the way the wind was blowing, sold off lands and possessions to families within the Pale, who often managed to strike a hard bargain in the circumstances. But the rapid demolition of some religious buildings seems to have been done in order for the building material to be sold off on the side by the vice-treasurer, William Brabazon. In 1539 the Priory of All Hallows – the future site of Trinity College – was granted to the citizens as recompense for damage sustained in Offaly's siege in 1534. The dissolution of the monasteries was the greatest physical

The 1539 charter granting the lands of All Hallows to Dublin by Henry VIII, in recognition of the city's resistance to Silken Thomas. (*Courtesy of Dublin City Library and Archive*)

A detail from Henry VIII's charter, in which the traditional three castles motif is visible. (*Courtesy of Dublin City Library and Archive*)

change in the sixteenth-century city, though traces remained, and indeed the old religious buildings of All Hallows would be used as a plague house in the seventeenth century (outbreaks of plague were a continuous fear). Religious houses had provided social services (two, St John of Jerusalem and St John the Baptist, acted as hospitals), and one consequence of the dissolution was that care for the poor would now devolve upon the secular rather than the religious authorities. Dublin's infrastructure, such as the Tholsel and its watercourses, was in disrepair by the sixteenth century. With an eye on economic growth, the 1548 charter granted by Edward VI ceded greater power to the twenty-four aldermen of the council. These were a self-selecting oligarchy drawn from the mercantile elite, with names such as Stanihurst, Sedgrave, Ball, Plunkett and Sarsfield all prominent. These were some of the great 'Old English' families of the Pale, many of whom had benefited greatly from the dissolution of the monasteries.

Dublin's trade began to increase towards the end of the sixteenth century, with Chester and Bristol still key trading partners. Hides and textiles left Ireland, while cloth, metal and coal arrived from England. Ireland's internal markets were, however, disrupted in the second half of the sixteenth century in the course of conquest and colonisation; a period in which Dublin's development seems to have stalled.

'First, in the name of God, the Mayor, Sherrifs, Recorder and Aldermen, accompanied with the number of three hundred horse, and above, of the citizens, took their way out at the Dame's Gate, turning presently betwixte the Dame's Mills and the city walls, and so to the river side of [Annelyffy], riding directly eastward by the waterside to the Rings End, and from thence eastward to Clarade, otherwise called the Clear Road, and now called Poolbeg, and from thence to Ranelagh, now called the Barr Foote, where the trumpet sounding the company came together, and, according to the ancient usage, Richard Fitzsimons, one of the water bailiffs, was called upon and commanded to rise as far into the sea eastward from thence as he could, being then low water, and thence to cast a spear as far as he could into the seas, which he did, and so far extended the franchises of the south side of the river and harbour of Dublin.' – The beginning of the traditional ritual known as the riding of the franchises in 1603, in which the mayor and alderman rode around the city boundaries, symbolically reasserting their authority. J. T. Gilbert and Rosa Mulholland Gilbert, *Calendar of Ancient Records of Dublin* (1889–1922), vol. i, pp. 190–1.

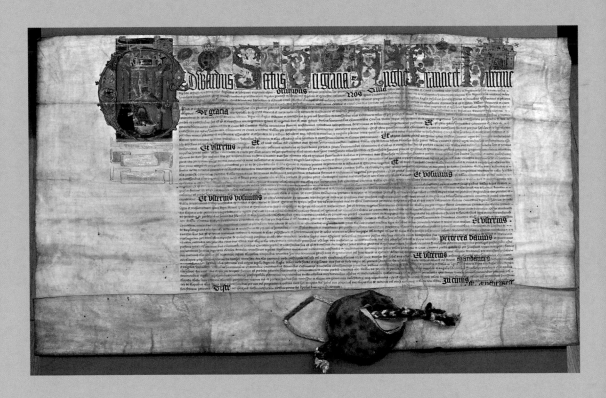

The charter granted to Dublin by Edward VI in 1548. (*Courtesy of Dublin City Library and Archive*)

in in regno nostro hist ine situati nobis ∞
rum sint Regum nram mutadere volen
os in omnibns exhibuerunt et patatos
s si nostros Ballim Communitas et cines

A depiction of a castle, from Edward VI's charter. This is broadly similar to the individual castles depicted on Henry VIII's charter, which may indicate a possible model. The flags are those of the Guild

In trading terms, Dublin was inferior to Drogheda, Waterford, Limerick and Galway, with a population of between 10,000 and 15,000. The Tudor conquests saw increasing arrivals of newcomers, and there was considerable concern about encroachment from the borderlands, increasing numbers of refugees on the outskirts and, of course, subversion from within. But Dublin benefited from the increasing involvement of the English authorities in Irish affairs, and the Elizabethan authorities consciously sought to foster trade; in 1577 Elizabeth issued a charter to the guild merchants, consolidating their power.

The rebellion spearheaded by James Eustace, Viscount Baltinglass, in the late 1570s and 1580s was important in many ways as the Catholic community of the Pale and Dublin came to be victimised by the authorities, often in a brutal manner. It was an indication that the traditional civic leadership of Dublin might yet be supplanted by the sectarianism that was becoming an increasingly significant part of Irish life. One of the more brutal instances of this repression came in 1584 when the Catholic archbishop of Cashel, Dermot O'Hurley, was tortured to death in Dublin Castle, using so-called hot boots (boots filled with oil that were placed into a fire). He was hanged by authority of martial law as part of the ongoing investigation into Catholic dissent in the Pale that stemmed directly from the Baltinglass Rebellion and its aftermath. Religious change was exemplified by the foundation of Trinity College on the site of the Augustinian Priory of All Hallows. The establishment of a new college was prompted in part by a desire to forestall the Irish going abroad for their education, which might lead to them being influenced by Catholicism. Equally, in some Irish quarters, the creation of this new college was viewed as simply creating another venue for teaching heresy. The college makes an appearance in the earliest existing map of Dublin, that of John Speed. Also appearing on that map is evidence of change, and indications of a dramatic event that may have prompted at least some of that change.

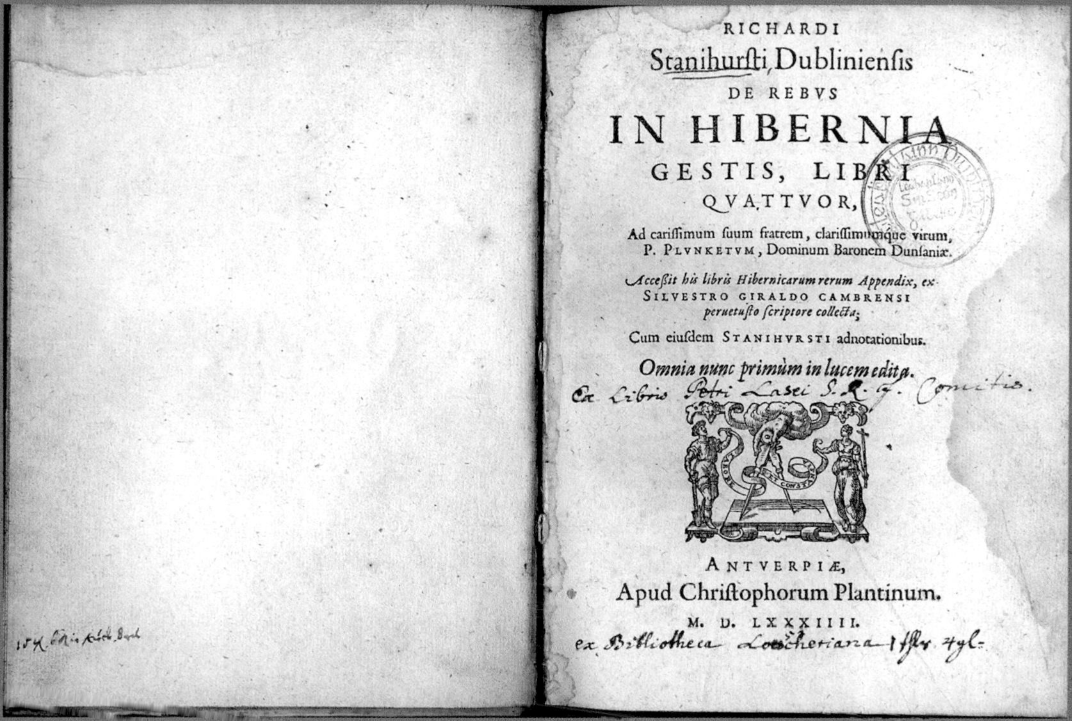

RICHARDI
Stanihursti, Dubliniensis
DE REBVS
IN HIBERNIA
GESTIS, LIBRI
QVATTVOR,

Ad carissimum suum fratrem, clarissimumque virum,
P. PLVNKETVM, Dominum Baronem Dunsaniæ.

Accessit his libris Hibernicarum rerum Appendix, ex
SILVESTRO GIRALDO CAMBRENSI
peruetusto scriptore collecta;

Cum eiusdem STANIHVRSTI adnotationibus.

Omnia nunc primùm in lucem edita.

ANTVERPIÆ,
Apud Christophorum Plantinum.
M. D. LXXXIIII.

Above: Richard Stanihurst's Latin history of Ireland, *De Rebus in Hibernis Gestis* (*Great deeds in Ireland*), written while he was in exile on the continent. Note his designation as 'Dubliniensis'; he came from a wealthy and established 'Old English' family in the city. (*Courtesy of Dublin City Library and Archive*)

Next pages: An image from John Derricke's The *Image of Ireland* (1580), which was written in praise of the Tudor viceroy Sir Henry Sidney. In this case, an English army departs from Dublin Castle; the spire of Christ Church can be seen in the top left-hand corner. (*National Library of Ireland*)

These trunckles heddes do playnly showe, eache rebeles fatall end,
And what a haynous crime it is, the Queene for to offend.

Although the theeues are plagued thus, by Princes trusty frendes,
And brought for their innormyties, to sondry wretched endes:
Yet may not that a warning be, to those they leaue behinde,
But needes their treasons must appeare, long kept in festred mynde.
Whereby the matter groweth at length, vnto a bloudy fielde,
Euen to the rebells ouerthrow, except the traytours yelde.

6

For he that gouernes Irishe foyle , prefenting there her grace,
Whofe fame made rebelles often flye , the prefence of his face:
He he I fay, he goeth forth , with Marfis noble trayne,
To iuftifie his Princes caufe , but their demenures bayne:
Thus Queene he will haue honored, in middeft of all her foes,
And knowne to be a royall Prince , euen in defpight of thofe.

The birth of the modern city

❧

1600-1730

I

On Christmas Eve 1592, Hugh Roe O'Donnell escaped from the Record Tower of Dublin Castle, having been kidnapped to guarantee his father's good behaviour. He and a number of others escaped by shimmying down a privy on a rope before travelling through the city, heading over the Wicklow Mountains in heavy snowfall to reach sanctuary at Glenmalure. Within a few years he was at war, and the outbreak of hostilities between Queen Elizabeth and Hugh O'Neill, the Earl of Tyrone – the 'Nine Years' War' – ensured that Dublin was a city on a war footing in the late 1590s. The city endured food shortages thanks to poor harvests and the presence of large numbers of troops; disease was also rampant. A force of forty nightwatchmen patrolled the walls, with another forty-four around the suburbs. Each household was to contribute at least one male member over sixteen to the watch, for a period at least; they were to be armed by the authorities. Taxes had been imposed upon the citizens to pay for these, along with repairs to the fortifications and supplies. These were largely to be directed at a potential enemy from outside. Soldiers were quartered in the city, from winter 1598 the gates were to be closed and locked at night, with the keys being given to the mayor, while by 1600 'suspicious' Irishmen entering the city were to be monitored and questioned.

To keep fighting, the English had to bring soldiers and weapons to Ireland, and they often arrived in Dublin. Because the Liffey was quite shallow and hard to navigate, smaller boats would bring the goods into the city from outlying ports such as Dalkey and Ringsend. This is what was happening on 11 March 1597, as barrels of gunpowder were being unloaded at Wood Quay. These would normally be taken away for safe keeping. But on that day, the dock workers refused to do this because they were unhappy at their low wages and bad working conditions. By the early afternoon of 11 March, there were 140 barrels of gunpowder sitting on the quays. At around 1 p.m. on a dry and windy day, they exploded. The damage was enormous: between twenty and forty houses were destroyed, with major damage in Cook Street, Fishamble Street and Bridge Street. The steeple of St Audoen's was badly damaged; there is a memorial to Stephen Sedgrave, the crane operator who was killed along with his family, in the church. The explosion caused the single greatest loss of life in Dublin's history: 126 were killed, fifty of whom were deemed 'strangers' to the city.

The cause of the explosion was never determined, but it was more likely to have been an accident than sabotage. The investigation revealed something, however. The barrels had been stacked on the quays in an unsafe way, as the labourers were on strike. The official in charge of the unloading, one John Allen, had absented himself from the scene before the explosion to go a merchant's house to 'drink a pot of ale'. But it seems that he had been prone to abusing and underpaying the casual labourers on the docks, hence the strike. Most of those labourers interviewed by the authorities in the course of their investigation had Irish names. Who were these Irishmen? Little is known about them other than their names, but they may well have been viewed with some hostility by the emerging British Protestant colonial order, and in turn, they may well have stood at odds to it themselves.

British colonialism, regardless of where it manifested itself, found expression in word and image as well as in deeds. John Speed, a tailor from Cheshire, took up cartography as a hobby and turned it into a career. In crude ideological terms, his *Theatre of the Empire of Great Britain* (1611) was imperialist propaganda, but in its desire to represent the dominions of the new British monarchy, it also contains the earliest surviving map of Dublin (though it is unclear whether or not Speed actually visited the city).

What does it reveal? It contains a great deal of detail about buildings, geographical features, earlier patterns of habitation and, by extension, processes of change. A close examination of the map reveals the city walls, the old castle, and the newer buildings on the north side of the River Liffey.

One can also make out the consequences of the 1597 explosion. Speed's map (see overleaf), dated 1610, suggests that the damage was not yet repaired; there are gaps between the buildings near the numbers 8 and 37 on the map, which presumably indicates the damage done by the explosion on 11 March 1597. But the map also indicates new expansion to the east. Did the reconstruction of the city after 1597 spill eastward over the walls, rather then being restricted to within their confines? At the right edge of the map is Trinity College. The buildings of the college are very different now, and today Trinity is in the city centre. But less than twenty years after its foundation it remained outside the city; after all, it was 'The college of the holy and undivided Trinity of Queen Elizabeth near Dublin'. Over the centuries, as Dublin expanded to the east, it slowly but surely swallowed up the college. Speed's map depicts the first buildings creeping eastwards, outside the old city walls. Significantly, it is not to scale; it suggests 600 houses within the wall and 300 outside. But the average width of the houses would have been 15–20 feet (4½–6 metres), a third of the sizes indicated on the map: could there have been as many as 1,800 houses within the walls? As for their residents, the population of Dublin in 1610 was anywhere between 5,000 and 20,000. Like so much else about this period, the precise details of life in the city remain uncertain.

II

In the early seventeenth century Dublin gradually reaped the benefits of the increasing power of the English state in Ireland. The viceroy, parliament, judiciary, commerce, finance and trade had all come to be centred in Dublin by the early seventeenth century, and by the 1640s the city's population was predominantly Protestant. This points to the increasing importance of religion, and religious division, in Irish life; and Dublin was not immune from this. Increasing tensions over religion, most especially with regard to relations between the government and the city's traditional Old English elite, could be discerned in the city in the first four decades of the seventeenth century. While the accession of James VI of Scotland as James I had been proclaimed at the High Cross near Christ Church on 5 April 1603 (with copious quantities of wine provided for

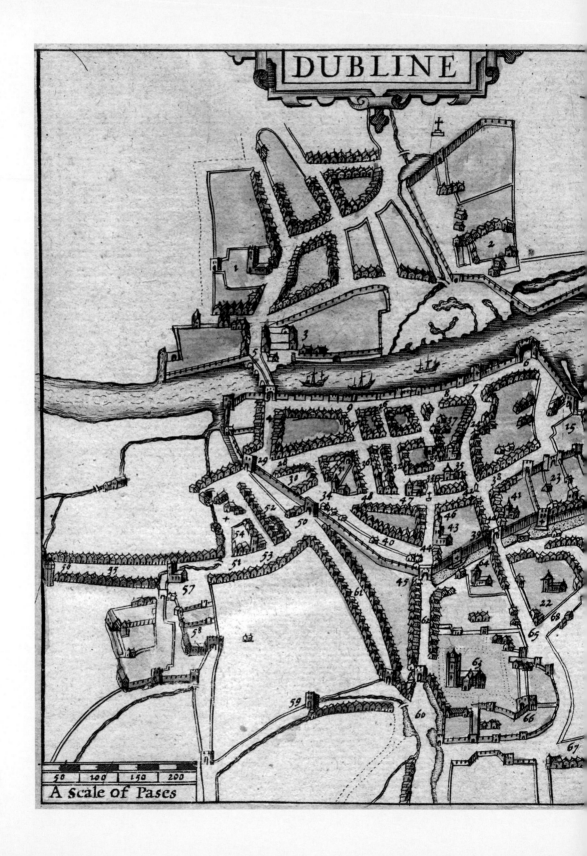

DUBLINE

A scale of Pases

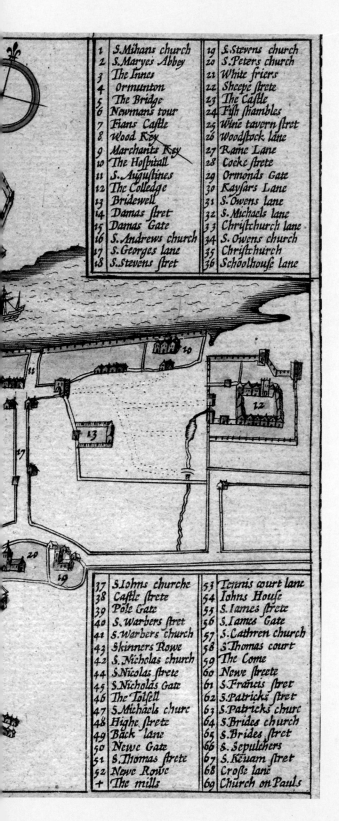

1	S.Mihans church	19	S.Stevens church
2	S.Maryes Abbey	20	S.Peters church
3	The Innes	21	White friers
4	Ormunton	22	Sheepe strete
5	The Bridge	23	The Castle
6	Newmans tour	24	Fish shambles
7	Fians Castle	25	Wine tavern stret
8	Wood Key	26	Woodstock lane
9	Marchants Key	27	Rame Lane
10	The Hospitall	28	Cocke strete
11	S.Augustines	29	Ormonds Gate
12	The Colledge	30	Kaysars Lane
13	Bridewell	31	S.Owens lane
14	Damas stret	32	S.Michaels lane
15	Damas Gate	33	Chrystchurch lane
16	S.Andrews church	34	S. Owens church
17	S.Georges lane	35	Christchurch
18	S.Stevens stret	36	Schoolhouse lane

37	S.Iohns churche	53	Tennis court lane
38	Castle strete	54	Iohns House
39	Pole Gate	55	S.Iames strete
40	S.Warbers stret	56	S.Iames Gate
41	S.Warbers church	57	S.Cathren church
43	Skinners Rowe	58	S.Thomas court
42	S.Nicholas church	59	The Come
44	S.Nicolas strete	60	Newe streete
45	S.Nicholas Gate	61	S.Francis stret
46	The Tolsell	62	S.Patricks stret
47	S.Michaels churc	63	S.Patricks churc
48	Highe strete	64	S.Brides church
49	Back lane	65	S.Brides stret
50	Newe Gate	66	S. Sepulchers
51	S.Thomas strete	67	S.Keuan stret
52	Newe Rowe	68	Crosse lane
+	The mills	69	Church on Pauls

The first map of Dublin: a hand-coloured version of John Speed's representation of the city. The numbers, and the key to the numbers, on the right of the map indicate that a lot of these place names are still in existence today, such as Mary's Abbey, Wood Quay, Back Lane and Winetavern Street. Some of them have changed: Sheep Street was now called Ship Street; beside it can be seen the last remnant of the original pool. (*Courtesy of Dublin City Library and Archive, Map Collection*)

the occasion by the city authorities), it was unclear whether or not the king's Catholic heritage would cause his government in Dublin to show at least some favour towards the old faith. The answer, especially after the crisis of the attempted assassination of James I in London in 1605, the so-called Gunpowder Plot, was to be a resounding no. This had implications, first and foremost, for the elite who governed the city. The holder of the office of mayor was drawn, on a rotating basis, from the ranks of the twenty-four aldermen (who were chosen for life from among the commercial elite, and who met in the Tholsel every Friday). But the office was declined with increasing frequency in the early decades of the century, due to the requirement that the incumbent swear the oath of supremacy, recognising the king as head of the Church. Dublin's civic leaders were generally Catholics who declined to attend the services of the Church of Ireland; they were naturally willing to facilitate Catholic worship discreetly. But the crackdown that followed the events of 1605 in London left Dublin's Catholic community under no illusion that the reformed faith was now the new, and official, dispensation, especially during the tenure of Lord Deputy Arthur Chichester, whose grandiose mansion on Hoggen Green later housed the Irish parliament. Sectarian tensions could be seen in disturbances such as a disputed election to parliament in April 1613, when the election of two Catholics was voided by the Protestant mayor, James Carroll. A second election saw an attempt to pack the vote with unfree citizens who normally could not vote, and which resulted in unseemly scuffles in the Tholsel. It boded ill for the political future of Dublin's traditional rulers.

While early seventeenth-century Dublin remains largely obscure, we get some glimpses of it in the accounts of contemporary visitors. In 1610 the former Elizabethan soldier Barnaby Rich, who had settled in Dublin, complained of the simmering hostility directed at soldiers and officials of the Crown, and profiteering, for 'they sell their drink in Dublin at double the rate that they do in London: and this commodity the aldermens wives and the rest of the women brewers do find so sweet, that master Mayor and his brethren are willing to wink at, and to tolerate those multitude of alehouses that themselves do even know to be the very nurseries of drunkenness … and many other vile abominations.'

The city in which such complaints were grounded was undergoing significant changes to its physical fabric. In 1599 one George Burroes was granted a lease on a substantial site near Hawkins Street to make bricks, which were used with increasing frequency in the early seventeenth century (unfortunately, virtually no structures remain from this era, though the impressive Boyle monument in St Patrick's Cathedral, erected by Richard Boyle, Earl of Cork, is a notable exception indoors). Cold weather in the early modern period led to greater risks of fire, and building in brick was a natural preventive measure. Thatch was banned in the suburbs in 1610, and by 1616 every fifth house was ordered to have lighting from 6 to 9 p.m. from 'Hallowtide' to 'Candlemas'. Darkness, after all, brought danger and mischief.

Dublin remained a modest-sized city, especially when compared to its British counterparts. For the Munster judge Luke Gernon, writing in 1620, Dublin was, of Irish towns, 'the most frequented, more for convenience than for majesty', given that this was where the lord deputy and council were based: a telling indication of the city's increasing importance as an administrative centre. But 'the buildings are of timber and of the English form, and it is resembled to Bristol, but falleth short'; perhaps an indication that elements of the medieval urban landscape were still to be seen in 1620?

Flashes of discontent survive; for example, the execution of the Catholic Bishop Cornelius O'Devanny in Arbour Hill in 1612 for allegedly conspiring with the exiled

'Before and during the reigns of Henry VIII, Edward VI, Mary and Elizabeth, most of the buildings for habitation here were of the cage work fashion, and only castles, towers, churches, monasteries, and other buildings appropriated to religious or charitable uses, were built of lime and stone ... In the reign of James I, upon the settlement of the nation after the rebellion of the Earl of Tyrone, the inhabitants of Dublin began to build their houses of lime, stone, or brick, and to cover them with slates of tiles, after a more elegant and convenient form than the cage-work houses before mentioned.' – John Warburton, James Whitelaw & Robert Walsh, *History of the City of Dublin: From the Earliest Accounts to the Present Time* (London, 1818), vol. i, pp. 78–9.

Earl of Tyrone saw Catholic citizens lining the route to the place of execution lamenting his fate. The gallows were ransacked for relics after the execution and became the site of masses on the night of his death, all accompanied by what one observer described as a 'heathenish howling'. While Catholicism had undergone something of a revival after the accession of Charles I in 1625, there were limits to official tolerance. The Old English of Dublin had strong links to Irish colleges on the continent, and another official crackdown took place in 1629, prompted by the prospect of a Jesuit college being established in Back Lane. The authorities were authorised to suppress Catholic activities in Dublin in April 1629. Yet this could be, and was, resisted at times. On 26 December 1629, during a raid on a Franciscan chapel in a house in Cook Street (led by the mayor, Christopher Gorster, and the archbishop of Dublin, Lancelot Bulkeley), soldiers tore down the altar, defaced images and seized paraphernalia such as vestments. They were driven out when the congregation, led by the 'Widow Nugent', turned on them. Matters got worse as the officials and soldiers were confronted outside by a group of pilgrims – this was St Stephen's Day – en route to the saint's traditional holy well, who began to stone them and pelted them with 'the durt of the kennel'. The bishop was forced to take refuge in nearby Skinner's Row and some of those involved (including Elinor Nugent, the 'widow' in question) were subsequently imprisoned.

In July 1635 William Brereton, who later served as a general in the parliamentarian army, visited Dublin and noted his impressions. Dublin was 'the metropolis of the Kingdom of Ireland, and is well beyond all expectation the fairest, richest, best built city I have met with in this journey', apart from York and Newcastle; it even surpassed Edinburgh. He noted the lack of shelter and the treacherous course of the Liffey, saying that most ships anchored at Ringsend, and that Howth Head was sometimes used for shelter. He counted thirteen churches, with St Patrick's pre-eminent, and mentions that James Ussher (the most senior cleric of the Church of Ireland, as archbishop of Armagh) still preached in St Audoen's, the parish of his birth. He was dismissive of the parliament house (Chichester House on College Green), and noted that the castle had guns mounted on its towers and battlements.

Brereton was looking at a city that had grown since Luke Gernon had dismissed it fifteen years earlier. By the 1630s Dublin's mercantile community was more powerful, but their wealth and status was based on the evolution of the city's role and status. Dublin was not yet foremost among Irish trading ports: Drogheda was more important for cross-channel trade, as were Galway and Waterford for European trade. But Dublin had, in the early seventeenth century, become the major port for *imports* into Ireland. (One unwelcome import was feared, however: Dublin was racked by outbreaks of plague in 1603–1605; and in August 1603 the city water bailiffs had been ordered to patrol the river to prevent the landing of English goods, which were presumably seen to be carrying more than they should.) Dublin had little in the way of an indigenous shipping fleet; most of the trade was carried out by foreign vessels. Indeed, among many immigrants to the city prior to the 1640s was a small but vibrant community of a few dozen merchants from Holland and Flanders. The Dublin merchants benefited from the upsurge in imports as agents, as the city benefited from the improved infrastructure of colonial Ireland; the construction of the first custom house, between Dame Street and the Liffey, pointed towards this growing trade. And with it came wealth: large numbers of craftsman and tradesmen seem to have been present in Dublin in the years prior to 1641, possibly indicating a level of economic growth, wealth and business that would be dramatically cut short by the chaos that erupted in the winter of 1641.

III

In October 1641 one Owen Connolly (or O'Connolly) revealed details of a plot by the Irish to rise up against the English who had conquered them. Connolly heard the details of this plot in an inn in Winetavern Street, and having left to go to the lodgings of one of the conspirators, he stopped and pretended to urinate, instead slipping away

'He (the examinant) came to Dublin about 6 of the clock this evening and forthwith went to the lodging of the said Hugh to the house near the boot in Oxmantown, and there he found the said Hugh and came with him into the town near the pillory to the lodging of the Lord Maguire, where they found not the lord within and there they drank a cup of beer and then went back to the said Hugh's lodging. He saith that at the said Maguires lodging the said Hugh told him that there were and would be this night great numbers of noblemen and gentlemen of the Irish and Papists from all parts of the kingdom in this town, who with himself had determined to take the castle of Dublin and possess themselves of all of his majesty's ammunition there tomorrow being Saturday, and that they intended first to batter the chimnies of the town and if the city would not yield then to batter the houses, and to cut off all the Protestants that would not join with them.' – The testimony of Owen O'Connolly, cited in Mary Hickson, *Ireland in the Seventeenth Century* (London, 1884), vol. i, p. 367.

'Thus was the town within the compass of the few days after the breaking out of this rebellion filled with the most lamentable spectacles of sorrow, which in great numbers wandered up and down in all parts of the city, desolate, forsaken, having no place to lay their heads on, no clothing to cover their nakedness, no food to fill their hungry bellies. And to add to their miseries, they found all manner of relief very disproportionable to their wants, the Popish inhabitants refusing to minister the least comfort unto them: so as those sad creatures appeared like living ghosts in every street.' – John Temple, *The Irish Rebellion: or, a history of the beginnings and first progress of the general rebellion raised in the kingdom of Ireland ... in the year 1641* (London, 1646), p. 62.

to alert William Parsons, one of the lord justices (the senior officials who governed in the absence of viceroys) at his lodgings on Merchants Quay.

The rebellion that Connolly spoke of did not break out in Dublin, but it erupted in Ulster within a matter of days when Catholic insurgents launched attacks on Protestant settlers, who responded in kind. Over the next weeks and months brutal sectarian warfare began to spread across Ireland as a whole. Dublin had a population of perhaps 20,000 in 1641, but this was soon swollen by Protestant refugees escaping the rebellion elsewhere (and often having their testimonies recorded before they departed); those who could not escape Ireland remained in Dublin over the coming months and years, and many died there.

The government in Dublin, led at this time by officials such as Parsons and John Borlase, held its fire until reinforcements arrived in December, after which they embarked on brutal campaigns within Dublin's hinterland. The traditional Catholicism of the Palesmen rendered them suspect and prompted the government's assault on the 'Old English'; Parsons, Borlase and their colleague John Temple (whose family later gave their name to Temple Bar) were zealously Protestant. With the subsequent formation of the Confederate Association, based in Kilkenny, to defend Catholics from the depredations of the government and its forces, and the descent into countrywide warfare that ensued, Dublin was cut off from much of the rest of Ireland, as the city's dwindling food supplies were augmented by fish and grain imports from Britain and Holland. There were attempts to erect an earthen rampart of sorts around the city by way of fortification; the city's defences had deteriorated drastically in the early seventeenth century, when many of the remaining medieval fortifications were eroded or rendered redundant by the city's expansion. Houses outside the perimeters of the old walls, however, would be destroyed throughout the 1640s.

Irish politics in the 1640s loosely mirrored the divisions of the British Civil War that had erupted at around the same time, though with crucial sectarian differences. Dublin remained a Protestant royalist (later parliamentarian) enclave throughout this decade. An attempted confederate siege was abandoned due to low supplies in 1646, but in early 1647 the royalist viceroy James Butler, Earl of Ormond (the Protestant scion of a traditionally Catholic dynasty of Norman descent originally based in Kilkenny) surrendered Dublin to the forces of the English parliament (rather than the confederates, despite their willingness to negotiate with King Charles II). Catholics began to be expelled from Dublin by the new parliamentarian authorities (many had already departed the city, whose population shrank below 9,000 in the 1640s). Ormond, however, returned at the head of an army in 1649. He intended to recapture the city, but in the Battle of Rathmines in August 1649 (which took place somewhere between modern Rathgar and Baggot Street) his forces were defeated by those loyal to the English parliament, which in turn paved the way for the arrival of Oliver Cromwell at Ringsend with 20,000 troops in the same month. And, to paraphrase one Catholic bishop, he passed through the land like lightning. Following Cromwell's devastating campaigns, by 1653 the parliamentarian army had defeated the remaining confederate and royalist resistance in Ireland.

Dublin in the 1650s was not in danger of attack, but it was stricken by shortages, disease, and fears of war returning. New Protestant faiths took root in the city: Presbyterians, Independents, Baptists – congregations whose members had emerged from the ranks of the Cromwellian army and enjoyed varying degrees of political support from the new regime though the stern discipline of parliament's New Model Army may have spared Dublin from the traditional excesses of soldiers. Throughout the 1650s, fear of Catholics (and even of the Irish language, which was often suspected of masking sedition) remained constant among the authorities and presumably many

'A high court of justice was erected in Dublin by the commissioner of the parliament, for the trials of such as were accused of the barbarous murders committed by the papists in the rebellion, in which Sir Phelim O'Neill and others were condemned and executed.' – Walter Harris, *The History and Antiquities of the City of Dublin, from the Earliest Accounts* (Dublin, 1766), p. 339.

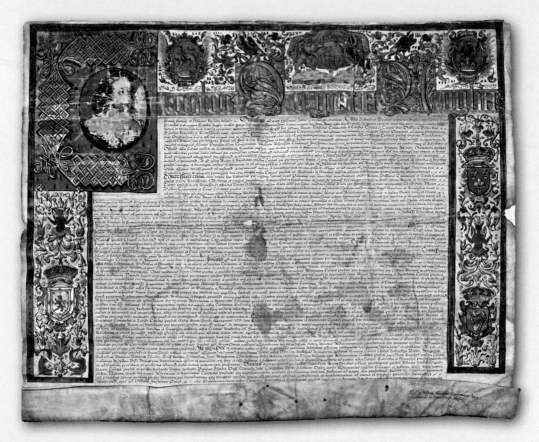

Charles I's charter to the city, dated 29 July 1641, which created the titles of Lord Mayor and Lady Mayoress; the civil wars and interregnum ensured that the provisions of the charter were not introduced until 1665. Note how the image of the king on the top left-hand corner has been defaced, possibly by parliamentarian supporters or officials. (*Courtesy of Dublin City Library and Archive*)

Protestant inhabitants, despite attempts to purge the town of both the Catholic clergy and Catholic laity, but the city retained an 'Irish' population. It was hoped that immigrant tradesmen might replace Catholics, which led to the extension of civic freedoms to many new arrivals from Britain and the continent under the commonwealth. One consequences was the increased prominence of a number of Dutch merchant families such as the Verscoyles and Westenras, who were sustained by international links: while they had been present in Dublin prior to the 1640s, they emerged as challengers to the traditional oligarchies in the 1650s. (Dublin had four Dutch lord mayors in the mid- to late seventeenth century.)

IV

After Cromwell's death in 1658 his regime slowly began to unravel, and in May 1660 Charles II succeeded his late father as king of England, Ireland and Scotland, restoring the Stuart monarchy. But the events that led to this began in Dublin, when in December 1659 a group of army officers seized control of Dublin Castle and overthrew the government there within two hours. These men knew that the days of the Cromwellian regime were numbered, and they struck first to preserve themselves should the monarchy be restored, as indeed it was. Having fought for parliament, they sought to avoid being called to account for their actions, and they especially wanted to maintain the huge gains they and others had made from massive confiscations of Catholic-owned land throughout the 1650s, which had been transferred into the hands of a newer, and supposedly loyal, Protestant elite. Dublin had become a disputed

'The defendant being found guilty of neglect of duty, it was ordered that he should ride the wooden horse for the space of an hour at Cornmarket with two muskets at each heel, and that he should carry the wooden horse from the main guard to the place where he is to ride as above said.' – A Cromwellian soldier in Dublin, John Baydon, falls foul of the severe internal discipline of the New Model Army in June 1652. The 'wooden horse' was a form of hurdle that the victim straddled, with one leg on each side; the muskets added weight to pull the victim down onto it, to maximise pain and discomfort. Heather MacLean, Ian Gentles and Micheál Ó Siochrú, 'Minutes of courts martial held in Dublin in the years 1651–3', *Archivium Hibernicum*, 64 (2011), 109.

and beleaguered bridgehead for much of the 1640s and 1650s, but the second half of the seventeenth century would see the city expand at an unprecedented rate. The foundations of the city that came to exist outside the limits of the old medieval walls were laid in the 1660s.

In 1660 the old order was restored. In May of that year the lord justices, the mayor and aldermen embarked on a ceremonial procession on horseback that ended at Dublin Castle to mark the Restoration of the English monarchy under Charles II (traditional official ceremonies such as the riding of the franchises continued in the reign of the new king). In 1661, St Patrick's Cathedral hosted a mass consecration of bishops of the established Church of Ireland. In 1662, grandiose ceremonials welcomed the return of Ormond to Dublin (now further ennobled as the first Duke of Ormond), who served again as viceroy between 1662 and 1669. He was the most powerful and influential nobleman in Ireland, occupying the most powerful and influential office in the country, and, following his return to Dublin in appropriately splendid style after an extended sojourn in exile on the continent, he apparently favoured the creation of an appropriately splendid capital city.

Dublin in the early years of the Restoration had perhaps 10,000 inhabitants (largely of English extraction), and still retained some of its medieval features. Many of the old gates and sections of the walls remained substantially intact, if not necessarily fit for purpose. Both public and private development left its mark on the city in this era, in what proved to be a time of unprecedented and remarkable growth. The demographic and physical expansion of Dublin after 1660 easily outstripped that of the rest of Ireland. The population of the city began to grow in the years after 1660, and was swollen by an influx of newly returned exiles who had fled Ireland during and after the 1640s. The population would continue to increase, and not purely from within.

During this period, the physical structure of the city began to be transformed. Dublin had long outgrown its medieval centre – while wealth was retained in the old city, the outer edges were scattered with cabins and the dwellings of the poor – but now it continued to expand both north and south of the (admittedly filthy) River Liffey. Private speculation and development began in earnest, with two developers in particular leaving a lasting imprint. The MP and government official Francis Aungier began to develop property that he owned to the south and east of Dublin Castle on former monastic land belonging to the Cistercian precinct of Whitefriars; the street that bears his family name was laid out in the 1660s. Of greater significance was the development by Sir Humphrey Jervis, who made his fortune as a merchant before becoming an alderman and property developer, in this case, on land formerly belonging to St Mary's Abbey, which caused the city to spill over onto the north banks of the Liffey. The quays themselves were redeveloped in earnest from the 1670s by figures such as Christopher Usher, as the Liffey slowly became the spine of an expanding city rather than a maritime routeway adjacent to it. Jervis was a key figure, as the growth of his new estates necessitated the construction of new bridges to get from one side of the Liffey to the other. There was one bridge across the river prior to 1670. The construction of a second bridge attracted the ire of ferrymen who perceived it as a threat; affrays that arose from their abortive attempt to destroy it (during which a number of apprentices were killed) saw the new crossing christened 'Bloody Bridge'. More bridges would follow, which had a major long-term impact on the growth of the city: bridges imposed restrictions on access to shipping traffic, which began to be pushed further eastward, in what proved to be an enduring pattern. The traditional east–west axis of the city south of the river would give to way to the river itself as the key geographical division, as Dublin expanded to the north and the west.

'Though the wind was full west, yet the fire gained so much towards Bermingham's tower where the records are kept, I ordered the blowing up that part of the building that joined to the chapel's, which had so good effect that we then mastered the fire, which without all peradventure was first occasioned by a piece of timber that lay under part of the hearth of that closet, as we conjectured upon looking on the ruins, and I believed had been on fire some considerable time before, though nobody perceived or smelt anything of burning. I thank God nobody has been killed or hurt upon this occasion. What damage your grace and I have suffered by this accident I cannot yet learn, but I find the King has lost nothing except six barrels of gunpowder, and the worst castle in the worst situation in Christendom, for his majesty's goods are saved from the fire, and for the value of the ground it stood upon, and the land belonging to it, his majesty may have a noble palace built, and I believed there are a hundred projectors at work already about framing proposals.' – Richard Butler, Earl of Arran, informs his father Ormond of the destruction of Dublin Castle in April 1684. *Historical Manuscripts Commission: Calendar of the Manuscripts of the Marquess of Ormonde* (London, 1902–20), vol. vii, p. 218–19.

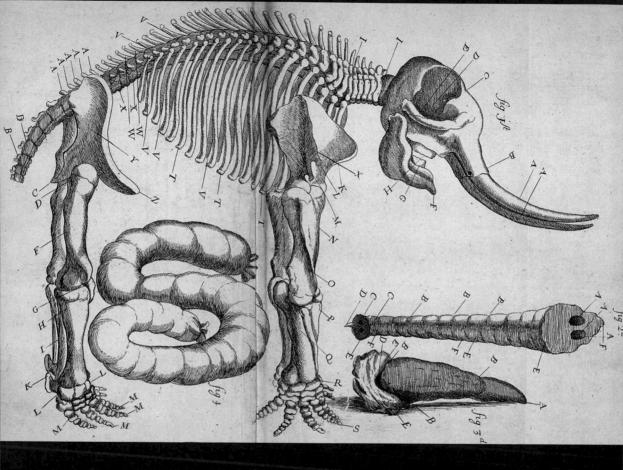

Alan Mullen's anatomical drawing of an elephant that had been on display in the vicinity of Parliament Street, but which was killed in a fire in 1681. According to Mullen, 'The circumstances of time and place were unfortunate, for the booth wherein the elephant was kept, took fire about three a clock in the morning, on Friday the 17th of June; upon this the city being alarmed, multitudes were gathered about the place: and when the fire was extinguished every one endeavoured to procure some part of the elephant, few of them having seen him living, by reason of the great rates put upon the sight of him' (*An Anatomical Account of the Elephant Accidentally Burnt in Dublin, on Friday, June 17 in the Year 1681* (London, 1682)). Mullen, sensing an opportunity, managed to persuade the elephant's 'manager' to let him examine the corpse. Apparently there was a tavern called the Elephant on Parliament Street until about 1770. (*Marsh's Library, Dublin*)

Street names bear testament to the public development and private speculation of the Restoration period: Aungier Street, Jervis Street, Capel Street, Ormond Quay, Arran Quay and Temple Bar. Smithfield (north of the Liffey near Oxmantown) and Newmarket (south of the Liffey near the Liberties) were laid out as new marketplaces in the 1660s and 1670s respectively, in order to move livestock markets out of the city centre. With the levelling of the old Viking Thingmount on Hoggen Green in 1681, the basis was laid for what would eventually become College Green. The 1660s had also seen the mapping out of St Stephen's Green on the south-east boundary of the city, partly in an effort to raise money by the cash-strapped corporation through opening up common land to private enterprise (though the eventual development of St Stephen's Green was to use brick and stone, lest Dublin experience its own version of the Great Fire of London). The green became a major promenade, another form of leisure in a city that had reacquired a theatre (Smock Alley) as early as 1662 and which by 1685 had over ninety breweries catering to nearly 1,200 alehouses and taverns.

Then there were the official projects that could magnify the presumed splendour of Ireland's rulers. Phoenix Park to the north-west was laid out as a royal demesne and deer park, though it narrowly avoided being pawned off on one of Charles II's mistresses in the early 1670s. Across from the park, on the south side of the river, was an area far removed from the fumes and industry of the city; and it was here, partly for the sake of the clean air, that the first of Dublin's great public buildings was erected between 1680 and 1684: the massive classical edifice of the Royal Hospital Kilmainham, built as a rest home for elderly soldiers, and inspired by Les Invalides in Paris. Ormond, who served as viceroy yet again between 1677 and 1684, oversaw its completion, and his coat of arms adorns the building. The actual administration of Dublin itself remained in the hands of the ancient corporation, remodelled in 1672 and meeting in the now-vanished Tholsel beside Christ Church Cathedral.

The Tholsel had been reconstructed between 1676 and 1685, complete with statues of the Stuart monarchs (which survive today in the crypt of Christ Church) and a clock tower (there had been a clock on the original building since 1466 which, along with church bells, informed Dubliners of the time). The formal post of lord mayor had been adopted in 1665, and the mayor, aldermen, sheriffs and guilds would seek to avoid numerous attempts to clip their wings and restrict their power throughout the Restoration; the 1670s was marked by running battles between the corporation and the government, as the latter sought to exert control over the former. But usually the corporation was concerned with more mundane realities: lighting, sanitation and even the traffic problems caused by the excessive number of hackneys (taxis) in the city.

appeare the sume of fifteene Guinyes

The Accomptant prayeth tobe allowed severall
Sumes of Money that was paid by him for the feast or
Entertainment made for his Grace the Duke of Ormond
& the Nobility & Gentry att the Thollsell after the same
had beene built new, And the particullars are as
followeth   (Vizt)

Paid Mr Baptist for Wine on that Occasion as appears by the bill
By the bill of particullars attested and allowed by ye
Comittee appointed by Act of Assembly to that purpose   } 34 : 04 : 00
and acquittance of the said Mr Baptist the sume of

Paid Mr William Ellcock for Wine on that occasion as
appeares by the bill attested by the Comittee aforesd being   } 10 : 00 : 00
22 Dozen bottles of Cahors Wine & the said Ellcocks acqt
thereupon appeares ——

Paid Mr Samuell Browne for Glasses &c Delivered
upon occasion of the feast given his Grace the Duke
of Ormond at the Thollsell as appeares by the bill   } 02 : 10 : 00
of particullars attested & allowed by the Comittee
aforesaid & the said Brownes acquittance appers

Paid William Hawkes the Lord Mayors Butler for
a silver spoone lost, and sweet water &c as ye bill of   } 01 : 10 : 00
particullars attested by the Comittee aforesaid & the
acquittance of the said Hawkes the sume of ——

Paid Richard Charter to be paid by him to Cookes &
Labourers as ye bill of particullars attested by the   } 30 : 15 : 00
Comittee aforesaid & the acquittance of the said
Charter the sume of ——

The bill for the entertainment hosted by the Duke of Ormond on the reopening of the Tholsel in 1676. (*Courtesy of Dublin City Library and Archive*)

THE THOLSEL

The reconstructed Tholsel, forerunner of the modern City Hall, as depicted by Charles Brookings in 1728. It was rebuilt between 1676 and 1685 in ornate style, complete with a clock tower. The statues of the Stuart monarchs that can be seen above the central arch have survived, and are held in the crypt of Christ Church Cathedral. (*Courtesy of Dublin City Library and Archive*)

St Patrick's Cathedral, as depicted by James Malton in the late eighteenth century. It was established in 1191 as a collegiate church, though the structure Malton sketched had been rebuilt in the fourteenth century. Note the early modern house style known as 'Dutch Billies', with their distinctive gables, to the left. Their design was often credited to continental immigrants, hence the name, which referenced William of Orange. Some relatively humble buildings can also be seen on either side of the cathedral. (*National Library of Ireland*)

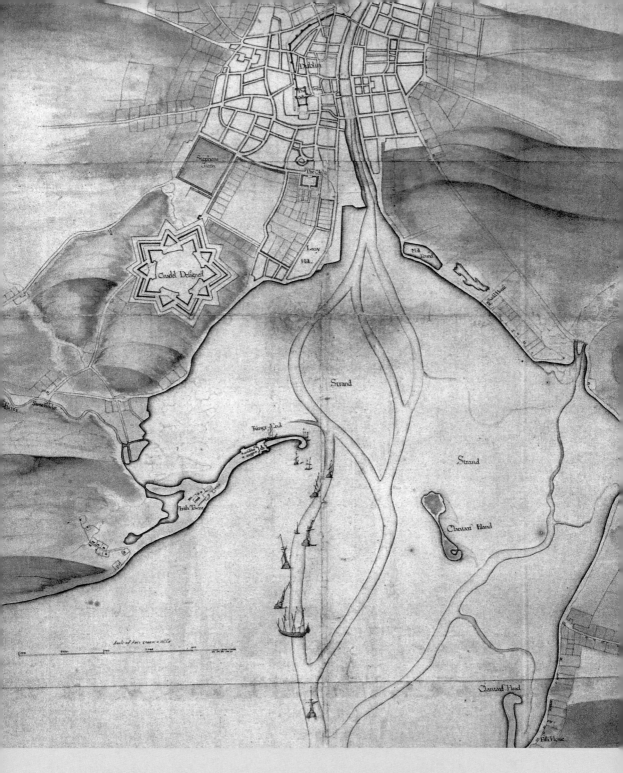

Thomas Philip's 1685 map of Dublin, which gives a sense of the growth that had taken place since 1660 beyond the boundaries of the old city walls. It was commissioned to give an indication of the defences that might be required to safeguard the city at a time of increasing international tension; hence the inclusion of a massive star-shaped fort to the south-east of the city, which was never constructed. (*Courtesy of Dublin City Library and Archive*)

'Newgate stands about the south point of the city. This is the city gaol or common house of correction, where the prisoners howl in the most hideous manner, when any coach or gentry pass through the same, like a den of wolves; and the poor women sing their ah! hone!, a hone [sic] with such a doleful sweetness, that it forces compassion from those who pass by. The way from Patrick Street to this gate is through Francis Street, beyond which southwards lies another large street called the Coombe, in which two streets all the worsted-spinners, weaver and mercers, who sell druggets and other Dublin stuffs (the chief manufacture of the town) do chiefly inhabit, who are generally nonconformists. These two streets lead into Thomas Street, the longest suburbs about all the city, which reacheth from Newgate to Kilmainham Hospital, about a mile long ... This is the longest and widest street about all the city. Kilmainham prison for the count [sic] stands at the foot of this street and close by the sessions house. The low end of the street is furnished every Wednesday and Saturday with kishes [sic] of Idough [Kilkenny] coals, peats, whins (which they call furs) and other fuel; the middle of the street with hay, straw, grass, herbs and salads according to the season; and a little higher is the corn market for all manner of grain, meal, malt; and in a cross street leading from Newgate to Ormond's gate, called New Row, where there is a market for leather, shoes, milk, both sweet and sour (for churned milk, which they call bony clabber, is the chief food of the common people both in the city and country). Within the gatesteed [sic] at Newgate seamsters sell all ordinary and course linen and lace. This gate opens to the High Street, where there is a stocking market every day in the week, as high as the end of Back Lane, which leads to St Nicholas Lane, a place inhabited by gentlemen of the long robe, chancery clerks and attorneys.' – Thomas Denton's account of the heart of the old city from a visit in the late 1680s. Angus J.L. Winter & Mary Wane (eds), *Thomas Denton: A Perambulation of Cumberland, 1687–1688, Including Descriptions of Westmoreland, the Isle of Man and Ireland* (Woodbridge, 2003), pp. 535–6.

Dublin's growth in the Restoration era was driven by its status as a national capital. The city was a hub: the main port and centre of finance, the seat of parliament (although it only met between 1661 and 1666 during this era) and the judiciary. Its proximity to Britain proved advantageous; Dublin in the 1660s accounted for as much as 40 cent of Ireland's total customs revenue, and the city developed into a major manufacturing base (especially for textiles) as industrial growth began in the ancient liberties to the south-west of the city, outside the medieval walls. Textiles were exported to Britain, with goods such as timber, wine, salt and spices being imported from the continent, with France and Spain being key sources. Dutch merchants remained prominent players in Dublin's overseas trade, possibly due to their vessels being more suited to the difficult conditions of Dublin Bay.

Urban expansion gave a renewed focus to distinct areas of the city that served, or would come to serve, specific purposes. The Liberties, for instance, became indelibly associated with the textile industry. From medieval times the area was extremely well irrigated by watercourses deriving from the Dodder and Poddle; the industries that would eventually set up here were industries requiring water. The location was agricultural land that became prime investment property in the late seventeenth century. The building boom saw the power of guilds associated with the building trade expand. An important addition to the area was a marketplace: Newmarket. The market itself was primarily agricultural, and was surrounded by 'Dutch Billies'; all have now been cleared away. This architectural style was brought by Northern European immigrants encouraged to settle here by William Brabazon, Earl of Meath, whose family acquired land here after the dissolution of the monasteries in the sixteenth century.

V

Dublin in 1685 was the largest town or city in Ireland, and second only to London in Britain and Ireland as a whole, with a population between 40,000 and 60,000, and a recognisable street plan bounded to the south-west by Trinity College and St Stephen's Green. The idea of refortifying the city had been floated during the Anglo-Dutch conflict of the 1670s, and was suggested again in 1681 amidst fears of either a Catholic rebellion or a French invasion. The contentious question of religion inevitably remained an issue in Restoration Dublin, as Catholics were slowly excluded from civic politics, and were eventually barred from being freemen of the city. Even Ormond became the subject of allegations at the height of the so-called Popish Plot in England, claiming that he indulged in late-night card games in the castle with members of the remaining Catholic gentry, rumours that were readily interpreted as being the prelude to a potential Catholic uprising. The ongoing commemorations of the outbreak of the 1641 rebellion on 23 October (and, indeed, the anniversary of the Gunpowder Plot on 5 November) by Protestants were a regular cause of sectarian conflict. The public and raucous nature of the celebrations – complete with bonfires, processions, and large quantities of drink – made them a perennial flashpoint, as they provoked a Catholic reaction.

This intensified under the Jacobite regime after 1685. The Catholic counter-revolution that followed the accession of James II to the thrones of England, Ireland and Scotland in 1685 was felt in the city. James himself was welcomed to Dublin in 1689, and Christ Church was converted to Catholic worship under a new dean, Alexius Stafford, who was later killed at the Battle of Aughrim; he had been forced to use wooden candlesticks after the cathedral plate was hidden.

The outbreak of full-blown war between James and his Dutch Protestant son-in-law William, who had already replaced him as the king of England (James was still legally king of Ireland), threatened to bring havoc to the capital city. Many of its wealthier Protestant inhabitants went into temporary exile in England to avoid the sectarian war they feared. Trinity College was used as a Jacobite prison, though its Catholic provost, Michael Moore, saved the library from the depredations of the Jacobite army. Little was done to defend the city against Williamite attack, though James was reportedly opposed to a suggestion by his French allies that the city be burned in the event of a Jacobite retreat.

In the end, when James and his followers abandoned Dublin, they did so rapidly after the Battle of the Boyne in July 1690. Arriving in Dublin on 5 July 1690, days after the battle, William was greeted rapturously by Dublin's Protestants, who viewed him as their saviour from destruction at Catholic hands. The chair that William supposedly sat in while attending a thanksgiving ceremony in St Patrick's Cathedral still remains there. On 4 November 1690 his birthday was celebrated rapturously in Dublin, with

'The day observed for the Irish Rebellion [23 October] was kept by some as formerly with making of bonfires and a certain number of soldiers going about and taking upon them to rebuke and chastise the authors were severely beaten about Nicholas Street, but on the Coombe the soldiers killed one or two tradesmen, upon which bonfires were forbid this day and for the future.' – An account of how conflict on a Dublin street in October 1687 prompted the banning of bonfires to mark the anniversary of the Gunpowder Plot on 5 November lest these be a flashpoint as well. Patrick Melvin, 'Letters of Lord Longford and others on Irish affairs, 1689–1702', *Analecta Hibernica*, 32 (1985), 40.

James II's 1687 charter, appointing his supporters, including Catholics, Anglicans, Presbyterians and Quakers, to the Dublin City Assembly. The crest on the left (top), is that of Richard Talbot, Earl of Tyrconnell, his Catholic viceroy from an Old English family near Dublin. He had long been a hate figure for Irish Protestants, who suspected him (with some justification) of seeking to roll back their relatively privileged position in favour of Catholics. (*Courtesy of Dublin City Library and Archive*)

A contemporary German pamphlet recording the Williamite victory at the Battle of the Boyne in July 1690, complete with a map of Dublin clearly based on that of John Speed. (*Library of Congress*)

a procession of troops and horse, pageantry, fireworks, bonfires and bells, and with copious quantities of wine being distributed to the citizens. William would, in time, give the name of his house to the Orange Order on the one hand, but also to Dublin's Nassau Street on the other, named as it was after his familial title. More prosaically, he also replaced the lord mayor's chain, which had been stolen by the Catholic Jacobite mayor, Terence MacDermot, when he fled to France after the Jacobite defeat. (The replacement chain subsequently presented by William was himself only replaced in 1988.) After MacDermot fled, no Catholic would hold the office, let alone the chain, until Daniel O'Connell did so in 1841.

VI

A key change in civic life after the Williamite victory was evident by 1692: regular meetings of parliament were now taking place in Chichester House, which had long-term implications, not least due to the passage by the Irish parliament of the 'popery' or 'penal' laws. By 1692 all freemen had to take an oath repudiating Catholicism, a stricture subsequently extended to all employees of the corporation in 1699 (and in 1695 there was a serious proposal to replace Catholic cleaners at the Tholsel with Protestants). Catholic businesses and merchants survived, however, though the Catholic Church itself was officially driven underground in a city whose public culture was increasingly, and aggressively, Protestant. This copperfastening of Protestant privilege applied to only one type of Protestant – those of the established Church of Ireland; there were others, in the form of Dublin's substantial dissenting congregations. Many British nonconformists had settled in Dublin earlier in the century, but the most eye-catching of these new faiths came in the form of the renewed, and much increased, influx of French Huguenots in the 1690s, partly due to the demobilisation of the Williamite army. Dublin had received a steady trickle of Protestant refugees from the continent, encouraged as they were to settle in Ireland since 1662, and Huguenots arrived here in earnest after the revocation of the Edict of Nantes, which had guaranteed toleration of their religion in France, in 1685. The Huguenot cemetery on Merrion Row, for example, dating from 1693, is testament to the influx of French Protestants who brought their skills and trades to Dublin; many were tradesmen, with gold- and silver-working being well represented. There were perhaps 400 Huguenots in Dublin before the Williamite war, but there may have been 3,600 by 1720; the Lady Chapel of St Patrick's Cathedral became the religious hub of Dublin's new francophone community.

Wee ministers and church Elders of the french congregation of St Bride Dublin, do accordingly certifie that Daniel Paul a Surgeon, Iean Iusol Silk waver, Paul adrien Tannour, daniel Raoul a surgeon, Isaac Terrieu Skinner, Iean So a tayllor, Iaques Sorbier Shoo maker, guy Sauvegrain a barber, Iean chamard a wells maker, matthew Bonlevgeant Ioynar, Etiene ferret a joyner, Iean Corneille Sarges waver, Raimond fabre apoticary, françois morgua shoo maker, were forced to leave tha Kingdom of france, by reason of the severe persecution against the Protestants there, and are all very fitt objects to receive the benefit of the above generous Act, of this honourable Citty, In favour of the said french persecuted Protestants. Dublin apvrill the 19th, 1694.

Bartholomew Balaguier, minister

A 1694 letter confirming the refugee status of some newly arrived Huguenots, all of whom were tradesmen. Such immigrants were often encouraged to come to Ireland by various financial incentives, including tax concessions; hence the need to confirm their status according to the relevant legislation. (*Courtesy of Dublin City Library and Archive*)

'If you expect an account of the people and place I say they are both without exception, they live in as great perfection as in London or, I believe, in Europe for eating and drinking … Their habits and coaches equal if not exceed London, especially the last for they have four score coaches that drive in the streets with 6 horses and 500 [hackneys]. The city itself is very small, but the suburbs and city together is said to be by some nine miles but by all seven in compass, the buildings brick and stately, the streets generally broader than those of London paved with small pebbles. There is no streets nor alleys but broad enough to pass a coach and their only fault is that sometimes in the middle of a curious well-built street is a single house or two that spoil the uniformity being defective in height or excellency.' – Rev. John Verdon of Norfolk records his impressions of Dublin in 1699. Rolf Loeber, David Dickson and Alan Smyth (eds), 'Journal of a tour to Dublin and the counties of Dublin and Meath in 1699', *Analecta Hibernica*, 43 (2012), 56.

On 1 July 1701, an equestrian statue of King William III by the famous English sculptor Grinling Gibbons was unveiled on Dublin's College Green. At 4 p.m. on the appointed day, the lord mayor, aldermen, sheriffs, common councilmen and other worthies of Dublin assembled at the Tholsel and marched to College Green behind musicians and companies of the Dublin Militia. The lord justices joined the procession at College Green as it went around the statue three times, with music playing from a stage before it. During the second circuit, the recorder read out a eulogy to William, 'expressing the attachment of the people of Dublin to his person and government'. Volleys of shots were then fired, and when the third circuit of the statue concluded, the lord justices, the provost and fellows of Trinity College, along with members of the aristocracy, went to a reception in a 'large new house' on College Green. After toasts, cakes were thrown to the crowd and, as promised, casks of claret were set up on stilts. The patrician elite retired to the lord mayor's residence to celebrate, and the streets were left to the populace at large: the revels continued through the night.

Gibbons' statue of William was based (perhaps ironically) on a statue of his Stuart predecessor Charles II at Windsor Castle, and depicted the 'glorious and immortal' saviour of Protestant Ireland in the guise of a classical emperor. The location of the

'I am now come to put a finishing stroke to my perambulations of Dublin and its suburbs in taking a view of St Stephen's Green, in my way to which in York Street stands an handsome but not over large tennis court with a tavern next door to it where, with the juice of the generous grape, gentlemen may supply those spirits which they exhausted in tossing their balls; the most remarkable house I saw in Dublin for an high door and lofty windows stands here but belongs to one of the littlest and crookedest men in Ireland, though a great virtuoso and of the Royal society in London.

'Stephens Green is a very large square piece of ground walled in, and contains about 13 acres of land. On every side there is a large gravel walk set on each hand with lime, sycamore, and ash trees, though on the fourth part they were spoiled for want of care in looking after ... This green lays in my way to Donnybrook which I visited one day when there was a fair at it, and a perfect Irish one too. There were a great many sorts of booths set up in which the ordinary citizens, as well as the country people, were very busy and merry with bagpipes and scrapers, muddy ale, sour wine and herring pasties went off very well. Here was frieze linen, ruffles for candle grease, hens and tobacco, good store with some few cows, hogs &c ... at my return home in the evening, I could not but smile to see the various humours and conditions (which I can not describe) of the drunken citizens and their wives.' – The English bookseller John Dunton explores Dublin in 1698, from Andrew Carpenter (ed.), *Teague Land, or, a Merry Ramble to the Wild Irish* (Dublin, 2003), pp. 149–50.

statue was crucial to its symbolic power, and added to the underlying message: it was originally intended for Cornmarket in the 'old' city, but College Green far outmatched it or any other location in symbolic resonance, given its proximity to such pillars of the Anglican establishment as the parliament house and Trinity College.

Admittedly, not all would view that symbolism in a positive manner: the statue was vandalised on numerous occasions throughout its existence, and not only by disenfranchised Catholics: a group of drunken Trinity students damaged it in 1710, and were forced to stand in the middle of College Green bearing plaques that publicly proclaimed their misdemeanours. But as late as the 1760s, the accepted practice on

The Statue of KING WILLIAM on COLLEDGE GREEN

Grinling Gibbons' statue of William III on College Green, as depicted on Charles Brookings' 1728 map of Dublin. (*Courtesy of Dublin City Library and Archive*)

> 'How nobly did our grateful city joyn
> To represent King William at the Boyn
> And yet their statue (we must all confess)
> Tho it speaks Dublin great, makes William less
> For, where are heaps of slain? Where streams of blood?
> Where do's it show how guardian angels stood?
> Watching to turn aside the fatal ball;
> And, in one royal person, sav'd us all?' –
>
> The city printer welcomes William's statue to Dublin in blood-curdling style.
> Cited in Robin Usher, *Protestant Dublin, 1660–1760: Architecture and Iconography*
> (Basingstoke, 2012), p. 102.

4 November was still for the lord lieutenant himself to proceed to College Green to salute the statue. It was a significant indication of the fact that Dublin in the eighteenth century was now the capital city of an officially Protestant kingdom.

Georgians

❧

1730-1780

I

Dublin was transformed in the first three decades of the eighteenth century, a process that can be seen in Charles Brooking's 1728 map. In the first quarter of the eighteenth century Dublin had acquired clusters of set-piece buildings and residential developments; new parishes were laid out with new churches to minister to them; merchants' houses continued to spring up along the quays; and many of the final fragments of the medieval city were swept away. In other words, a new city was taking shape, and adopting a style usually classed as 'Georgian'.

'Georgian' is a term taken as shorthand for the 'long' eighteenth century; the period from the accession of George I as king of Britain and Ireland in 1714 to the death of King George IV in 1830. In terms of Dublin's history it is the era in which the city acquired

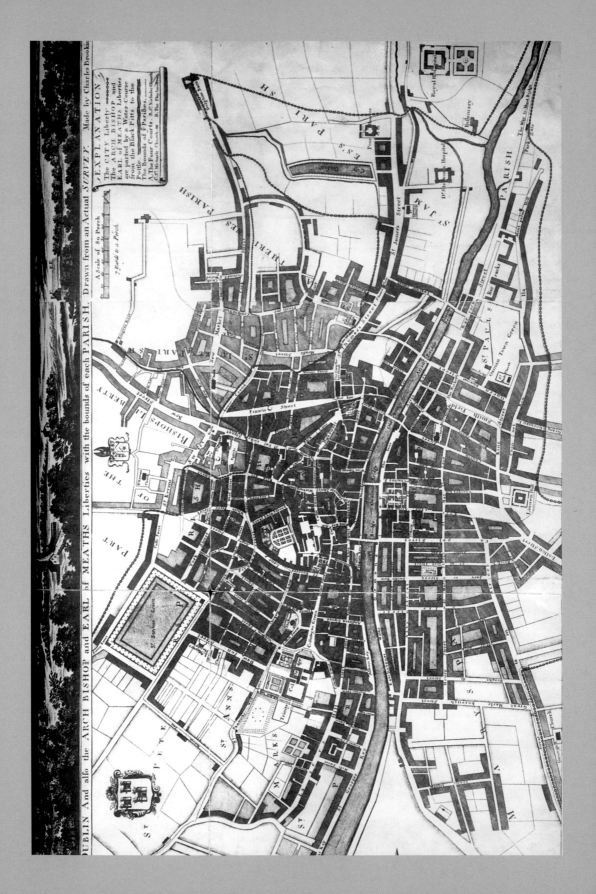

DUBLIN And also the ARCH BISHOP and EARL of MEATHS Liberties with the bounds of each PARISH. Drawn from an Actual SURVEY. Made by Charles Brooking

EXPLANATION

the character and layout that remains largely intact to this day. Yet the foundations for this change were being laid long before the accession of George I. Aside from the transformation of the streetscape, by the 1730s the foundations of an enduring social geography had also been established. The location of industries told a story of its own. Along with textiles, brewing and its associated industries such as cooperage came to be concentrated in and around the old Liberties, while consumer goods and metalworking remained clustered around the castle and the heart of the old city.

To the east, developers such as Sir John Rogerson (who, like Humphrey Jervis, was a merchant, MP and alderman) continued to reclaim lands along the Liffey and build up the quays, while north of the river new suburbs began to be developed by enterprising developers such as the MP and revenue official Luke Gardiner. Henrietta Street was originally laid out by Gardiner in the 1720s and was apparently named after either the Duchess of Grafton or the Duchess of Bolton, both of whom were called Henrietta. It was located on the edge of the vast estates the Gardiner family would develop in the north inner city. Like much of the land in this area, it had once belonged to St Mary's Abbey prior to the dissolution of the monasteries in the sixteenth century.

A similar process could be seen south of the Liffey, in the area bounded by Trinity College and St Stephen's Green, where developers such as Joshua Dawson left their own mark. Despite Ormond's pretensions to grandeur in the reign of Charles II, the fact that Dublin lacked the overwhelming power and splendour of a resident monarch opened the door to the more fragmented developments of private speculators. Wealth was becoming concentrated in the eastern parishes of the city, as the western areas remained poorer and saw their populations swollen by waves of new migrants to the city.

Alongside these changes in its social geography, Dublin also acquired a number of major public buildings in the early eighteenth century, many of which were designed by the architect Thomas Burgh. Among the most impressive was the Royal Barracks near Oxmantown, completed in 1710; it was the largest contemporary barracks in Europe, and the largest public building constructed in Ireland or Britain in the reign of William of Orange. It was built on land sold by the second Duke of Ormond (who had succeeded his grandfather to the title) and was prompted by the necessity to move away from the traditional practice of billeting soldiers in private residences and premises. Its westerly location was originally to have been defended by a massive

Opposite page: Charles Brooking's 1728 map of Dublin, with an unusual perspective looking from north to south. Nevertheless, it depicts an early version of what remains a recognisable streetscape in the twenty-first century. (*Courtesy of Dublin City Library and Archive, Map Collection*)

THe LORD MAYOR,
to prevent the Calamities that may happen by Fire, has Ordered Publick Notice to be given,

THAT *John Oates*, WATER-INGINEER to the Honourable City of *DUBLIN*, living in *Dame-ſtreet* at the Sign of the Boot, is directed by his LORDSHIP to aſſiſt with Two *Water-Ingines* on the firſt Notice that ſhall be given him, when any Fire breaks out in this City or Suburbs.

☞ Note, *That the ſaid* John Oates *makes all Sorts of* Water-Ingines *at Reaſonable Rates, and to as great Perfection as in* London, *having already made One for the Honourable C I T Y of* DUBLIN.

Printed by *John Ray* in *Skinner-Row,* Printer to the Honourable City of D U B L I N, 1711.

A notice for early eighteenth-century firefighting. (*Courtesy of Dublin City Library and Archive, Postcards and Views Collection*)

The Royal Barracks, seen from the south banks of the Liffey. This was, when completed, the largest barracks in Europe and was one of a major network of barracks constructed in eighteenth-century Ireland. Apart from providing for Ireland's security, these barracks helped the British government to sidestep British suspicions of the maintenance of permanent standing armies that might be used to coerce the population in peacetime (as opposed to forces raised specifically in wartime) by keeping such forces out of sight and out of mind in Ireland. (*National Library of Ireland*)

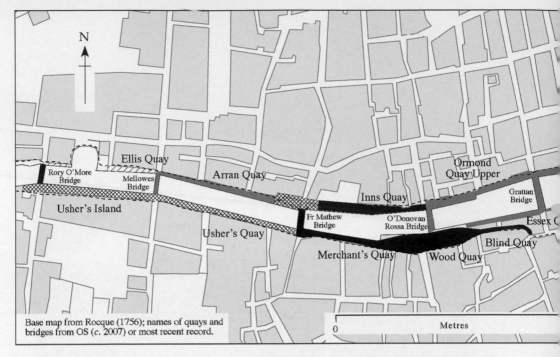

The development of bridges and quays on the River Liffey, 1610–1756. (Royal Irish Academy, *Irish Historic Towns Atlas*)

fort in the Phoenix Park, but this was never built; the later Magazine Fort, built in the 1730s, was a smaller alternative.

The Royal Barracks was grandiose purely in its sheer size. At the other end of the scale was a more modest building with a very different purpose: Marsh's Library, built at the behest of Narcissus Marsh, the Church of Ireland archbishop of Dublin, which was intended to compensate, to some degree, for the inadequacies of Trinity College's library. The new library was to be squarely aimed at 'graduates and gentlemen'; it was not intended for the use of the general public, even though literacy would have been increasing throughout this era. Its precise audience remains unclear, but the composition of the library that bears Marsh's name, reflecting to some degree its founder's interests in science and languages, points towards intellectual pursuits.

Between these two extremes came a range of other new buildings: Tailors' Hall, Dr Steevens' Hospital and the Lying-In Hospital, the Linen Hall near Constitution Hill, the 'Old Library' of Trinity College Dublin and, most impressive of all, the grandiose Parliament House on College Green. The construction of the latter was seemingly instigated by the speaker of parliament, the Donegal-born William Conolly, possibly to help boost the economy during the recession of the 1720s. It replaced Chichester

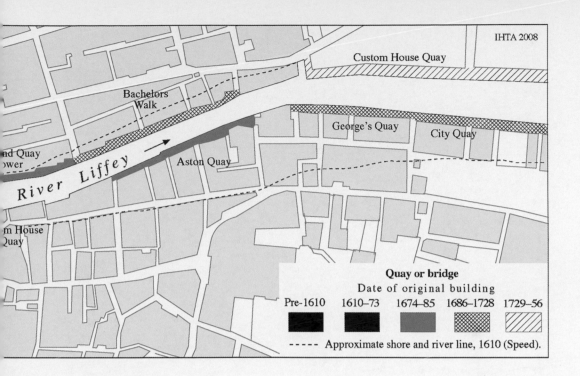

Custom House Quay

Bachelors
Walk

George's Quay

City Quay

nd Quay
ower

River Liffey

Aston Quay

m House
Quay

Quay or bridge
Date of original building
Pre-1610   1610–73   1674–85   1686–1728   1729–56

----- Approximate shore and river line, 1610 (Speed).

House and was apparently the first purpose-built parliament building in Europe. The new building marked the emergence of College Green (formerly Hoggen Green) as a focal point for development outside the old city; it had begun as a place of assembly in the Viking period, and throughout the Middle Ages continued as a public space just outside Blind Gate, the most easterly gate in the city.

The Parliament House, designed by Edward Lovett Pearce (who died before its completion), was begun in 1729. It was built rapidly: the plans were confirmed in March 1728, the foundation stone was laid in February 1729 and it opened in October 1731. The front is a mixture of Portland stone (the columns) and granite (the walls), with the imperial arms on the portico offering the main decorative motif. (The statues of, from left to right, Fidelity, Hibernia and Commerce that adorn the roof today are later additions, from 1809.)

The building is symbolic of 'Protestant ascendency'; a common, and often misused, term to describe the eighteenth-century Protestant landowning elite. The phrase was not used before the 1780s, and even then it described the composition of Irish society as defined by the discriminatory Penal Laws, which underpinned and maintained Protestant status in Ireland, rather then a distinct social group. The use of the term

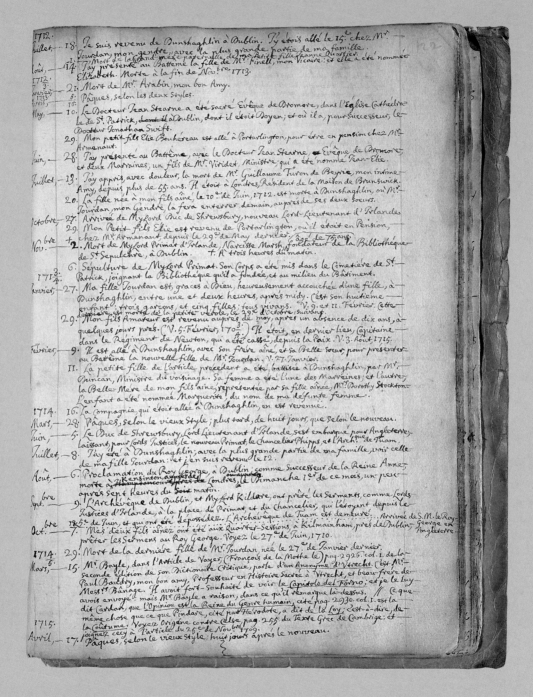

A page from the diary of Elias Bouhéreau, the first librarian of Marsh's Library and a Huguenot refugee born in France. Near the top of the page he records the death of Archbishop Narcissus Marsh, the founder of the library. (*Marsh's Library, Dublin*)

Tailors' Hall in the 1950s. It was originally built as a guild hall in the early 1700s. (*Courtesy of Dublin City Library and Archive, Fáilte Ireland Tourism Photographic Collection*)

The Parliament House on College Green. This was originally a place of assembly outside the city, and was occasionally used for public executions, but was redeveloped from the 1680s onwards. (*National Library of Ireland*)

'A girl of about eight years of age, who stepping on a little before them, turned about suddenly, and, with uplifted hands and horror in her countenance, exclaimed, *Are there any of those bloody papists in Dublin?* This incident, which to a different hearer would be laughable, filled the doctor with anxious reflections. He immediately inferred that the child's terror proceeded from the impression made on her mind, by the sermon preached that day in Christ-Church, whence those ladies proceeded; and having procured a copy of the sermon, he found that his surmise was well founded.' – The Catholic physician and writer John Curry, while walking through Dublin Castle, overhears a reflection of one of the traditional sermons preached by Church of Ireland clerics annually on 23 October to mark the anniversary of the 1641 rebellion. From Charles O'Conor, 'Account of the Author,' in John Curry, *An Historical and Critical Review of the Civil Wars in Ireland, from the Reign of Queen Elizabeth to the Settlement Under King William* (Dublin, 1810), np.

'ascendancy' emerged at a time when there were increasing calls to relax or repeal the Penal Laws. Eighteenth-century Dublin was dominated by property developers, the mercantile elite and, perhaps most important, the landed gentry: the Protestant ruling class who had emerged victorious from the wars of the seventeenth century.

The eighteenth-century city was reshaped under the auspices of the aristocracy, and at least part of its growth was related to their needs: as the exclusively Protestant Irish parliament sat every two years from the 1690s onwards (even before the opening of the Parliament House), the gentry now had a reason to spend extended periods of time in the city, and needed to be housed. Much of Dublin's life came to be driven by the spending power of the Protestant aristocracy and their presence during the 'winter season', as much as by its successful professional and merchant classes (many of the latter were Catholics who sidestepped the discriminatory Penal Laws). The city that was emerging was, in effect, the capital city of Ireland's Protestant elite.

The statues of monarchs that had been erected in Dublin after 1690, beginning with that of William of Orange on College Green, illustrate the manner in which the power of the British monarchy could be displayed on an Irish streetscape. As the century wore on William was joined by George I (on Essex Bridge, near the centre of commerce and the eighteenth-century port) and George II (in St Stephen's Green, near the centre of style).

Yet these statues were far less prominent in symbolic terms than the statue of William: here was the defender of a Protestant Ireland conveniently located outside the building that most obviously embodied Protestant rule. Alongside such official markers of the Protestant state in Ireland were annual commemorations that reinforced the point at a more populist level, such as the commemoration of the Battle of the Boyne on 1 July (according to the old-style calendar), the 1641 rebellion on 23 October or even the Gunpowder Plot on 5 November. After 1690 the sectarian elements of such celebrations became more pronounced, even respectable, with bells, bonfires, drinking, often elaborate fireworks, parades and, in the case of 1641, bespoke annual sermons preached by the clerics of the Church of Ireland to remind their congregations of what their ancestors had faced.

One obvious witness to the changes wrought in this era was perhaps the most famous cleric of the Church of Ireland in the period: Jonathan Swift, who was born in Hoey's Court near Dublin Castle in 1667 and spent much of his career as Dean of St Patrick's Cathedral. But while his career spanned the early decades of the eighteenth century, and he himself became a fixture in the life of the capital, Dublin itself was peripheral to Swift's literary works. 'The Dean' rated Dublin as little more than a provincial capital, when compared to the metropolis of London that remained his cultural and political lodestar, yet which remained tantalisingly out of reach to him. After all, his most famous creation, Lemuel Gulliver, began and ended his travels in London.

If the Church of Ireland was a fundamental part of Dublin's official culture, there was still room for other denominations to maintain a foothold. A wide range of 'dissenting' congretions remained vibrant in Dublin. A Lutheran Church was to be found on Poolbeg Street, with an earlier venue having been established on Marlborough Street; the latter seems to have roots in the Williamite Army, as it was founded by Esdras Marcus Lichenstein, a Lutheran chaplain from Hamburg who returned to Ireland after the Peace of Ryswick was signed with the French in 1697. 'Dissenting' Protestants were found throughout the city, with the Huguenots being the best known to posterity. As time went on, Methodists and Moravians were to be found, with a Moravian Church opening on Kevin Street in 1760 ('Protestant Row' remains the name of a lane around the corner, off Camden Street). Some Huguenots worshipped according to the rites of the Church of Ireland in St Patrick's Cathedral, and, unlike Presbyterians, Methodists and Moravians did not have doctrinal issues with the established Church. As time went on, 'dissenters' benefited from a good deal of official tolerance, even if they were barred from state office and political rights. Yet aside from their relationship with the state, there could certainly be tensions between the various dissenting congregations: the opening of an elaborate new Presbyterian

Prospect of the Custom House, and Essex Bridge, DUBLIN. Vüe de la Doüane, et Dupont d'Essex à DUBLIN.

London, Printed, for Robt Sayer Map & Printseller at the Golden Buck near Serjants Inn, Fleet Street.

Essex Bridge and the original Custom House. The first bridge on this site collapsed during a flood in 1687, killing a hackney driver and a horse. It was rebuilt, and in 1722 a statue of George I by John van Nost the Elder was erected on a conjoining pedestal; it can be seen on the right of the image. Alas, the pedestal on which the statue rested altered the flow of the Liffey, causing the river to erode the foundations of the bridge. In the 1750s the statue was removed and the bridge was rebuilt under the direction of George Semple. Until the construction of Carlisle (now O'Connell) Bridge in 1795, Essex Bridge was the last bridge on the Liffey; ferries took people across the river, which was open to traffic from this point on. (*National Library of Ireland*)

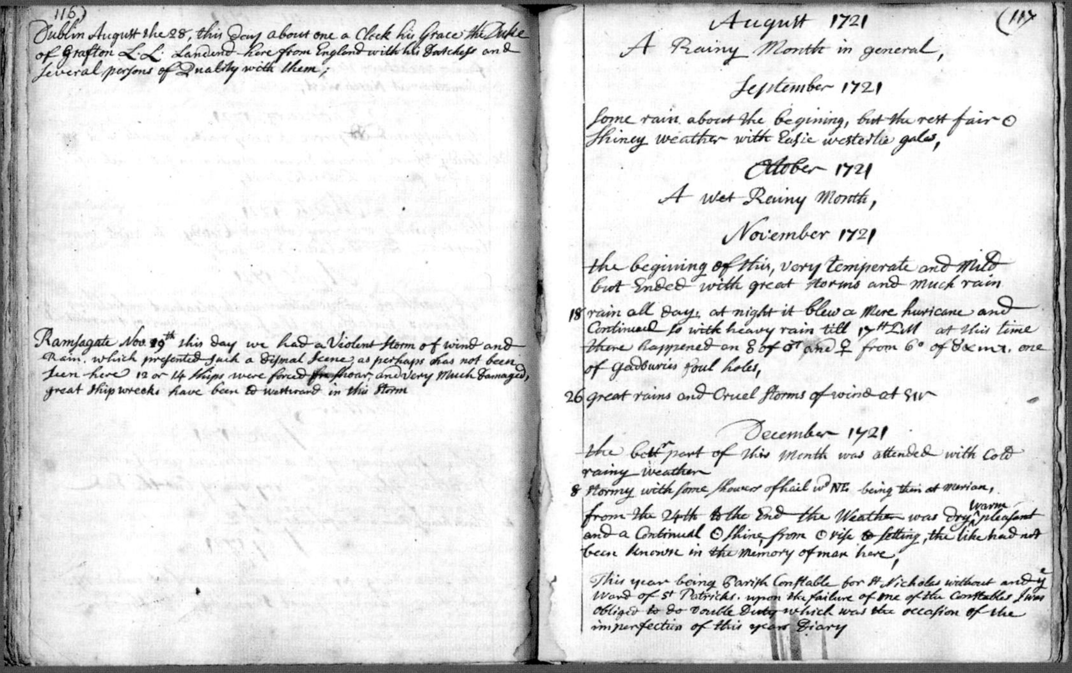

116)
Dublin August the 28, this Day about one a Clock his Grace the Duke
of Grafton L L Landed here from England with his Dutchess and
Several persons of Quality with them;

Ramsgate Nov 29th this day we had a Violent Storm of wind and
Rain, which presented such a Dismal Scene as perhaps has not been
seen here 12 or 14 ships were forced from shoar and very much damaged,
great Ship wrecks have been to wuthward in this Storm

(117)

August 1721
A Rainy Month in general,

September 1721
Some rain about the begining, but the rest fair &
Shiney weather with Easie westerly gales,

October 1721
A Wet Rainy Month,

November 1721
the begining of this, very temperate and Mild
but Ended with great Storms and much rain
18 rain all day, at night it blew a More huricane and
Continued so with heavy rain till 17th Dit at this time
there happened on 8 of ♂ and ♀ from 6° of ♒ one
of Gadburies foul holes,
26 great rains and Cruel Storms of wind at SW

December 1721
the best part of this Month was attended with Cold
rainy weather
8 Stormy with some Shower of hail wd Ne being thin at Meridian,
from the 24th to the End the Weather was dry warm pleasant
and a Continual ⊙ Shine from ⊙ rise to setting, the like had not
been knowne in the memory of man here,

This year being Parish Constable for St Nicholas without and
Ward of St Patricks, upon the failure of one of the Constables I was
obliged to do double Duty which was the occasion of the
imperfection of this years Diary

A page from a diary kept by Isaac Butler in the wet autumn and winter of 1721. Butler was a keen amateur scientist, with a particular interest in botany and meteorology, and was also parish constable of the parish of St Nicholas Without; he notes that the duties involved in this position had impeded his recording of the weather in his diary. (*Courtesy of Dublin City Library and Archive*)

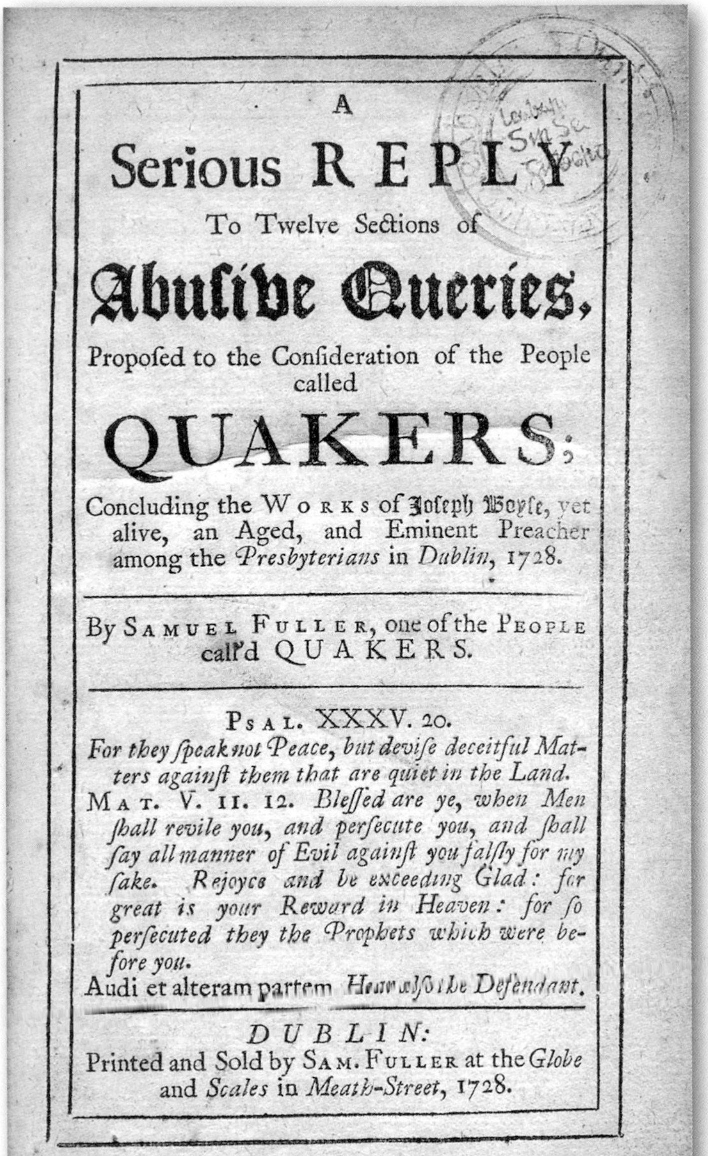

A

Serious REPLY

To Twelve Sections of

Abusive Queries,

Proposed to the Consideration of the People
called

QUAKERS;

Concluding the Works of Joseph Boyse, yet
alive, an Aged, and Eminent Preacher
among the *Presbyterians* in *Dublin*, 1728.

By SAMUEL FULLER, one of the PEOPLE
call'd QUAKERS.

PSAL. XXXV. 20.
For they speak not Peace, but devise deceitful Mat-
ters against them that are quiet in the Land.
MAT. V. 11. 12. *Blessed are ye, when Men*
shall revile you, and persecute you, and shall
say all manner of Evil against you falsly for my
sake. Rejoyce and be exceeding Glad: for
great is your Reward in Heaven: for so
persecuted they the Prophets which were be-
fore you.
Audi et alteram partem *Hear also the Defendant.*

DUBLIN:
Printed and Sold by SAM. FULLER at the *Globe*
and *Scales* in *Meath-Street*, 1728.

A small salvo in a paper war between Quakers and Presbyterians. Dissenting Protestants were discriminated against by the Penal Laws, but this did not guarantee solidarity: different denominations were quite capable of squabbling among themselves on matters of doctrine. (*Courtesy of Dublin City Library and Archive*)

meeting house on Eustace Street in Temple Bar near an older Quaker meeting house prompted one of the latter to observe that 'where there is so much vanity without, there cannot be much religion within'. (The presence of both the Quaker and Presbyterian meeting houses in close proximity lends itself to the modern name Meeting House Square.) The 1757 version of John Rocque's famous map of Dublin depicted at least seventeen meeting houses belonging to Presbyterians, Quakers, Moravians, and the Dutch and French Reformed Churches. It revealed what was otherwise discreetly hidden.

And then there were the Catholics. The population of Dublin in the late seventeenth and early eighteenth century was predominantly Protestant, but the Roman Catholic Church retained a presence there to cater for its flock, despite instances of repression in the first few decades of the eighteenth century. Fears that Jacobites – Catholic supporters of the exiled James II and his descendants – might remain active in the city often prompted a harsh official response, and public disorders in the city might often be blamed on Catholics (in the case of a riot in St Stephen's Green in 1725, the authorities may have had a point, as it took place on the birthday of James's son James Francis Edward, better known to history as the 'Old Pretender'). The Catholic population of Dublin *circa* 1710 was perhaps 30,000 out of a total of 80,000, and was ministered to surreptitiously in chapels found in warehouses, stables and a variety of unlikely locations. The closure of such unofficial venues was the bread and butter of official discrimination against Catholics. But the collapse of a 'mass house' in Pill Lane in February 1744, resulting in the deaths of ten people, prompted a level of discreet toleration to be extended to Catholics by the authorities. As Dublin's population grew, from perhaps 89,000 in 1715 to over 180,000 by 1800, its religious composition shifted. At some point in mid-century, Catholics became the majority in an ever-expanding city.

II

The 1730s saw venues for musical performances open outside the traditional limits of the castle and the cathedrals, beginning with the opening of Crow Street Music Hall in 1731. This points towards a burgeoning demand for more and more varied forms of entertainment, and it is worth considering the nature of Georgian Dublin's cultural and intellectual life. The presence of the gentry accounted for the higher end of cultural life, or at least for the conspicuous consumption that could accompany it. The peak of their winter season ran from November to March, tailing off somewhat in April and May. Given that parliament met only every second year for between five and eight months, the gentry season was not automatically intertwined with it.

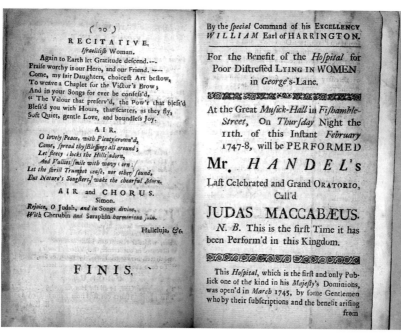

Top: A nineteenth-century depiction of the music hall on Fishamble Street, the venue for the most famous cultural event of Georgian Dublin, when the German composer George Friedrich Handel's ten-month stay in Dublin reached its zenith with the premiere of his *Messiah* on 13 April 1742; bottom: an advertisement for the Irish premiere of Handel's *Judas Maccabeus* (written to celebrate the defeat of Scottish Jacobites at the Battle of Culloden) in the same venue in 1748; like many such performances (including that of the *Messiah*) it was harnessed to a charitable purpose. (*Courtesy of Dublin City Library and Archive*)

Dublin Fireworks

This Perspective View, of the Illuminations and Fire-Works, to be Exhibited at S.t Stephens Green, at Dublin in Ire on the Thanksgiving Day for the GENERAL PEACE Concluded at Aix la Chapelle. 1748.

Preparations for a fireworks display in St Stephen's Green in the mid-eighteenth century. (*National Library of Ireland*)

Both the gentry and upper classes were treated to a regular diet of musical and theatrical performances in venues such as Smock Alley (though Dublin theatres very much took their cue from London). Alongside these events, balls, outdoor concerts, often with fireworks, and promenading were important parts of social life. Over time St Stephen's Green and later constructions such as the Sackville Mall became popular venues for promenades, as did Marlborough Bowling Green (complete with tea rooms and space for musicians) and the Rotunda, Ranelagh and Coburg Gardens. Outdoor activities of another kind could also be witnessed on Dublin streets, in the form of sports: cock-fighting was common at Cork Hill, bull baiting occasionally took place on Oxmantown Green, and there are hints of hurling, football and wrestling taking place in open spaces in the city in the early to mid-eighteenth century. For the elites, domestic entertainment was also vitally important; many of Dublin's eighteenth-century houses, especially those on and around the six squares that had been built by the end of the century, were designed to accommodate such entertaining. Polite society reflected a combination of derivative insecurity and patriotic confidence.

The social and cultural worlds of the classes beneath the elite can be harder to discern, but many of the features found towards the top of the social ladder were also found en route to the bottom. Taverns came into their own: at mid-century, Dublin was estimated to have 3,500 venues for the consumption of alcohol, from the ubiquitous tavern to more obscure and fleeting dram-shops.

'I remember Doctor Swift told me, he once dined at a persons house, where the part of the table cloth, which was next to him, happened to have a small hole in it, which, says he, I tore as wide as I could; then asked for some soup, and fed myself through the hole. The Dean, who was a great friend to housewifery, did this to mortify the lady of the house; but, upon my word, by the general love of scandal and distraction in Dublin, one might reasonably imagine they were all to feed themselves through the holes, which they had made in the characters of others.'
– A recollection of Jonathan Swift by Laetitia Pilkington, whose own turbulent personal life had been a source of scandal and gossip after her husband, a clergyman, divorced her for infidelity; ironically, Swift himself turned on her after the divorce. *The Third and Last Volume of the Memoirs of Mrs Laetitia Pilkington, Written by Herself* (London, 1754), p. 4.

Coffee houses were also present in Dublin from the 1660s onwards. These dealt in beverages, games and, crucially, newspapers. This required natural light, so they were often located in upstairs premises. They often had a commercial function, especially for visiting merchants and ships' captains, and as venues for 'sociability' and news, they also had close links to bookselling and printing; Richard Pue and Edward Lloyd were good examples of entrepreneurs who dabbled in both. The Guild of St Luke the Evangelist, representing cutlers, painters and stationers, had been established in 1670, and the number of booksellers in Dublin trebled between the 1690s and 1760s, with more than 165 newspapers being published in the first half of the century and supplying both foreign and domestic news. The nature of Dublin's commercial economy required literacy and information; coffee houses were convivial venues for obtaining the latter. The clusters of coffee houses in and around the quays were a testament to Dublin's status as a port town; and these locations often overlapped with the centre of Dublin's book trade, which from the later seventeenth century lay in and around Essex Quay, Ormond Quay and Dame Street (near Trinity College). Over time this shifted to Grafton, Capel, Sackville and Abbey streets. Different areas had different emphases: Catholic printers could be found near High Street, with their

Quaker counterparts near Meath Street. Many bookshops had reading rooms, but there were stalls on the quays and no shortage of pedlars and hawkers adding their wares to the raucous street life of the city.

The intertwined growth of coffee houses and the periodical press could be seen to constitute a public sphere. While there were more elevated cultural and intellectual organisations, in the form of learned societies – the Dublin Philosophical Society and, later, the Royal Dublin Society and Royal Irish Academy – humbler institutions such as coffee houses and their associated industries accounted for a good deal of Dublin's intellectual life from the 1730s to the 1770s. Coffee houses went into decline in the second half of the century due to competition from taverns, hotels, and dedicated commercial and cultural spaces and institutions. Some evolved into restaurants; many limped on into the nineteenth century. Dublin's cultural life was a male-dominated world at all levels: elite women could carve out a niche as hostesses, but they were excluded from taverns, coffee houses and such learned societies as existed.

III

Between 1700 and 1800 Dublin's population tripled, making it one of the largest cities in Western Europe. Change was also aesthetic; the existing urban fabric of much of the city is a legacy of this era. The Georgian architecture of the public buildings, along with that of residential districts like Mountjoy Square on the northside and Merrion Square and St Stephen's Green on the southside, are easily some of the most famous features of the city that exists today. As the century wore on, other major buildings appeared: King's Inns, the Four Courts, Custom House and, probably the most elegant of all, the City Hall, built as the Royal Exchange in the 1770s. One reason for the enduring Georgian character of Dublin is the fact that the buildings used materials that would endure, the perishable wood of the Middle Ages had given way to stone and, crucially, brick. The use and manufacture of the latter expanded rapidly and became ubiquitous over the next century (the Guild of Bricklayers and Plasterers was founded in 1670) due to urban growth; by 1771 parliament legislated to move brickfields and their kilns out of the city as a health and safety measure. Outlying districts such as Clontarf and Baldoyle on the north of Dublin Bay became areas for their manufacture, but the canals could also be exploited to bring bricks from further afield – they were a major good transported on the Grand Canal, for instance.

A snapshot of Dublin at mid-century is provided by the famous map of John Rocque, a Huguenot cartographer whose family fled France after the revocation of the

Dublin's north inner city, as depicted on a hand-coloured version of John Rocque's famous and richly detailed map. Dunghills are visible at the top left, and the open space of St Mary's Church at the centre can be contrasted with the Catholic chapel (indicated by a cross) tucked away at the corner of Mary Street and Bull Lane, and indeed the Meeting House on Mary's Abbey. The street plan shown in Rocque's map largely survives today. (*Courtesy of Dublin City Library and Archive, Map Collection*)

Edict of Nantes. Primarily based in London, he created a number of maps of major European cities (Rome, Paris, Berlin), usually working from earlier maps. However, his 1747 map of London was an original work (as were most of his maps of British towns), and so too was his map of Dublin. He lived in Dublin between 1754 and 1760, and was originally based in lodgings across from Crane Lane, in the centre of Dublin's de facto publishing district; the map of Dublin was in progress from September 1754, and was published in November 1756.

Dublin expanded from the urban framework depicted by Brookings in the 1720s. It had, since then, continued to grow eastwards, which – unusually – meant the windward side. The old artisan areas of the Liberties, along with the Phoenix Park, made it difficult to grow westwards, though the development of the Grand and Royal canals from the 1750s and 1790s respectively opened new routes to the west of the city later in the century.

Two major residential districts had emerged in the early decades of the eighteenth century, thanks to the efforts of developers such as Joshua Dawson and the ubiquitous Gardiner (who took over the mantle of earlier developers such as Aungier and Jervis). One was centred on Gardiner's developments on Henrietta Street and Dominick Street, north of the River Liffey; the other was around Dawson Street and St Stephen's Green, where Leinster House, the elegant townhouse of the Duke of Leinster, stood out after its construction in the 1740s. While large mansions such as this were built to specifications, many were simply bought as completed from the developers themselves.

The location of Trinity College was another magnet for prestige, and the eventual creation of Fitzwilliam and Mountjoy squares also reflected the eastward shift onto higher ground. Peers and MPs eventually tended to be clustered around Rutland Square, Henrietta Street, Sackville Mall and St Stephen's Green. Likewise, luxury goods tended to be sold in and around Capel Street, Henry Street, and especially Dame Street, Grafton Street and College Green. But the residential districts were not just the preserve of the aristocracy. As the traditional civic elite gave way to the aristocracy, mercantile interests and office holders, the emergence of a recognisable, non-aristocratic middle class could be seen.

The distinctive plain-fronted townhouses that dominate the eighteenth-century squares were only one type among many. A great deal of architectural diversity was on display in Georgian Dublin, often deployed with ingenuity. The relative lack of exterior decoration (in stark contrast to frequently elaborate stucco interiors) on often-uniform terraces may have been an aesthetic driven by commercial considerations. Brick remained the dominant building material, with stone (often calp limestone) quarried from County Dublin or elsewhere in Leinster.

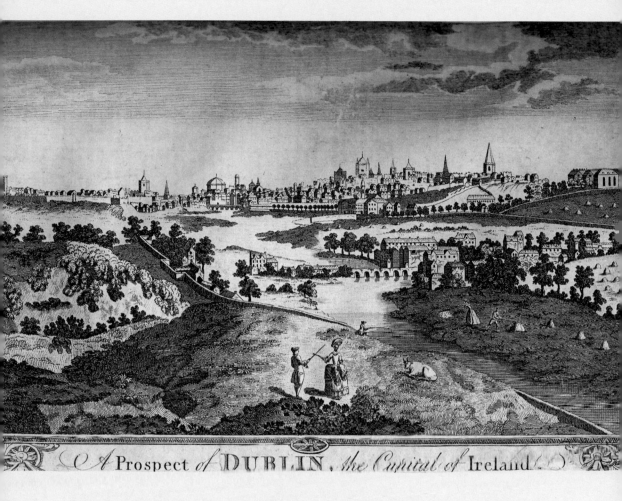

A Prospect of DUBLIN, the Capital of Ireland

Dublin from the Phoenix Park, *circa* 1780. This engraving, by one 'F. Cary', or versions thereof, appeared in a wide range of popular publications in the late Georgian era. The Liffey is clearly visible, as are landmarks such as the cathedrals and the Royal Hospital. (*Courtesy of Dublin City Library and Archive, Postcards and Views Collection*)

LEINSTER HOUSE, DUBLIN.

Leinster House, as depicted by James Malton. Built in the 1740s, it became a focal point for more exclusive developments in the area of St Stephen's Green, thereby fulfilling the Duke of Leinster's apocryphal claim that where he would build, fashion would follow. (*National Library of Ireland*)

The real transformation came between the 1750s and the 1790s, with the Wide Streets Commissioners clearing away much of the congested streetscape that had survived from the Middle Ages. The 'Commissioners for wide and convenient streets' was established in 1756; it was a uniquely powerful body which would deliberately reshape Dublin's streetscape over the course of the next century, in an effort to weave together the disparate developments that made up the city centre, to deal with long-standing problems of congestion and to facilitate further growth. The members of the Wide Streets Commission were MPs, property owners and various other worthies, but they were by no means philistines, and the commissioners did not serve a purely utilitarian function, important as that was (though lanes and yards were singled out as especially pernicious hubs of 'anti-social' behaviour).

Beginning in the 1760s with the development of Parliament Street, leading from Essex Bridge, the commissioners remodelled the city centre, with City Hall, the Parliament House and Trinity College all becoming focal points for set-piece vistas. By the end of the 1770s Dame Street had been widened, with a newer, more uniform aspect linking the Royal Exchange to College Green. By the 1780s D'Olier Street and Westmoreland Street had been laid out as development turned towards the Liffey, followed by the creation of North Frederick Street and Carlisle Bridge in the 1790s to forge another link between the gentry estates on the northside with the centres of commercial and political power south of the river. It is an eighteenth-century streetscape that defines much of the inner city to this day.

Urban development came in phases, and around 1770 the focus of development began to shift north of the river. Parnell Square was originally Rutland Square, and is the earliest of Dublin's 'Georgian' squares, created in its current form between 1751 and 1785, when the gardens were named after the duke of Rutland, the then lord lieutenant. It was laid out from the 1740s by Bartholomew Mosse, who had established pleasure gardens on the site of what is now the Rotunda Hospital, which was built very soon afterwards; one was intended to fund the other. The garden was always the centrepiece, as it was the unique focus for the construction of the square. Another source of income for the hospital was a tax on sedan chairs: covered chairs carried by two people, and used as a means of transport by the better-off, many of whom lived in the vicinity. The original idea was to have the hospital facing directly on to Sackville Street, but this was prevented, possibly by a dispute with Luke Gardiner, who had sensed an opportunity and laid out Cavendish Street on the east side to link the new square to Sackville Mall. The east side was built first, and the construction of Charlemont House in the 1760s ensured that it became a very high-profile address. It

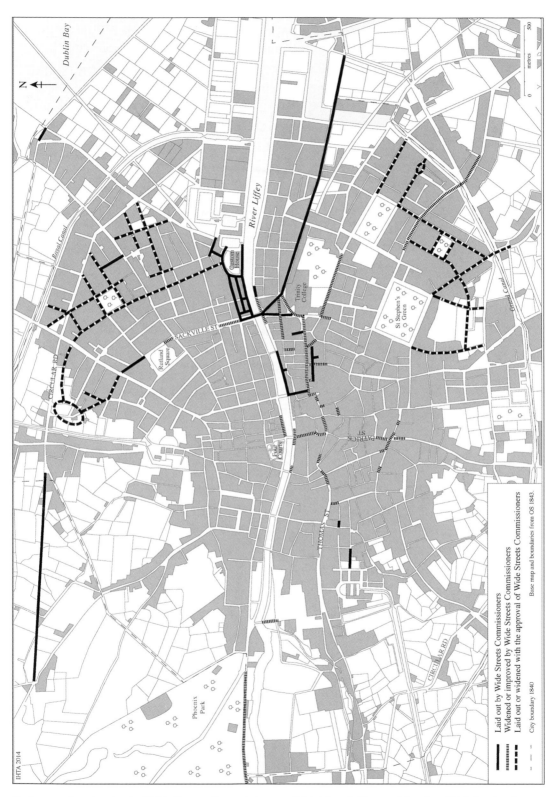

Projects undertaken by the Wide Streets Commissioners. (Irish Historic Towns Atlas, *Royal Irish Academy*)

VIEW FROM CAPEL-STREET, LOOKING OVER ESSEX-BRIDGE — DUBLIN.

Essex Bridge leading to the Royal Exchange (later City Hall), as depicted by James Malton. This was one of the first major set piece vistas laid out by the Wide Streets Commissioners. (*Library of Congress*)

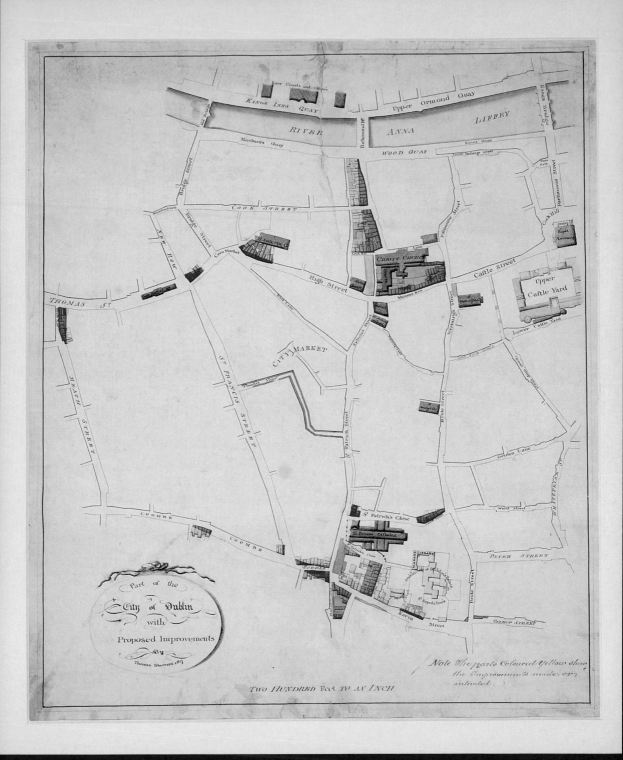

Some of the maps drafted by the Wide Streets Commissioners from the 1790s to the 1840s, indicating the precise changes being suggested for individual streets and localities. (*Courtesy of Dublin City Library and Archive*)

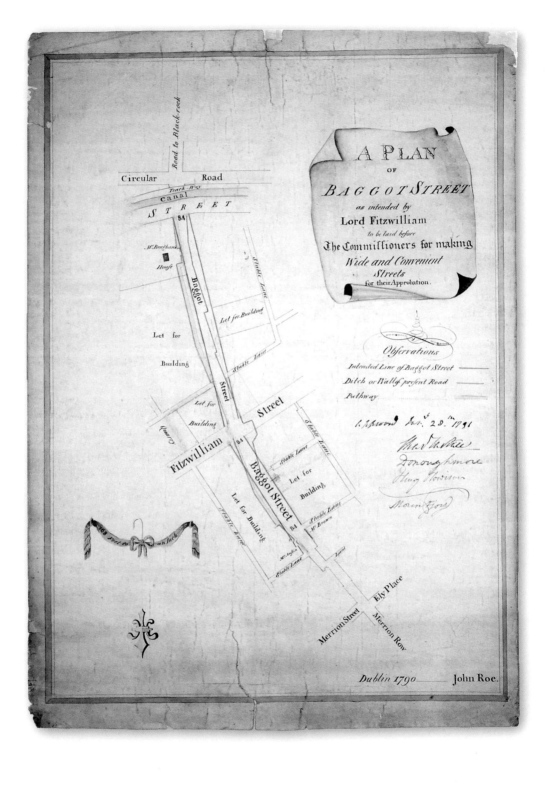

A PLAN
OF
BAGGOT STREET
as intended by
Lord Fitzwilliam
to be laid before
The Commissioners for making
Wide and Convenient
Streets
for their Approbation.

Observations

Intended Line of Baggot Street
Ditch or Wall of present Road
Pathway

Road to Black-rock

Circular   Road

Track Way

Canal

STREET

84

Mr Bingham's

House

Stable Lane

Baggot

Let for Building

Let   for

Stable Lane

Building

Street

Let for

Street

Building

Clanwilliam

Stable Lane

Fitzwilliam

84

Stable Lane

Baggot Street

Let for

Building

Let for Building

84

Stable Lane

Mr Brown

STABLE Lane

Mr Inglis

Lane

Stable Lane

Ely Place

Merrion Street

Merrion Row

Dublin 1790 ———— John Roe.

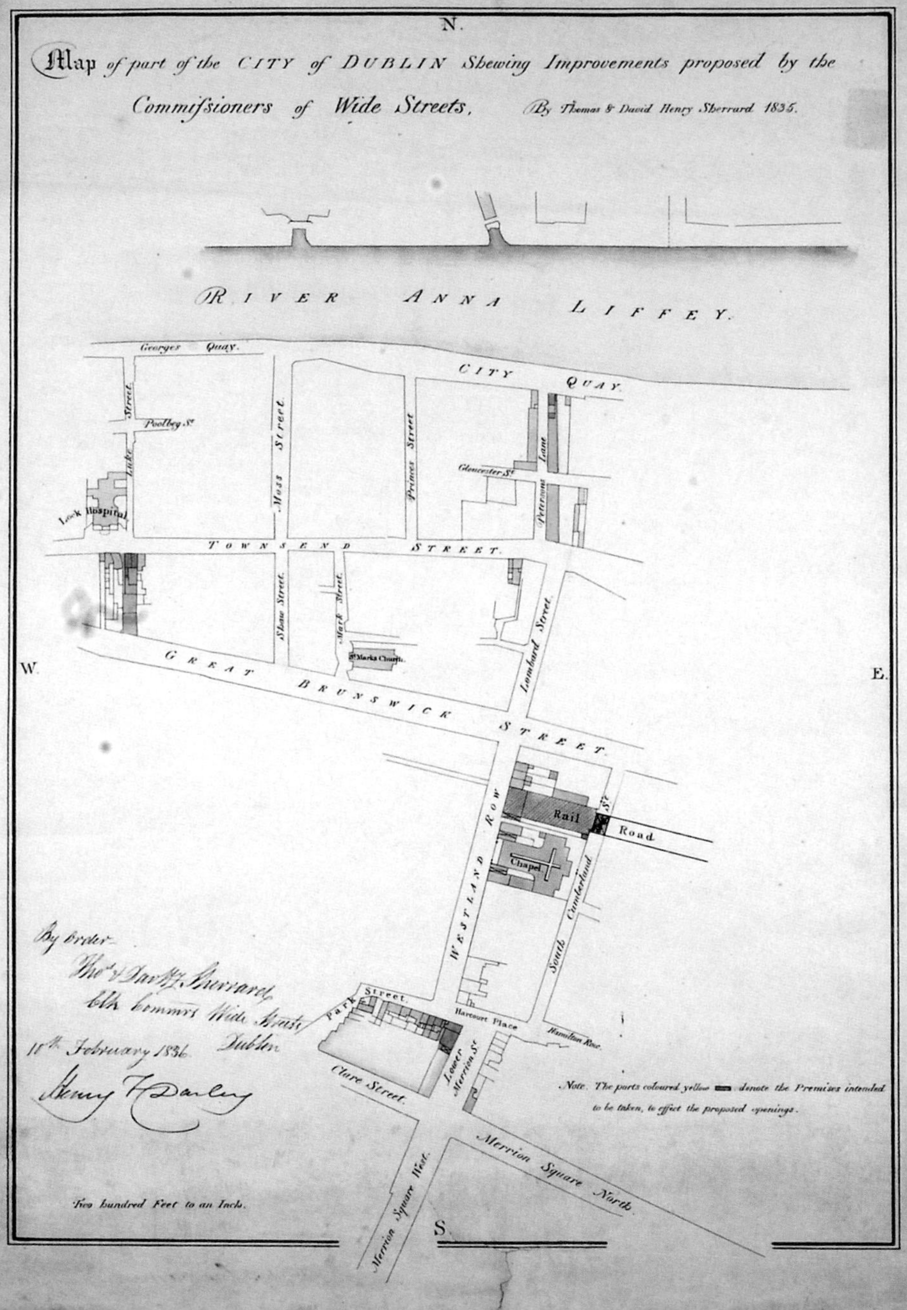

N.

Map of part of the CITY of DUBLIN Shewing Improvements proposed by the Commissioners of Wide Streets,

By Thomas & David Henry Sherrard 1835.

RIVER ANNA LIFFEY.

Georges Quay.

CITY QUAY.

Poolbeg St.

Luke Street

Moss Street

Princes Street

Gloucester St.

Princes Lane

Lock Hospital

TOWNSEND STREET.

W.

Shaw Street

Mark Street

Lombard Street

E.

St Marks Church.

GREAT BRUNSWICK STREET.

WESTLAND ROW

Rail St. Road

Chapel

Cumberland Street

South Cumberland

By Order

Thos & David H. Sherrard,
6th Commrs Wide Streets,
Dublin

18th February 1836.

Henry F. Darley

Park Street

Clare Street

Harcourt Place

Hamilton Row

Lower Merrion St

Note. The parts coloured yellow ▬ denote the Premises intended to be taken, to effect the proposed openings.

Merrion Square West

Merrion Square North.

Two hundred Feet to an Inch.

S.

was built for James Caulfield, Earl of Charlemont, who also built the Casino Marino; a youthful excursion on the 'grand tour' bred a lifelong interest in the arts, which was reflected in the neoclassicism of his townhouse.

The boulevard that the new square looked down upon had been laid out in the 1740s by Luke Gardiner. It may well have been a conscious decision to move the centre of gravity north of the Liffey further east, away from the old Jervis estate. Gardiner's trademark was wide streets, as seen in his development of Henrietta Street, and the new mall was no exception: relatively new buildings were demolished on what was then Upper Drogheda Street to make way for a mall that was over 150 feet (45 metres) wide and 1,050 feet (320 metres) long, extending from the Rotunda Hospital to the junction of Drogheda Street and Henry Street. Gardiner had served in the government of Lionel Cranfield Sackville, first Duke of Dorset and Lord Lieutenant of Ireland on two occasions. The name had a certain cachet that presumably appealed to Gardiner's intended market, and so Sackville Mall came into being.

It was an immediate success. The mall was completed by the 1770s, as the last vacant lots were filled with new houses, but even before then it had attracted a reasonable cohort of MPs and 'persons of quality'; it was easily one of the most prestigious addresses in the city (as indicated, amongst other things, by the large numbers of sedan chairs owned by some of the residents). Yet even before the turn of the century, its social and physical character had started to change, in ways that were interrelated. By 1785 the Wide Streets Commission had redeveloped Drogheda Street and, in doing so, had brought the mall down to the river. By 1795 Carlisle Bridge had been constructed, part of a streetscape designed to permit a grand entrance to the Parliament House on College Green for those members, amongst others, who were coming from the northside. In doing so the enclosed mall became transformed into a bustling thoroughfare, as slowly but surely the professional classes – merchants, lawyers, doctors – began to make their homes and locate their businesses there. Other, newer developments beckoned to the gentry, though the slow but sure aristocratic exodus that followed after the Act of Union in 1801, which abolished the Irish parliament and integrated it into its British counterpart, ensured the transformation of the old mall into a commercial and professional centre. But in the first half of the nineteenth century at least, it kept much of its original prestige.

Mountjoy Square was another creation of the Gardiners, being laid out from the 1780s, possibly in response to the development of Merrion Square south of the Liffey. Developed by Luke Gardiner (grandson of the Luke Gardiner who laid out Rutland Square, and who was killed serving with government forces at New Ross in Wexford

CHARLEMONT HOUSE, DUBLIN.

James Malton del. et Sculp.

London Pub. by J. C. Malton & G. Cowen, Dublin June 1795.

Charlemont House on Rutland (now Parnell) Square. The building now houses the Dublin City Gallery The Hugh Lane. (*Library of Congress*)

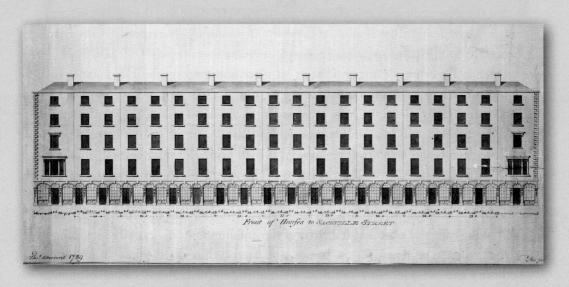

A profile depiction of Sackville Street in 1789, as recorded by Thomas Sherrard for the Wide Streets Commissioners. (*Courtesy of Dublin City Library and Archive*)

The Four Courts and environs, 1807, as depicted from the south-east. The ruins of Coal Quay bridge can be seen in the foreground. (*National Library of Ireland*)

A late nineteenth-century postcard image of the Custom House (*Courtesy of Dublin City Library and Archive, Postcards and Views Collection*)

east end of the crescent consisted of warehouses adjacent to a dock, since filled in. The building itself was the first Irish project of the prolific English architect James Gandon, and was completed in 1785; it is regarded as his finest work. (The scale of the construction necessitated the importation and employment of English workers, who acquired an unenviable reputation for drunkenness.) The building was meant to be seen from all sides; the massive Doric south front is 375 feet (114 metres) wide. A statue of Hope rests upon the dome, but a notable feature is the carved keystone heads, representing Ireland's rivers, of which Anna Livia – the Liffey – is the only female head.

Along with these vast and elaborate edifices came developments of a more modest nature: the reconstruction of churches and the development of more residential areas, often in new styles. What were the economic foundations of a city that saw such growth, and the extremes of wealth and poverty it contained? The presence of the gentry, parliament, the university and judiciary gave Dublin a unique cluster of social groups and associated institutions, but its pre-eminence in eighteenth-century Ireland was based on the simple realities of its location and its size.

IV

Dublin underwent rapid growth in the mid-eighteenth century and came to dominate the Irish economy. The volume of its shipping trade increased over the course of the century: from 58,000 tons to 258,000 tons, though coal made up a substantial proportion of this (Dublin depended on British coal throughout the Georgian era). It was an entrepôt for external trade, and a distribution hub for internal commerce. Sugar

'Out of Dublin, and its environs, there is scarcely a single capital picture, statue, or building, to be found in the whole island. Neither is music cultivated out of the abovementioned limits, to any degree of perfection; so that nothing is to be expected in making the tour of Ireland, beyond the beauties of nature, a few modern-antiquities, and the ignorance and poverty of the lower class of the inhabitants.' – The waspish judgements of the English travel writer Richard Twiss prompted outrage when published in his *A Tour in Ireland in 1775* (London, 1776), p. 10. In fairness to the rest of Ireland, Twiss was left unimpressed by Dublin as well.

An advertisement for a Dublin grocer. Even aside from the other wares on sale, Dublin (along with Cork) provided the greatest variety of consumer goods in Ireland; in this case, alcoholic beverages are especially prominent among Boyd's wares. (*National Library of Ireland*)

refining was a major industry earlier in the century, though brewing and distilling later eclipsed it. Speaking of alcohol, Dublin was the main import point for French wine (a bewildering variety of beverages was available in the city for the tables of the gentry and upper classes).

Dublin's eighteenth-century industries largely consisted of processing and refining rather than manufacturing, especially for the domestic market: glass, metalworking, textile and furniture production, and leatherworking were all prominent. But the most important export from eighteenth-century Dublin was a product more usually associated with Ulster: linen. The capital dominated the Irish trade for much of the early to mid-eighteenth century, hence the presence of the Linen Hall near Constitution Hill, and the cluster of streets around it named after locations in Ulster. Linen was sourced from Ulster but processed in Dublin (and goods went back the other way along the north–south routeways). Cotton and wool took over as the century wore on, and linen processing shifted back to Ulster. Then there were the administrative and cultural economies of bureaucracy, banking, the law, government, medicine and publishing, and the constant supply of food and migrants from Dublin's Leinster hinterland, who travelled to the city via the increasingly sophisticated infrastructure of turnpike roads and, by the second half of the century, the Royal and Grand Canals.

Yet the growth of both the population and the physical environment of the city had other consequences: by the end of eighteenth century could a social topography be seen? Wealth was concentrated in the eastern parishes of the city, as the western areas remained as older, poorer, artisan areas, the populations of which were being swollen by waves of new migrants to the city. Three zones could be loosely identified: upmarket residential to the east; middle-class and commercial in the central districts; and a more industrial and proletarian region on the western fringes. Alongside the lives of the elites, a substantial underclass had emerged who, from the point of view of many in authority, needed to be corralled and controlled.

To the VERY RESPECTABLE the LINEN MERCHANTS and MANUFACTURERS of Ireland, The CONDUCTORS of that GREAT and BENEFICIAL STAPLE of our COUNTRY; This Perspective View of the Linen Hall in Dublin with the Bears and Bales of Linen nearly Exportation, the Emblems of their Industry, Is Dedicated by their obedient humble Servant, Wm Hincks.

The Linen Hall at Constitution Hill. This was located adjacent to a spur of the Royal Canal, which was later filled in. The Linen Hall later became a military barracks but was destroyed by fire during the Easter Rising of 1916. The streets around its old location are named after locations in Ulster, thus highlighting the link to the heartlands of the eighteenth century linen industry. *(Library of Congress)*

Protest, rebellion and union

1780-1820

I

Dublin's official culture and ruling elite was, to put it crudely, Protestant and wealthy. Even leaving aside religious divisions, class and social distinctions were acute. Traditionally, Church of Ireland parishes dealt with the relief of poverty, often raising money by intermittent levies or collections (which became a regular feature in the eighteenth century). Yet the system was open to abuse; as early as the 1680s, there had been calls for beggars to wear badges to identify themselves.

A concrete means of separating the genuine poor from imposters was the creation of dedicated institutions for that purpose. The original Dublin workhouse was built in 1705 to tackle the increasing numbers of the poor, from Dublin and elsewhere, who were to be found on the streets of the growing capital. It was located in Mount Brown, south of the River Liffey between the Royal Hospital at Kilmainham and the modern location of James's Hospital (across the road from the intriguingly named Murdering Lane). But it was beset by financial problems from the outset. As early as May 1706, concerns were being raised that the parish churchwardens who were supposed to provide at least some monies were remiss in doing so. Prior to the creation of the workhouse, charity was the responsibility of individual parishes; it is tempting to think that after the establishment of the workhouse, the city parishes may have assumed that poverty was a problem for others to tackle. Some of the workhouse's income came from cloth processing; in November 1706 it could at least pay the wages of its manager, but in June 1710 the workhouse was still in arrears. The implications of this ongoing problem can be guessed at from a list of its occupants. As of 20 March 1726, it held 222 inmates, from virtually every parish in the city. Ninety-seven were male and 125 female. Their ages ranged from five to ninety, with the higher and lower age groups making up most of the inmates: 111 were under the age of fifteen, and sixty were over fifty. The reasons for their admission were listed as, variously, 'superannuated', 'infirm', 'bedrid', 'king's evil' (scrofula), 'mad', 'fools', 'blind', 'dumb', 'fits', 'lame', 'washers', 'sound children' (there were ninety-three in the last category, which was by far the largest). Some were detained for combinations of these problems, though no reason was given for the admission of John Howard, aged thirty-four, other than that he was, or had been, a 'schoolmaster'. The list gives little indication of the human stories that lay behind the names, but hints of tragedy come through. What is one to make of the admission of John Dunn, aged eight and 'infirm', or Jane Meredith, aged thirteen and afflicted by 'the evil'?

Less than three weeks later, the number of the workhouse's inhabitants had been reduced to 211, but even those who remained were in a precarious position, thanks to the perennial lack of funds. A list of 'observations on the present state and condition of the workhouse, 6 April 1726' wearily refers to 'the usual deficiencies in the parish money for several years past'. It was in arrears to the tune of £1,635, and was owed £1,040, mainly from the city parishes, but also from licences granted to coaches, chairs, carmen, brewers, and various rentals that were supposed to supply funds to the workhouse. By 1750 the Dublin workhouse was essentially a foundling hospital, having never overcome the problems of finance and mismanagement that had beset

'O'Shauchnesee Esqr, a beggar in Dublin', one of the vast army of Dublin's poor, as depicted by the engraver Edward Harding from an original picture by James Nixon. (*National Library of Ireland*)

it from the start. It was to be expected that if the means to tackle poverty were to be disregarded, the problem of poverty would survive. A recurring, if unedifying, thread in Dublin's history is the manner in which the appalling poverty of its poorest inhabitants retained the capacity to shock and appal observers down through the centuries.

II

On 22 August 1734 the constable Paul Farrell was taken from custody by a mob, paraded to the Coombe, where he was beaten, mutilated with knives, castrated, and then hanged from a tree. Arrests followed, but two trials ended in acquittals. Farrell had both upheld the law and broken it – he was in custody, after all – and at some point may have incurred the wrath of weavers from the Liberties (possibly after helping to arrest a few of them the previous May). Public order was traditionally enforced by watchmen attached to each city parish. These had been reformed in 1715 to exclude Catholics from their ranks and to operate 365 days a year; they were equipped with lamps, staffs and halberds, paid for by taxes. As for punishment, Dublin had a variety of prisons, most notoriously Newgate (the 'Black Dog') and Marshalsea, with a set of stocks on Bride Street from 1665 (they were moved there from Ship Street) for minor offences and vagrancy, and the gallows for capital crimes. Further reforms in 1723 saw constables appointed to oversee the watches (Catholics and innkeepers were barred from these new posts). In the 1720s Dublin had perhaps 2,000 constables, but these were often involved in crime themselves. Many of them had been sacked after a ten-month period of unrest in 1729 (which had also prompted an inquiry into the extortion of prisoners by jailers in prisons such as Newgate). Farrell seems to have survived this purge, at least for a few years.

The watchmen and constables were tasked with the prosecution of crime in a broad sense. For example, the west end of Temple Bar was in the parish of St John, which in 1770 was described as 'remarkable for the number of infamous brothels that were in it'. But it was equally notorious for prosecuting vice. The parish watchmen were based on Wood Quay and in October 1732 they held four prostitutes and a pimp overnight in a cage there: the idea was to teach them a very public lesson before they were sent to prison, for as one newspaper delicately put it, the prostitutes and the pimp had been caught in 'the public performance of their duties'. Eighteenth-century Temple Bar was notorious for prostitution. The fact that it was part of a port, was filled with taverns and pubs and was also located between Dublin Castle and the Parliament House meant that it became a haven for the world's oldest profession.

Prostitution had a social scale of its own, and brothels were often well connected; some operated in conjunction with other criminals and even the soldiery. Alcohol sales, among other legitimate businesses, were used as cover for brothels, with licences often obtained by bribery. Some madams were enormously successful, most famously Margaret Leeson ('Peg Plunkett'). She had operated a brothel catering to wealthy and well-known men, and her memoirs, written after her release from debtors' prison, proved an inevitable bestseller. Brothels were scattered throughout the city and different establishments catered for different clienteles (the barracks was naturally a magnet for vice, and soldiers a reliable source of crime in general), but Temple Bar had a very high concentration. One madam of Copper Alley, Margaret Flood, was publicly whipped for brothel keeping in 1747, while unofficial justice was dispensed in January 1796 when a brothel on Kennedy's Lane was reportedly damaged in a riot prompted by rumours that innocent passers-by were being kidnapped and forced into prostitution. The authorities viewed prostitution as a danger to both public morality and health (the existence of the Westmoreland Lock Hospital on Townshend Street was a morbid testament to the prevalence of sexually transmitted diseases). Wherever there was prostitution, there were also attempts to stamp it out.

'The gownsman step'd in wid his book
and spoke him so neat & so civil
Larry tipt him a Kilmainham look
and pitchd his big wig to de devil
den raising a little his head
he took a sup out a de bottle
and sighing most bitterly said
Oh de hemp will be soon round my throttle
and squeeze my poor windpipe to det.' –

From 'De nite afore Larry was stretch'd' (1780s), an anonymous ballad from late eighteenth-century Dublin. The 'Kilmainham look' was a reference to Larry's place of execution; from 1682 Kilmainham Gaol to the west of the city had become the principal venue for executions. Cited in Andrew Carpenter, *Verse in English from Eighteenth-century Ireland* (Cork, 1998), p. 432.

'Mr Crosbie ascending in his air balloon on Wednesday the 19th of January 1785.' As related by J.T. Gilbert, Crosbie ascended from Leinster Lawn in a balloon at 2.30 p.m., and drifted out over the Irish Sea. The balloon apparently crash-landed, but fortuitously did not sink, and the balloon acted as a de facto sail. Having been inclined to eat 'a morsel of fowl', Crosbie was 'rescued' and the balloon was towed back to Kingstown, though not before briefly ascending again with a terrified sailor who was trying to secure it. The scion of minor gentry from Wicklow, Crosbie had apparently been a member of a gang comprising Trinity College students known as the 'Pinkindindies', who in 1779 had ransacked Margaret Leeson's brothel on Drogheda Street; Leeson suffered a miscarriage after being assaulted in the incident and sought to have Crosbie prosecuted for murder. She was persuaded to drop the charge but successfully had him imprisoned and fined for the damage to her premises. (*National Library of Ireland*)

Throughout the eighteenth century public unrest and disorder were a recurrent feature of Dublin life, across the full range of the social spectrum: from the city's small army of pickpockets and footpads, to the aristocratic drinking club known as the Hellfire Club, with its premises in the Eagle Tavern and an unenviable reputation for violence and sexual assault; to the Trinity students who shot dead a fellow of the college on campus in 1734; to the so-called Liberty and Ormond boys and their running affrays throughout the middle decades of the eighteenth century. The standard punishments were fines and imprisonment, with whipping, the pillory and even the gallows for greater offences. But the machinery of justice was not without manifest flaws.

The constabulary in Dublin in the eighteenth century were apparently highly corrupt, and the system continued without any alteration from the 1730s to the 1770s. A degree of oversight had been established in 1778, with committees consisting of parish vestry members and members of the council being set up, and the first police force in Ireland or Britain was established in Dublin in 1786, at a time of considerable unrest in the wake of the American Revolution; a fact that suggested that sometimes the necessity to maintain law and order had other ramifications than merely containing crime. Public disorders were often blamed on Catholics, which carried the hint of deeper issues, and ensured that Catholics were firmly excluded from any role in the maintenance of law and order. But unrest in eighteenth-century Dublin could also be prompted by more basic realities that had little or nothing to do with religion. At noon on 3 December 1759 a crowd assembled in the Liberties and marched to College Green, led by a drummer and collecting more numbers at specified points along their route. MPs were harassed as they entered the parliament, and a mock gallows was erected outside: the harassment was not indiscriminate. It culminated in a forcible entry of the House of Lords, and the installing of a pipe-smoking old woman in the speaker's chair before the crowd was dispersed by troops that night. Their point of origin was important. Dublin's workforce had a marked 'artisan' complexion, with the textile industries being especially important. Their economic grievances were often intertwined with political grievances; in this case, concerns that a union was to be foisted on Ireland, a measure that it was felt would be economically ruinous. The riot was triggered by legislation that reduced the period of notice to be given for the calling of a parliament from forty days to fourteen, which was seen as the prelude to an underhand move to abolish it.

There were hints of cross-class solidarity in what happened and its aftermath: juries refused to convict those arrested, and Trinity students had provided the drum. The

Catholic Church distanced itself from the riot, which might suggest that Catholics had indeed been involved. And this brings us to Dublin's Catholic question. Business and the professions remained dominated by Anglicans, but a substantial Catholic (and dissenter) middle class was emerging from the mid-century, avoiding the Penal Laws as it did so, in a city marked by profound inequality and a remarkable dependence on the Ascendancy in economic terms, as key consumers of goods and employers of labour in the city. This might have implications in and of itself, in terms of law and order. Disorder could be prompted by economic factors: artisans and tradesman were known to attack imported goods.

There was a definite preference among the upper classes for high-end luxury imports, and this inclination towards foreign goods could prompt unrest at times of economic uncertainty. In 1734 weavers from the Liberties had attacked wool drapers on High Street whom they suspected of selling imported goods, and such grievances did not abate. Dublin had, after all, became increasingly politicised towards the end of the eighteenth century. The constituency of 'freemen' was too big to allow for the dominance of the landed gentry, the vast bulk of whom retained their seats of power and influence outside the capital. The network of guilds and a thriving print culture were key to the politicisation of previous decades. Catholics were excluded from official power, and had been for generations, but a Catholic mercantile elite had emerged in Ireland's towns and cities in the second half of the eighteenth century. Guilds were a different matter. By 1750 Dublin had twenty-five trade guilds, with the right to nominate (and, after 1760, to elect) representatives to the common council. 'Half freedom' was extended to Catholics, who lacked these political rights. The controversy that arose in the 1740s thanks to the stance taken by the alderman Charles Lucas points to the politicisation of the guild system, and gives a concrete example of how these issues might come to a head.

Dublin's Common Council was made up of ninety-six representatives of the guilds, forty-eight sheriff's peers, and two sheriffs; an upper house was comprised of the lord mayor and twenty-four aldermen. Lucas, whose statue is in City Hall, was originally from Clare. He became an apprentice apothecary in Dublin and, having risen through the ranks of his profession, was in 1741 one of the nominees appointed by the Guild of Barber Surgeons to sit on the city's Common Council. In the late 1740s he began to agitate for reforms based on the assumption that the council was not governing in the interest of the citizens, and was actively breaching the rights enshrined in the older charters. In 1749 he stood for election as MP, and his campaign stepped up a notch: he established his own campaigning newspaper, *The Censor*, and eventually had to flee

The arms of some of the Dublin trade guilds. (*Courtesy of Dublin City Library and Archive*)

Ireland after the House of Commons ordered his arrest. He fled to Paris, advanced his medical career in London, and eventually returned to Dublin in 1760.

III

Lucas had touched a nerve. If, as he argued, the Protestants of Ireland were entitled to the same rights and privileges as their British counterparts, then the British parliament, and British administrators, had no right whatsoever to govern Ireland. This was an issue that became especially relevant during the American Revolution. In 1776 the British had placed an embargo on Irish exports (especially dairy, salted meat and

'The glorious, pious and immortal memory of the great and good King William – not forgetting Oliver Cromwell, who assisted in redeeming us from popery, slavery, arbitrary power, brass money, and wooden shoes. May we never want a William to kick the **** of a Jacobite! And a **** for the bishop of Cork! And he that won't drink this whether he be a priest, bishop, deacon, bellows blower, gravedigger, or any other fraternity of the clergy; may a north wind blow him to the east! May he have a dark night – a lee shore – a rank storm – and a leaky vessel to carry him over the river Styx! May the dog Cerberus make a meal of his rump and Pluto a snuff box of his skull! And may the devil jump down his throat with a red hot harrow, with every pin tear out a gut, and blow him with a clean carcass to hell! Amen!' – The elaborate opening toast of 'The Aldermen of Skinner's Alley', as recorded in Jonah Barrington's *Personal Sketches of His Own Time* (London, 1830), vol. i, pp. 250–1. The toast was apparently made at the beginning of meetings in the presence of a bust of William of Orange ('which they regarded as a sort of deity'), and was drunk on the knees, each member having unbuttoned his breeches. They Aldermen was originally a loyalist political club, named after aldermen ejected from power in the reign of James II. Over time they adopted many of the concerns of eighteenth-century 'patriots' (during protectionist campaigns they were quite concerned with consuming only Irish drink). They mainly met at the Weavers' Hall in the Coombe, being one of innumerable societies of this kind. They split in the 1790s over the 'Catholic question'; some were also members of the United Irishmen, but the original name was retained by a loyalist remnant active well into the nineteenth century.

The *Dublin Chronicle*, 6 December 1787, one of Georgian Dublin's many newspapers. The proliferation of newspapers in the eighteenth century was vitally important for the transmission of all kinds of commercial, cultural and political information. Over time they also played a major role in fostering political debate. (*Courtesy of Dublin City Library and Archive*)

linen) to the colonies. This proved highly unpopular as it came during an economic downturn and was blamed (perhaps unfairly) for restricting Irish trade: it became a focal point for discontent. Indeed, in 1779 an embargo on English imports was launched at the Tholsel, and was policed by members of the newly-formed 'Volunteer' movement. The Volunteers were founded across Ireland against the backdrop of the American Revolution. The British required manpower and were by now unconvinced of the vitality of the Catholic threat, so were intent on recruiting Irish Catholics into their army: the beginning of the repeal of the Penal Laws was the quid pro quo. As troops were withdrawn from Ireland to fight in America, the Volunteers began to emerge to take up the slack, and the most famous depiction of them in action is set on College Green.

Francis Wheatley's famous painting of College Green, first exhibited in Dublin in 1780, depicts a Volunteer rally on 4 November 1779 (the birthday of the figure represented in the statue, William of Orange, which associated the Volunteers with loyalism) commanded by a variety of landowners, parliamentarians, wealthy businessmen and members of the urban bourgeoisie. Wheatley sanitised the scene by leaving out the various placards and banners that were present on this occasion. These included 'Free Trade or Else' and 'Relief to Ireland' draped on the statue itself, and 'Free Trade or Speedy Revolution' on a placard hanging from a cannon. Eleven days after the Volunteer rally depicted by Wheatley, a crowd of five to six thousand people from the Liberties descended on College Green in protest; MPs were manhandled, and magistrates allegedly refused to call out troops to disperse the crowd. The authorities viewed this kind of activity as ominous. Mob or crowd violence had been a common feature of Dublin life for decades, but the increasingly politicised climate of the late 1770s meant that economic and political issues were intertwined: Ireland's prosperity was seen to be the victim of British policy; even though, at this time, there was no argument for leaving the British sphere of influence, the terms of Ireland's involvement in that world were at stake. The campaign spearheaded by the Volunteers involved many who were normally outside the formal political sphere: women, the mercantile middle classes, and, of course, Catholics. By 1784 it was quite obvious that the Dublin Volunteers were admitting Catholics (a fact that was by no means welcomed by all). April 1784 saw a renewed anti-importation campaign, as weavers from the Liberties who were feeling the pinch directed their ire at those who were importing English goods (or who were suspected of doing so). Such fears were not groundless: the number of Dublin's silk weavers, for instance, had declined from 800 in 1730 to fifty in 1765. On 19 June 1784 a crowd of 300 attacked the home of one

Alexander Clark of Chancery Lane before dragging him (almost naked) to the tenters' fields in Blackpitts, and tarring and feathering him. The 1784 campaign was more violent than that of 1779, as high unemployment raised the stakes and prompted calls for further protectionism. Yet it was not until the 1790s that urban unrest took the form of attempted revolution.

IV

The Dublin Society of United Irishmen was founded in the Eagle Tavern on Eustace Street – now the Quaker Meeting House – in November 1791. This came a matter of weeks after the society was famously founded on Cave Hill, just outside Belfast. The United Irishmen began, arguably, as one of the innumerable clubs or societies that emerged in eighteenth-century Ireland and, like many others, they had been energised and created in the wake of the French Revolution. The society was the brainchild of William Drennan, a Belfast-born physician of liberal Presbyterian stock. Educated in Edinburgh, he had lived in Newry since 1782, where he had become involved in the Volunteer movement. In the 1780s he conceived of an organisation that would act as a hard core of radicals within the Volunteers: as he put it, 'a plot for the people'. He moved to Dublin in 1789 and, like many others, he arrived at the conclusion that the political reforms demanded by the radicals of the 1770s and 1780s could never succeed without the involvement of Catholics, and he proposed the formation of a new organisation to press for such reforms. This sentiment was shared, and it was most famously articulated in a tract entitled *An Argument on Behalf of the Catholics of*

'Called at Moira House. Apprehend I am out of favour there for holding Democratic principles; cannot be helped. "'Tis but in vain, &c, &c."' – Theobald Wolfe Tone wonders if his principles have offended his hosts, September 1792. Moira House, on Usher's Island, had been built in 1752 as the townhouse of the earls of Moira. Tone need not have worried; less then a fortnight later he called there again and was 'most graciously received. Introduced to Lady Granard, who takes charge of my letter to Col. Barry. Dinner and a great deal of wine. Frivolous day! Generally drunk – fine doings twice running.' – T.W. Moody, R.B. McDowell and C.J. Woods (eds), *The Writings of Theobald Wolfe Tone, 1763–98* (Oxford, 1998–2007), vol. i, pp. 290, 301.

'Tarring and feathering, the reward of the enemies of Ireland': a late eighteenth-century depiction of one of the more extreme measures taken against those suspected of importing English goods in Dublin. (*Library of Congress*)

Ireland, written by a young Dublin Anglican barrister called Theobald Wolfe Tone. The tract was hugely successful, and in the wake of its publication Tone was invited to Belfast to attend the inaugural meeting of the new society. It was he who came up with the name for the Dublin branch, of which Drennan was the first president. At the beginning, however, the real centre of its radicalism was among the Presbyterians of Belfast: the Dublin society was relatively moderate. That would change after the Dublin United Irishmen were suppressed by the authorities in May 1794: a pro-French group could never be acceptable after the outbreak of war with revolutionary France.

The United Irishmen in Dublin were composed of the middling to upper ranks in society, and it was by no means a dominant voice in the radical underground of the 1790s. Other organisations, such as the Defenders, the Freemasons and the Catholic Committee, also had very strong, if occasionally surreptitious, profiles. But it is the United Irishmen who became revolutionaries. Having been founded in November 1791, by March 1793 the Dublin United Irishmen allegedly had at least 350 members, with many drawn from the professional classes: attorneys, barristers, doctors, printers, textile manufacturers and cloth merchants. Of these perhaps only 150 or so were active, with a roughly even division between Catholic and Protestant. Notable members included the barristers Henry and John Sheares, born in Cork, who had witnessed the execution of Louis XVI before returning to Ireland in the company of the young Daniel O'Connell, to whom they boasted that they had helped as guards at the execution. They joined the Dublin society, in which they were seen as notably militant, and even established a branch in Cork. Then there was the Donegal-born Presbyterian merchant Oliver Cromwell Bond, whose name speaks volumes about one tradition the United Irishmen drew from. Prior to their dissolution they usually met in the Music Hall in Fishamble Street for debates and to conduct their business.

'Nothing very particular except our great regret for poor Napper [Tandy] whose health we drank with three cheers as also our friends the Catholic Committee, national assembly of France, independence to old Ireland and perfect equality and unity to the people, etc.' – The government informer Thomas Collins reports on a meeting of the Society of United Irishmen at the Music Hall on Fishamble Street in February 1792. R.B. McDowell (ed.), 'Proceedings of the Dublin Society of United Irishmen', *Analecta Hibernica*, 17 (1949), 15.

From 1793 Britain was at war with revolutionary France, and the United Irishmen became interested in forging some kind of link with the French. Throughout the 1790s Paris was a regular port of call for Irish radicals, with the abortive Bantry Bay expedition of 1796 being the fruit of Wolfe Tone's labours. It was this engagement with the French that made the United Irishmen so dangerous, and this is why it was suppressed. In the mid-1790s, as the United Irishmen went underground, its natural radicalism became streamlined as it was transformed into a conspiratorial revolutionary movement, intent upon rebellion, and by 1796 focused on Dublin rather than Belfast.

Nominally, from January 1797 the United Irishmen had adopted a national structure, with provincial committees, which in practice meant Leinster and Ulster. The layers of organisation provided a degree of security that even today remains difficult to disentangle. By June 1797 plans were in place for an insurrection throughout Leinster, with Dublin as the epicentre (though at this time the Dublin United Irishmen lacked arms and organisation).

The framework of the plan was quite simple: the seizure of key locations in Dublin; risings in outlying areas to establish a rebel cordon (the seizure of the scheduled mail coaches from Dublin and their subsequent non-arrival was to be the signal); finally, the rising was to spread out across the country. At the time of the rising on 23 May 1798, the nominal membership of the United Irishmen had risen from 1,500 in January to 10,000 in the city, with another 9,000 in the county. In the city, the areas with the highest memberships were the artisan areas of the west. In the early months of 1798 the west of the city became disturbed, and was swollen with refugees fleeing the repression in the countryside.

On 2 March 1798 Lord Edward Fitzgerald, the colourful son of the Duke of Leinster and a veteran of the American War of Independence, whose military experience had led to him being given a key role in formulating the United Irishmen's military plans, narrowly avoided arrest, but by 21 March the authorities knew of the plans for an uprising. The United Irishmen were to attack the castle (from Ship Street and Hoey's Court), a bank on Mary Street, Trinity College and the Custom House, though many of the precise details remained obscure at this time. In mid-May weapons were found, along with a proclamation in the possession of the Sheares brothers. On 11 May the authorities concluded that a rising was imminent and on 19 May Fitzgerald was arrested by the notorious town major, Henry Sirr, who had already arrested the Sheares brothers and who shot Fitzgerald as they struggled: the wound was not fatal, but an infection from the wadding killed him. On 22 May the Dublin Yeomanry were called out: houses on Thomas Street were searched and ransacked; those where weapons were found were

Dublin and its surrounding counties, from Daniel Augustus Beaufort, *Memoir of a Map of Ireland* (London, 1792). These were to be the epicentre of the national rising planned by the United Irishmen for 1798; the seizure of mail coaches from Dublin and their subsequent non-arrival at their destinations was to be the signal for the rebellion to begin. In the end, the rising in most of the surrounding counties was swiftly and brutally dealt with by the authorities. (*Courtesy of Dublin City Library and Archive, Dublin and Irish Collections*)

burned. On 23 May there was still uncertainty about whether the rising was to take place that day, and the form it might take: would there be fighting in the city, or would risings in Meath and Kildare draw the military away from Dublin? But at 9 p.m. on 23 May, Samuel Neilson instructed fifteen 'colonels' to occupy key posts, most notably at Smithfield and Newmarket – open spaces that could be occupied by large numbers of men. By 10 p.m. word had reached the castle and the Yeomanry were called out.

Ironically, given that troops and cavalry were crammed into Smithfield, this would have been a golden opportunity for pikemen to attack. But their very presence dissuaded any would-be attackers; pikes and other weapons were allegedly found abandoned in the streets around the market. Neilson himself had intended to attack the nearby Newgate prison – Green Street – to free Fitzgerald, Oliver Bond and others, but was captured before he could do so when the jailer recognised him. Newmarket was also occupied by the yeomanry; weapons were found abandoned around it too. The Liffey bridges were then barricaded, splitting the city in two, and checkpoints established at the approach roads to the city and along the canals. City Hall was used as a prison, a curfew was imposed from 9 p.m. to 5 a.m., and executions began at gibbets erected along the Liffey bridges (some unfortunately tardy lamplighters were killed too): the bodies supposedly lie at Croppies Acre, the open space in front of the Royal (now Collins) Barracks. The Sheares brothers became the first United Irish leaders to be executed for high treason, being hanged outside Newgate Prison on 14 July 1798: the bodies were decapitated and were interred in St Michan's Church.

'A new, disgusting, and horrid scene was next morning publicly exhibited after which military executions commenced, and continued with unabating activity. Some dead bodies of insurgents, sabred the night before by Lord Roden's dragoons, were brought in a cart to Dublin, with some prisoners tied together; the carcasses were stretched out in the Castle yard, where the Viceroy then resided, and in full view of the Secretary's windows; they lay on the pavement as trophies of the first skirmish, during a hot day, out and gashed in every part, covered with clotted blood and dust, the most frightful spectacles which ever disgraced a royal residence, save the seraglio. After several hours exposure, some appearance of life was perceived in one of the mutilated carcasses. The man had been stabbed and gashed in various parts; his body was removed into the guard-room, and means were taken to restore animation; the efforts succeeded, he entirely recovered, and was pardoned by Lord Camden; he was an extraordinary fine young man, above six feet high, the son of a Mr. Keough, an opulent landholder of Rathfarnham; he did not, however, change his principles, and was, ultimately, sent out of the country.' – Jonah Barrington records the aftermath of the suppression of the 1798 rebellion. *Rise and Fall of the Irish Nation* (Dublin, 1853), pp. 297–8.

But the associated risings around the edges of the city did take place, in Wicklow, Kildare, Meath and north Dublin. Some of the mail coaches had been stopped, which was the signal to rise. Some of the outlying United Irishmen managed to get into the city, but with the leaders imprisoned the vacuum was insurmountable. The focus of the rebellion soon shifted away from Dublin. Many – most – of the United Irishmen's forces in the city collapsed, but in the Liberties, one of the city's four rebel 'divisions' they remained active under the leadership of an ironmonger of Thomas Street called James Moore, and contemplated a second attempt. Indeed, on 24 May hundreds had assembled near Blackpitts in anticipation of this, and in the following weeks there were attempts to organise a march on Dublin from Wexford, but defeats there and in Wicklow put paid to that.

What seems to have happened in the meantime is that United Irish members from south Dublin streamed further south into Wicklow and Wexford, and fought there, in the thick of the action. Many later surrendered and were of a low enough rank to receive amnesty; of those, between a third and a half were weavers from the Liberties.

The failure to capture Dublin may have been crucial. It robbed the rebellion of a focal point from the outset and, indeed, 1798 really consisted of a series of localised rebellions that were contained before they were dealt with. But the United Irishmen did not go away, despite their defeat: they would make a second attempt at rebellion in 1803, under the leadership of Robert Emmet.

Between 1798 and 1803, however, came a distinctive milestone in the history of the capital. This was the first attempt to compile a comprehensive census of the city, which was carried out by James Whitelaw, the Church of Ireland vicar of St Catherine's in the Liberties, a particularly impoverished district. In 1798 he embarked on a census of the city with the blessing of the authorities: his task was made easier in the aftermath of the rebellion, as the Lord Mayor had instructed that lists of inhabitants be placed at the door of every house in the city. The repressive response to 1798 may have cowed the inhabitants of the city somewhat; Whitelaw met little resistance. His estimate of the total population of Dublin was 182,370. The census was conducted over five months in 1798 and the results were published in 1805 (unfortunately, the original returns were destroyed in the Four Courts in 1922).

V

Whitelaw's research indicated that population density varied enormously from parish to parish: St Michael's (beside Christ Church) recorded 439 people per acre, while St Thomas (between O'Connell Street and Gardiner Street) recorded 87 per acre. Whitelaw subdivided the population of the city into three categories: the upper and middle classes made up 21.8 per cent of the population; servants made up 10.7 per cent; while the largest group by far, the 'lower class', made up 67.4 per cent of Dublin's inhabitants on the eve of the Act of Union.

Here was a city in which the haves were greatly outnumbered by the have-nots. What made Whitelaw's census unprecedented was its combination of statistical information and his own descriptions of what he had witnessed in the course of obtaining it (see page 159). Whitelaw also noted that landlords were oblivious to the squalor, and every Saturday night extracted their rent 'with unfeeling severity'.

Descriptions such as this would recur with disconcerting regularity throughout the nineteenth century, and as time went on, were often linked by observers to the consequences of the second milestone to appear in the aftermath of 1798: the Act of Union of 1801. The abolition of the Irish parliament in 1800, and the incorporation of Ireland into a new, expanded United Kingdom, had been vociferously opposed by

'In the ancient parts of this city, the streets are generally narrow; the houses crowded together; the rears or back yards of very small extent, and some without accommodation of any kind. Of these streets a few are the residence of the upper class of shopkeepers and others engaged in trade; but a far greater proportion of them, with their numerous lanes and alleys, are occupied by working manufacturers, by petty shopkeepers, the labouring poor, and beggars, crowded together to a degree distressing to humanity ... This crowded population, wherever it obtains, is almost universally accompanied by a very serious evil; a degree of filth and stench inconceivable, except by such as have visited those scenes of wretchedness. Into the backyard of each house, frequently not ten feet deep, is flung, from the windows of each apartment, the ordure and other filth of its numerous inhabitants; from whence it is so seldom removed that I have seen it nearly on a level with the windows of the first floor; and the moisture that, after heavy rains, oozes from this heap, having frequently no sewer to carry it off, runs into the street, by the entry leading to the staircase. One instance, out of a thousand that might be given, will be sufficient. When I attempted, in the summer of 1798, to take the population of a ruinous house in Joseph's Lane, near Castle Market, I was interrupted in my progress, by an inundation of putrid blood, alive with maggots, which had, from an adjacent slaughter yard, burst the back door, and filled the hall to the depth of several inches.' – James Whitelaw, *An Essay on the Population of Dublin* (Dublin, 1805), pp. 50–3.

commercial interests in Dublin (especially those in the textile sector). The debate on the union in the College Green parliament was famously characterised by a dramatic intervention by the veteran MP Henry Grattan, one of the leaders of the 'patriot' campaigns of the 1770s, who rose from his sickbed to plead with his fellow MPs to retain Ireland's separate parliament. His plea proved to be in vain. The Act of Union was ultimately passed with the aid of substantial bribery, and integrated the Irish parliament with its British counterpart. Ireland, and Dublin, formally became part of the United Kingdom of Great Britain and Ireland.

'The last parliament of Ireland': an 1874 lithograph (seemingly based on an earlier engraving) of the Irish House of Commons. (*Library of Congress*)

'A very large collection of automata, amongst in the whole above an hundred, and some them extremely curious ... a small number are so ingeniously contrived as to utter any speeches that may be prepared for them by the purchaser.' – A satirical notice of an 'auction' at 'the museum, College Green', castigating those Irish MPs willing to vote for the Act of Union, in *The Anti-union*, 9 February 1799.

VI

Before the full implications of the union could be fully discerned came another failed rebellion, as the United Irishmen attempted one last throw of the dice. The significance of Robert Emmet's rebellion of 1803 is twofold: it was a continuation of the United Irish conspiracy; and it provided a pretext for arguably the most famous speech in Irish history. The Emmets were a prosperous family living at 110 Stephen's Green; the father, Robert, was the state physician. His son Thomas Addis Emmet was a Dublin lawyer who had joined the United Irishmen in 1792. He was close to many of the senior figures, defending them in court and providing legal advice as required. His younger brother Robert had been active in the United Irishmen since 1796, and was expelled from Trinity College for his pains. He had attended a meeting in Abbey Street on 23 May 1798, awaiting instructions that never arrived.

The rebellion Robert later attempted to plan was a direct response to the failure of 1798. As early as January 1799 the United Irishmen began to regroup, and to plan for a renewed offensive on a smaller, more disciplined scale, and with the assistance of a foreign power. In April 1799 Robert Emmet's arrest was ordered as the government suspected that he was involved in a new conspiracy, but he fled to Hamburg, and then to France, where he tried to get French assistance for another rebellion. By now the French were uninterested in an Irish rebellion, save as a bargaining chip as they came to terms with England, and, disillusioned, Emmet returned to Ireland in October 1802. Emmet began to link up with the old United Irish networks; he inherited a considerable sum on the death of his father in December 1802, which he ploughed into the rebellion. His plan was shaped by the failure of 1798. The rebellion of 1803 was to be a smaller but more purposeful affair, concentrated on Dublin, and it would involve a much tighter and smaller band of conspirators; there was to be no repeat of the attempted mass insurrection of five years earlier. Like its predecessor, however, the rebellion of 1803 was originally to have been predicated on French assistance.

Dublin was the key, and there were ambitious plans to decapitate the government by killing or capturing the viceroy and privy council, and by capturing Dublin Castle itself. The preparations began in March in 1803, with the assistance of a number of veterans of 1798, and went largely unnoticed by the new post-union administration in Ireland. Intent as they were on making a break with the discredited past, the new regime in Dublin Castle had run down the intelligence network that had proved so troublesome for the United Irishmen in the 1790s. Emmet established a weapons depot on Marshalsea Lane South behind Thomas Street, with another at 26 Patrick Street, where rockets were developed. Other locations were, apparently, Smithfield, Winetavern Street, Capel Street and North King Street. The plans involved the use of rockets and explosives – logs packed with black powder and with pieces of metal and nails bound to their exterior – to clear troops off the streets. There was an emphasis on urban warfare: other weapons included folding pikes and specially commissioned guns that could be concealed easily.

The second element of the plan involved insurgents from neighbouring counties flooding into Dublin; Emmet, perhaps naively, expected nineteen counties to be involved. Outlying towns and villages such as Dunshaughlin and Lucan were to be occupied; and indeed, roads were closed off by rebels at Maynooth, Phibsborough, Sandymount and a number of other places on the night of 23 May. However, prior to this, a large explosion took place at the Patrick Street depot on 16 July, killing two. This forced the date for the insurrection to be brought forward, to 23 July.

The almost farcical nature of what happened next is in stark contrast to the extent of the preparations. Rebel forces did assemble at a number of points in the city – Wood Quay, Townsend Street, Irishtown, Smithfield, with the Magazine Fort and the Royal Barracks to be targeted. Cornmarket, near the heart of the old city, was to be a particular focal point, given its proximity to the weapons depots. In the end, at around 9.15 p.m., Emmet called off the rebellion by firing a rocket into the air, and most of those around the city stood down. Rebels arriving in the city from Kildare left when they realised that there were not enough weapons, and the eighty or so who assembled at Cornmarket were drunk. Emmet led a group on an attack on Dublin Castle after reading out extracts from his proclamation. The prominent politician and judge Arthur Wolfe, Lord Kilwarden, was piked to death along with his nephew that evening. Emmet himself was captured in Harold's Cross on 25 August and was tried in Green Street courthouse on 19 September. During his trial he made a speech in which

"WHEN MY COUNTRY TAKES HER PLACE, AMONG THE NATIONS OF THE EARTH, THEN, AND NOT TILL THEN, LET MY EPITAPH BE WRITTEN: I HAVE DONE!"

COPIED FROM THE ORIGINAL.

EXECUTION OF ROBERT EMMET.

IN THOMAS STREET. 20TH SEPTEMBER 1803.

Entered according to act of Congress
in the year 1840 by FIRM & Co Buffalo, N.Y.
in the Office of the Librarian of Congress
at Washington, N.Y.

The execution of Robert Emmet outside St Catherine's Church on Thomas Street. While a memorial marks the spot, Emmett's final resting place is famously unknown. (Library of Congress)

he famously suggested that his epitaph remain unwritten until Ireland took its place among the independent nations of the earth. Emmett was executed on Thomas Street the next day. His final resting place remains unknown.

VII

In 1811 an anonymous pamphleteer known as 'Solomon second-sight' revealed a dream to his readers in which he was taken on a walk around Dublin by a mysterious man dressed in white robes emblazoned with red crosses, and holding a rosary. Solomon's journey around his dream city began at Christ Church, where friars belonging to the 'established church' were conducting a ceremony to purify the cathedral after centuries of Protestant occupation. Going past Dublin Castle, he learned that a French viceroy now resided there. It was with difficulty that Solomon made his way down Dame Street, for it was clogged with members of a bewildering range of Catholic orders – Franciscans, Carthusians, Dominicans, Benedictines – and he was repeatedly obliged to kneel before processions of the host. At College Green he visited 'the National Bank' (formerly the Bank of Ireland, which had moved into the vacated parliament building after the Act of Union). In Solomon's vision, it was now being converted into a new 'conservative senate', due to arrive from France very soon. The building had been stripped of its statues of Plenty, Commerce and Justice, for, as Solomon's guide put it, 'we had no further occasion for them'. Protestant merchants had been driven out of the country, as Ireland went from 'royal' to 'republican' to 'imperial'. Before reaching Trinity College – now 'that great and fruitful seminary of the Catholic religion established in Ireland' – Solomon surveyed College Green and noted a striking absentee. 'Where', he asked his guide, 'is the statue of King William?' Grinling Gibbons' statue of William III had stood on College Green since 1701; Solomon envisaged that the victor of the Boyne would have disappeared a hundred years later. In the dream, Dublin had been remoulded into a Catholic capital. And it got worse. As Solomon's guide put it, 'in 1773, when the Catholics of Ireland were first enabled to acquire an interest in land, the doom of Protestantism was sealed', for 'yet the last concession was ever turned into an argument for something further'. Now Catholics controlled Dublin's city council, and the mayor was due to present an address to Napoleon himself. A proclamation warned of Protestant spies in the city ('heretics, calling themselves Protestants'), and threatened those Protestants who had not taken the 'oaths of allegiance and of the papal supremacy' with expulsion or death. Protestants were to surrender their weapons, on pain of death. They were subject to curfew, and could not gather in groups of more than five, again under pain of death. The proclamation concluded: 'GOD SAVE THE EMPEROR AND THE HOLY CHURCH.'

If that was not ominous enough, at the Four Courts Solomon was assured that 'the attaint of English blood, though diluted over six centuries with the holy waters of our Shannon, can never lose its original impurity'. While digesting this, he saw a great procession to greet a papal nuncio, here to enforce 'the strict payment of Tithes to the Holy See'. But had not 'our peasantry exclaimed against tithes, as a system of the cruelest injustice'? Here a traditional grievance against Protestant 'ascendancy' was turned on its head. Finally, Solomon and his companion came to Smithfield, which was to be put to the same use that had made its London counterpart so notorious in the reign of Queen Mary: Protestant prisoners were about to be burned alive at the stake. It was too much for Solomon: 'God of mercy, is this Ireland?' A voice cried, 'Seize on the heretic!', but Solomon awoke before meeting the horror of the fate that surely awaited him. 'Oh how glad I waked, to find it but a dream!'

It is impossible to know who 'Solomon second-sight' was, but his politics could be categorised as 'ultra-Protestant'. As Dublin had expanded in the eighteenth century, much of the symbolism of its built environment had become emblematic of Protestantism, in the form of the established Church of Ireland. What Solomon was doing was turning this world upside down, in an account that purported to reveal how the traditional symbols and venues of Protestant 'ascendancy' – the statue of William, Trinity College – were to be appropriated by a new, Catholic 'ascendancy'. True, it was written during the Napoleonic Wars, which reinvigorated traditional fears of Catholic France, but the reference to the Catholic Relief Act of 1773 suggests that Solomon was tapping into a deeper set of Irish Protestant fears; that their status was being slowly but surely overturned. Not only had the concordat of 1801 restored the Catholic Church in France after the devastation of the revolution, but the lingering prospect of Catholic emancipation in Ireland after the Act of Union kept a fervent sectarianism alive in some quarters. By evoking his vision of Dublin as a Catholic capital, Solomon was simply reviving a traditional form of anti-Catholic polemic. In this he was not alone; but he was certainly more ingenious than most.

The Act of Union is usually, and justifiably, seen as a watershed. Without the parliament, the Irish aristocracy began to focus their attention on London rather than Dublin. Their elegant townhouses were gradually abandoned (a century later, many would be squalid slums). They took much of their spending power with them, so the services industries and consumer culture that had developed around the parliament were also stripped away. And the end of the Napoleonic Wars in 1815 was another

'In so populous a city as Dublin it is unreasonable to suppose that there will be no depredations committed, or that it is unnecessary to caution strangers against characters that always lurk in every metropolis ... persons who go to the four courts in term time, should carefully avoid taking any thing valuable in their pockets, as they are in danger of having them picked ... Hackney coach-men and car-men are in general, in Dublin, very apt to impose on strangers, by demanding much over the fare ... mock auctions, in which a variety of incredible frauds are practised upon the unwary, ought to be cautiously avoided. They are generally in alleys, where a few puffers, who have some articles to dispose of, attend to bid when strangers enter.' – *The Picture of Dublin*, 1811 (Dublin, 1811), pp. 56–7.

blow: Ireland and Dublin had done extremely well while the British were cut off from European markets during the war with France, but that changed with the coming of peace after the Battle of Waterloo. The last years of the Georgian era saw the start of Dublin's long decline from the professed second city of the British Empire to a provincial centre within the United Kingdom.

The early years of the nineteenth century witnessed a sense on the part of some that Protestantism was under siege, and was being forced into retreat (hence the hysterical vision of Solomon second-sight). The loss of the Irish parliament forced Ireland's ruling elite slowly but surely to turn their attention to London, as the seat of the parliament that governed Ireland as well as Britain. Dublin was to become less a destination in its own right than a transit point en route to London. Dublin's importance as a city prior to 1800 rested on a number of factors: it had the largest population on the island of Ireland and was the leading port and commercial distribution centre; it was the centre for printing and remained dominant in terms of financial services; essentially it had a monopoly of professional services, such as banking, education, and law; it also benefited from being the location of the Irish parliament, and from the social status granted by the presence of the Viceregal Court and the landed classes. The abolition of the Irish parliament, in which so many of them sat, by the Act of Union deprived the city of a key institution, one with a great deal of economic and social significance; it had acted as a magnet for the Anglican ruling elite, and after its abolition they gradually began to focus their attention elsewhere. But Dublin in the early nineteenth century was still a regional capital, and despite the assumption of decline in the early

OPENING of the NEW DOCKS on St GEORGES DAY 1796.

~ Yacht entering Camden Lock.
~ Ringsend.
~ Tent where Earl Camden breakfasted.
~ S heads of Clontarf.

~ Gondola that Earl Camden saild in
to name the Docks and Locks.
~ A Ship on the River Liffey.

The opening of the new docks on the Liffey in 1796, arising from the necessity for deep-water berths east of the Custom House; Dublin's docks would continue to expand eastwards throughout the nineteenth century. (*National Library of Ireland*)

A View of the BRIDGE on the Grand CANAL at the Circular Road near DUBLIN.

Publish'd by W.m Allen N.o 32 Dame Street Dublin

The bridge over the Grand Canal at South Circular Road. The canal had been fully completed by 1804.
(*National Library of Ireland*)

nineteenth century, building and development continued well into the Victorian era, though perhaps not on the scale of the eighteenth century.

After 1798, the impending Act of Union had provoked a range of responses: the customs union would be disastrous for the economy; Westminster's rule would be too far removed to care about Dublin. But the city still retained most of the attributes that had made it pre-eminent prior to 1800. It still acted as a distribution centre for consumer goods; and it still, at least in the early decades of the nineteenth century, retained the huge artisanal manufacturing base that had been built up in areas such as the Liberties in the previous century. It also continued to be developed, as building projects continued after 1800: the Four Courts, Carlisle Bridge, the General Post Office (GPO) (1818), and King's Inns (1820), along with the renewed development of Phoenix Park from 1832 and the ambitious cluster of institutional buildings in and around Grangegorman, to name but a few. The creation of buildings such as the Chapel Royal and the GPO, both designed by Francis Johnson, the development of Phoenix Park, the laying out of Chesterfield Avenue, the creation of the Commission of Education's place in Marlborough Street, and even later prisons such as Arbour Hill and Mountjoy, remain as impressive monuments to what is often presumed to be an age of unremitting decline. Indeed, the streetscape continued to attract the favourable comments of visitors to the city after 1800, with the public buildings often compared favourably to their British counterparts. Visitors' reactions after 1800 could be broken into three categories: a positive impression of Dublin's physical appearance; bemusement at the post-union departure of so many of the aristocracy; and unmitigated horror at the scale of poverty and degradation to be found on the Irish capital's streets.

'The truth is, amidst much noisy loud-tongued nationality, the people of Ireland, and in an especial manner, the people of Dublin, are as provincial a people as perhaps are anywhere to be found. On no subject of taste, nor (with the exception of politics) scarcely on any of literature, have they an opinion of their own. As good, as fashionable, as beautiful as in England, is the climax of praise; nor has any thing a chance to be reckoned either good, or fashionable, or beautiful, unless it comes from England, or has been approved there.' – **Strabane native and physician John Gamble gives a caustic account of Dublin's chattering classes in** *Sketches of History, Politics and Manners in Dublin and the North of Ireland, in 1810* **(London, 1826), p. 35.**

Yet the perception of Dublin as a city that declined after the union is broadly true, even if it has to be qualified in terms of causes and effects. The social topography of the eighteenth century became entrenched in the nineteenth; Dublin never became geographically segregated along sectarian lines, although some of the outlying suburbs that developed later in the century could have a marked Protestant and unionist complexion). Property prices prior to the Great Famine of the 1840s confirmed this pattern: for example, the wealthiest areas *circa* 1830 remained around St Stephen's Green. A decline in property valuations could be seen between *circa* 1840 and 1854, when the average tenement valuation went from £29 12s 6d to just under £25.

There was, as time went by, a degree of deindustrialisation; or, more properly 'de-skilling', as the gradual abolition of import tariffs between 1808 and 1824 opened the door to cheaper, better-quality British imports, produced by employers with far more substantial financial resources; a lethal development for the artisan industries of areas such as the Liberties. Certainly, some employers and employees felt this to be the case at the time: the collapse of the textile trade in the Liberties, for example, was due to a combination of tariffs being removed, a British recession that deprived Dublin of a market, and the introduction of steamboat services across the Irish Sea, thus enabling the produce of Britain's industrial revolution to penetrate the Irish market with greater facility.

The latter hints at something that has to be weighed in the balance against the sense of decline after 1800: the development of major, indeed defining, infrastructural projects. The one that had the most profound impact on the physical geography of Dublin lay out in the bay: the Bull Walls, built as a solution to the long-standing problem of the shifting silt of the bay, caused in large part by the discharge of the rivers Tolka and Dodder. The South Bull wall had been finally completed in 1795, but its northerly counterpart was not built until 1820–23; they exploited the tidal motion in the bay to create a clear channel naturally scoured of silt. One consequence was the extensive building up of silt to the north of the wall, inadvertently creating Bull Island over time. Moving north again, Howth Harbour was built on the Irish Sea itself between 1807 and 1813 as a solution to the low depth of water at the Pigeon House, which was causing mails to be delayed on Irish Sea crossings. It opened as mail packet station in 1818 but never took off, and that function was transferred to another new harbour at Kingstown (now Dún Laoghaire) in 1826, which had been built between 1817 and 1860 to replace an earlier harbour that was meant to serve as a refuge in bad weather. Leaving behind these new additions to the bay and moving into the city via the River Liffey, a range of new infrastructural developments sprang up along the

A view of Barrack Bridge, looking west, with the dome of the Four Courts visible. This was the location of the original 'Bloody Bridge', though the structure depicted here was built in 1704. The gatehouse to the right of the picture was later moved to the western gate of the Royal Hospital Kilmainham. The bridge was replaced in 1861 by the cast-iron Victoria (now Rory O'More) Bridge. (*Courtesy of Dublin City Library and Archive, Postcards and Views Collection*)

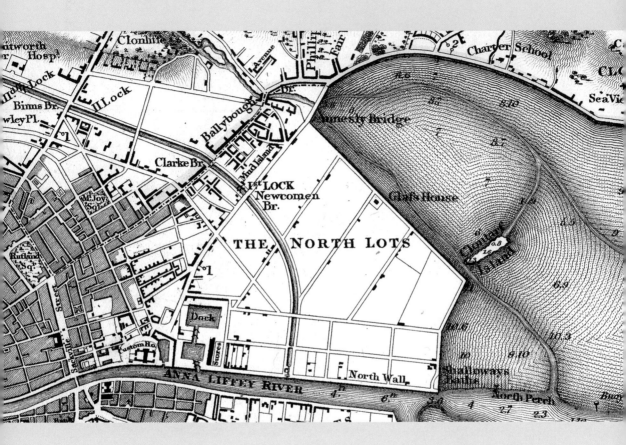

William Duncan's 1821 map of the north-east of Dublin city and the docks. Rutland and Mountjoy squares can be seen to the left, and the inexorable expansion of the docks is also evident. Yet what is not depicted is also revealing; the map also indicates how small Dublin still was, even at this stage in its history. Born in Scotland, Duncan was the principal draughtsman to the Quartermaster General's department of the British army, and was commissioned to devise a series of maps covering all of County Dublin, including the city. The coloured boundaries indicate administrative divisions. (*Courtesy of Dublin City Library and Archive, Map Collection*)

Liffey, as the quays began to be extended further eastward from the 1820s to facilitate deep-water berths.

But these cannot compensate for the negative legacy of the Act of Union, both in terms of loss of status and, perhaps more important, the loss of the particular consumer economy that was predicated on the presence of the parliament. In 1801, 271 peers and 300 MPs had residences in Dublin; by 1821 these numbers had been reduced to, respectively, thirty-four and five. There was a gradual aristocratic exodus, the impact of which was offset by wartime prosperity prior to the ending of the Napoleonic Wars in 1815. The development of gentlemen's clubs and hotels such as the Shelbourne indicates that the aristocracy did not abandon the city entirely, even if they became more peripatetic in their relationships with it, but for most of the nineteenth century the top rungs of Dublin's social ladder would be inhabited by the resident professional and business classes rather than the aristocracy.

Victorians

❧

1820-1880

The fears that Solomon second-sight articulated so hysterically in 1811 continued to fester throughout the early decades of the nineteenth century. Yet despite Solomon's concerns (to put it mildly) that Dublin's streetscape was to become a gigantic set of monuments to Catholicism, prior to 1850 it had acquired some very substantial monuments to Protestantism and loyalism, most obviously Nelson's Pillar, built in 1808 to commemorate British victory at the Battle of Waterloo. This could be seen as representing a form of imperialism that was not automatically sectarian, an important consideration as the state in Ireland began to detach itself from more openly sectarian commemorations. An imperial identity was potentially a more inclusive replacement for the Protestant ascendancy of a previous era.

'A view of College Green, Dublin, Westmoreland St, part of Sackville St and Carlisle Bridge', by J. Bluck and Thomas Roberts, 1807. The Parliament House and Trinity College are clearly visible. (*National Library of Ireland*)

'Many years ago, a clergyman belonging to St Catherine's church in Dublin resided at the old castle of Donore, in the vicinity of that city. From melancholy, or some other cause, he put an end to his existence, by hanging himself out of a window near the top of the castle, so small that it was a matter of surprise how he was able to force his body through it. That he had supernatural aid in accomplishing the deed is the belief of the neighbourhood; for, besides the smallness of the window, there is the farther evidence that, to this very day, the mark of his figure is seen on the wall beneath it, and no whitewashing is able to efface it. After his death, a coach, sometimes driven by a horses without heads, was frequently observed at night driving furiously by Roper's Rest, as the castle was called from him.' – Thomas Crofton Croker, *Fairy Legends and Traditions of the South of Ireland* (London, 1828), vol. i, pp. 110–22.

I

The essential backdrop to these changes was the slow but sure resolution of the Catholic question. Certainly, Catholic emancipation – in the form of granting Catholics in Ireland and Britain the right to sit in parliament – was discussed in a more encouraging climate by 1820 in Westminster, with the premiership of Robert Peel seeming to represent a thaw in official attitudes towards the issue. By 1821 the only major obstacle to emancipation remained George IV who, like his father, was deeply unenthusiastic about it, though the royal visit in August 1821 was met by huge and enthusiastic crowds in Dublin; a popular belief that the king was in fact amenable to Catholic emancipation probably helped in that regard. Yet despite burgeoning sympathies towards emancipation on the part of successive lord mayors, and the presence of a sympathetic (and Irish-born) viceroy appointed later that year (Sir Richard Wellesley, formerly a member of the Volunteers, Governor-General of Bengal, and foreign secretary, not to mention the Duke of Wellington's brother), an undercurrent of ultra-Protestant hostility to emancipation was still evident in the city.

On 12 July 1822 it took a familiar form. On that day, as was traditionally the case, Dublin Orangemen had decorated the statue of William of Orange on College Green as usual, though various people voiced their dissatisfaction throughout the day. At 9 p.m. an Orangeman was assaulted, at 10 p.m. the lamps around the statue were smashed, and a number of young men mounted the statue and tore down the

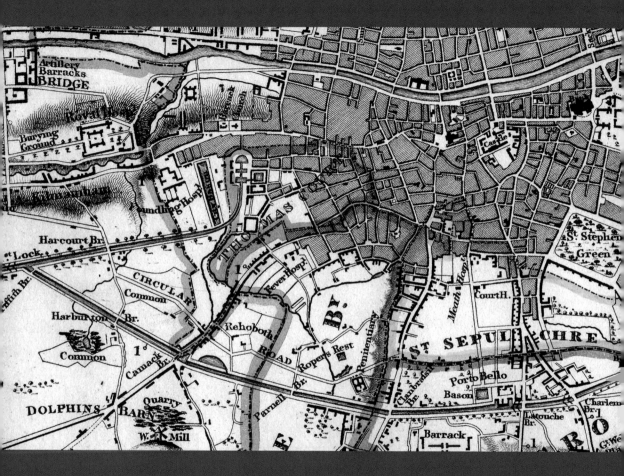

William Duncan's 1821 map of the south-west of the city; Roper's Rest can be seen in the centre, near the bottom of the map. (*Courtesy of Dublin City Library and Archive, Map Collection*)

George IV is welcomed into Dublin in 1821; note the triumphal arches. The painting was presented to the city by the king during the visit. (*Courtesy of Dublin City Library and Archive*)

'orange insignia', throwing them to the ground. The Orangemen then surrounded the monument and began to demand that passers-by take off their hats in respect to the statue, and the memory of King William. The police were eventually deployed, and the decorations were 'quietly' removed. The crowd had 'peaceably separated' by 11 p.m. At around the same time, the yeomanry removed what was left on the statue, which was then taken to a tavern on Werburgh Street. Numerous people had been injured, and so to avoid a repeat of such scenes on 4 November – William's birthday, the other major date in the Orange calendar – guards were placed around it the night before to prevent access to the statue, with dragoons on standby. On 4 November itself, the statue remained under guard. Unrest simmered in the evening, but was dealt with by the police. A mob assembled in Nassau Street, roaming around, breaking windows and 'demolishing' street lamps, and twice appeared outside the Mansion House, where they were kept at bay. But according to *The Freeman's Journal*, whose offices on Trinity Street gave a bird's-eye view of the proceedings, Orangemen later appeared on College Green 'In as strong force as before, and were even more riotous and ruffianly in their conduct. No individual was suffered to pass by without making obeisance to the idol of those wretches. When a passenger was unfortunate enough to come within view of the statue, he was immediately surrounded and huddled by fellows, who cried out "Down on your knees—a groan for the Lord Mayor—and Damn the Pope."'

It should be noted, however, that these disturbances seem not to have been one-sided. Anti-Orange slogans were also reported (such as 'down with the b----y Orangemen' or 'I'll send your Orange soul to hell's flames'), while streetlamps and windows were smashed in the area of Grafton Street and St Stephen's Green, as were some of the windows of the Archbishop of Dublin's palace on Kevin Street. The activities of the Orangemen would appear to have prompted a hostile response; but this was the high-water mark of such disturbances. The traditional Orange ceremonies around the statue on College Green, and the disorders that could accompany them, seem to have faded away rapidly thereafter.

Not all disorders in Dublin were prompted by differing beliefs. In August of the same year, 1822, *Saunder's Newsletter* reported on some of the unsavoury occurrences that invariably accompanied the annual Donnybrook Fair. Donnybrook itself lay just outside the city, and may have been the location of a medieval monastery. In the late thirteenth century a charter granted the corporation the right to hold a fair, which was then sold to the Ussher family in the 1690s to raise funds. In the 1750s the Madden family inherited the rights, and retained them until the fair was eventually suppressed. While livestock was an important part of the fair, as with so many others,

A relatively civilised scene from Donnybrook Fair, as sketched by William Brocas in the early nineteenth century. (*National Library of Ireland*)

To be Set,

From the 25th Day of March last,

For such Terms as shall be agreed on,

THE TWO HOUSES

ON the East Side of Jervis-street, Nos. 34, and 35, and the House at the Corner of Jervis-street and Britain-street, No. 36—Also the Houses and Ground in Britain-st. adjoining thereto, Nos. 17, 18, 19, and 20, extending to Chapel-lane—Also the four Houses in Britain-street adjoining the Widows' Alms House, on the East Side, and extending to Denmark-street, Nos. 22, 23, 24, and 25—and the several Houses and Ground in Denmark-street, extending from Britain-street to the Parochial-school of the Parish of St. Mary, Nos. 21, 22, 23 and 24, the Property of the Trustees of the Widows' Alms House in Britain-street.

PROPOSALS in Writing (POST PAID) sealed up, and directed To the TRUSTEES OF THE WIDOWS' ALMS HOUSE in Britain-street, will be received by JAMES BARLOW, Esq. No. 4, North Great George's-street.

April 25th, 1822.

'College St – Donnybrook, being in this division, there were made of the occasions of the fair the customary number of complaints for broken heads, black eyes, bloody noses, squeezed hats, singed, cut and torn inexpressibles, jocks, and upper benjamins, loodies, frocks, tippets, reels, and damaged leghorns, together with sundry assaults, fibbings, cross buttocks, chancey lodgements, and ground floorings, too numerous to mention.' – *Saunder's Newsletter*, 28 August 1822, cited in Séamas Ó Maitiú, *The Humours of Donnybrook Dublin's Famous Fair and its Suppression* (Dublin, 1995), p. 25.

its proximity to Dublin ensured that Donnybrook Fair became a fixture in Dublin's social calendar.

By the early nineteenth century the fair green at Donnybrook was a sprawling and raucous affair, with travelling theatres; tents and stalls selling food and drink (often set up by Dublin publicans) and arranged into mock thoroughfares bearing the names of streets and squares in the city; and sporting events (especially boxing and horseracing). Arguably the fair effectively began at St Stephen's Green, which was the obvious starting point for hackney cabs taking people out to it. Over time, however, the fair's reputation for drunken violence and sexual licence began to overtake its fame as one of Dublin's seasonal wonders. This had long been an issue, but the gradual expansion of the city out towards Donnybrook gave it an added impetus; despite restrictions being imposed, and the best efforts of the authorities, sabbatarians and temperance advocates, the charter that established the fair lent it a degree of legal protection. The death of the proprietor, John Madden, in 1850 proved fatal to the fair, his sister sold the patent and, despite the best efforts of his nephew, the censure of the authorities, respectable society and the Churches – not to mention the imposition of severe restrictions on the sale of drink – consigned the fair to history in the 1860s. When a new Catholic church was constructed in Donnybrook, the first mass, held there in August 1866, was presided over by the Catholic primate, Cardinal Paul Cullen, whose subsequent sermon pulled no punches in hailing the demise of the fair and the opening of the church as a victory over the forces of darkness. The last gasp of Donnybrook Fair came in 1868, when it was a shadow of what it had once been. It was never held again.

By the time that Cullen preached his sermon in Donnybrook, Catholic churches had become an established part of Dublin's streetscape. As early as 1749 Dublin had

'I remember looking up at the old cage work wooden house that stood at the corner of Castle Street and Werburgh Street, and wondering why, as it overhung so much, it did not fall down – and then turning down Fishamble Street, and approaching the Four Courts, that then existed, through what properly was denominated Christ Church Yard, but which popularly was called Hell. This was certainly a very profane and unseemly sobriquet, to give to a place that adjoined a cathedral whose name was Christ Church; and my young mind, when I first entered there, was struck with its unseemliness. Yes; and more especially, when over the arched entrance there was pointed out to me the very image of the devil, carved in oak, and not unlike one of those hideous black figures that are still in Thomas Street, hung over tobacconists doors ... I can assure you, reader, that there are relics of this very statue to this day; some of it was made into much esteemed snuff boxes – and I am told there is one antiquarian in our city, who possesses the head and horns, and who prizes the relic as the most valuable in his museum. At any rate, hell to me, in those days, was a most attractive place, and often did I go hither, for the yard was full of shops where toys, and fireworks, and kits, and all of the play things that engage the youthful fancy, were exposed for sale. But hell was not only attractive to little boys, but also to bearded me: for here were comfortable lodgings for single men, and I remember reading in a journal of the day, an advertisement, intimating that there were "To be let, furnished apartments in Hell. N.B. They are well suited to a lawyer." – *Dublin Penny Journal*, 27 October 1832.

nineteen Catholic chapels, all of which operated relatively unhindered. The relaxation of the Penal Laws brought the Catholic Church back onto the streets of Dublin more openly. The construction of St Teresa's on Clarendon Street from 1793 onwards was a new departure, but the construction of new, and prominent, Catholic churches in the early years of the nineteenth century was seen as an expression of a new confidence. St Mary's Pro-Cathedral was built between 1814 and 1825 on the site of another aristocratic townhouse to a Greek revival design by an unknown architect, and possibly based on a Parisian model. This was the largest church of any kind built in Dublin since the Middle Ages, and was a testament to the increasing assertiveness of the Roman Catholic Church in the early nineteenth century, as the repressive Penal

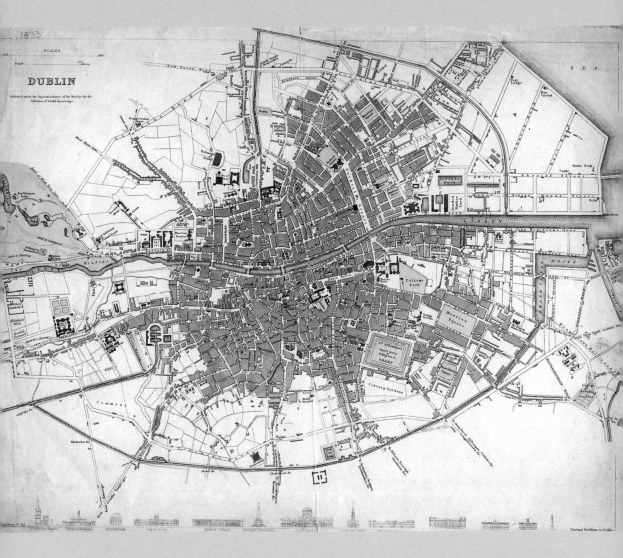

Dublin, as depicted in an 1833 street directory map produced by the Society for the Diffusion of Useful Knowledge, which had been founded in London in 1826 to promote and support education to the widest possible audience via inexpensive and accessible publications. (*Courtesy of Dublin City Library and Archive*)

Laws fell into abeyance. It is striking that the Pro-Cathedral is located away from the main thoroughfare of Sackville Street, though this probably has more to do with the land that was then available for its construction. The project was spearheaded by John Troy, the assertive Catholic archbishop of Dublin at the time. As the parish church of the archbishop, it was and is the de facto Catholic cathedral in Dublin, though it was not – is not – officially a cathedral.

The trend continued. In August 1841 a sermon delivered in St Audoen's name-checked a number of new Catholic churches – St Andrew's on Westland Row, SS Michael and John's on Blind Quay, St Francis Xavier on Gardiner Street, St Michan's, St Paul's and the Pro-Cathedral itself – as 'trophies of the glorious sacrifices of the Irish people for their religion'. There was a certain element of triumphalism in some of these constructions, most evident in the construction of the enormous new Catholic church of St Audoen's, which loomed over its adjacent medieval (and Protestant) counterpart. The new Catholic infrastructure continued to be embedded into the streetscape (though the building of churches such as that of the Three Patrons in Rathgar was deemed provocative by some shades of Protestant opinion, given the composition of the locality). And the creation of Goldenbridge and Prospect (later Glasnevin) cemeteries, while not explicitly Catholic, was intended to fend off the last remnants of the popery laws by providing places of burial outside the stricture of the established Church, in a modest but firm challenge to the lingering power of the Protestant establishment.

This is not to say that the Church of Ireland was on the back foot: witness the construction of new churches such as the 'Black Church', officially St Mary's Chapel of Ease (a secondary church within a parish). It took its nickname from the colouring of the calp limestone from which it was built, which darkens when wet. It originally opened in 1830, at a time when the long decline in the socio-economic status of the north inner city had not yet fully begun and the professional classes who lived on the Gardiner estates had not migrated to the suburbs and townships south of the city. It was designed by John Semple, who was the architect for the Board of First Fruits in Dublin and who, according to Maurice Craig, pioneered his own distinctive Gothic style of architecture, characterised by deep-set windows, pinnacles and a generally severe style (Semple also designed distinctive churches in Rathmines and Monkstown, among others). There is one apocryphal tale attached to Semple's churches, namely, that their solid and impressive structure arose from the fears of the then Church of Ireland archbishop of Dublin, William Magee, who was convinced in the early nineteenth century that the Protestant population was in danger of being massacred

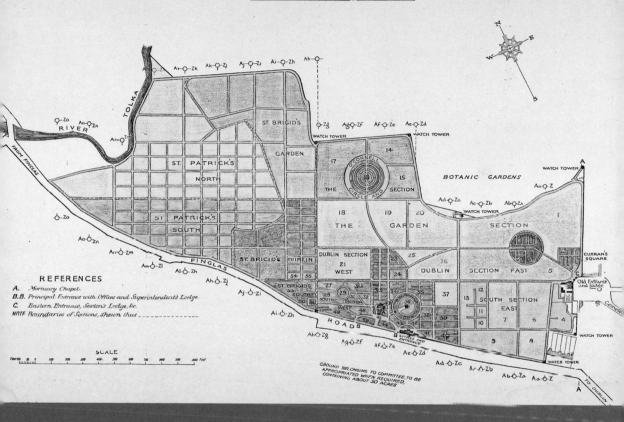

Prospect (Glasnevin) Cemetery around the turn of the twentieth century. The original cemetery consisted of the small section known as Curran Square, on the right of the map. Having opened in 1832 it grew dramatically in the Victorian era, being landscaped as a so-called 'garden' cemetery. By the second half of the century it had become increasingly associated with the interment of a range of prominent figures, most notably Daniel O'Connell, who had founded the original committee that established the cemetery and who was re-interred in 1869 beneath an enormous replica of an early Christian round tower. (*Glasnevin Trust*)

John Semple's St Mary's Chapel of Ease – the 'Black Church' – photographed in 1964 in the course of urban redevelopment. The vantage point from which the photo was taken is now occupied by a Dublin Corporation flats complex. (*Courtesy of Dublin City Library and Archive Dublin City Council Photographic Collection*)

'My Uncle Ludlow – Tom's father – while we were attending lectures, purchased three or four old houses in Aungier Street, one of which was unoccupied ... The house, to begin with, was a very old one. It had been, I believe, newly fronted about fifty years before; but with this exception, it had nothing modern about it. The agent who bought it and looked into the titles for my uncle, told me that it was sold, along with much other forfeited property, at Chichester House, I think, in 1702; and had belonged to Sir Thomas Hacket, who was Lord Mayor of Dublin in James II's time. How old it was then, I can't say; but, at all events, it had seen years and changes enough to have contracted all that mysterious and saddened air, at once exciting and depressing, which belongs to most old mansions.

'There had been very little done in the way of modernising details; and, perhaps, it was better so; for there was something queer and by-gone in the very walls and ceilings – in the shape of doors and windows – in the odd diagonal site of the chimney pieces – in the beams and ponderous cornices – not to mention the singular solidity of all the woodwork, from the bannisters to the window-frames, which hopelessly defied disguise, and would have emphatically proclaimed their antiquity through any conceivable amount of modern finery and varnish.' –
A fictional account of urban decay, from Joseph Sheridan Le Fanu's 'An account of some strange disturbances in an old house on Aungier Street', *Dublin University Magazine*, December 1853, p. 721.

by their Catholic neighbours. Consequently, he supposedly insisted that any new churches be capable of being fortified and defended.

II

The 1840 Municipal Reform Act had opened the door to a nationalist and Catholic presence in Dublin's political and public life by establishing Dublin Corporation as an elected body. Consequently, repealers – supporters of Daniel O'Connell's campaign to repeal the Act of Union – had won a majority on the corporation in 1841, with the towering figure of Daniel O'Connell himself becoming Lord Mayor. Yet liberal Protestants also held office in the 1840s and thereafter, in a conscious gesture to what was now a Protestant minority. The increasingly public emphasis on Catholicism in

Dublin began to intensify during the tenure of Cardinal Paul Cullen from the 1850s onwards. This was a very deliberate move by Cullen, who wanted schools, churches and religious orders to become a key part of the public life of the metropolis; it was also seen as essential to have Catholic foothold in charity, education and politics. This was essentially an attempt to redress structural imbalances. In 1834, Dublin was 73 per cent Catholic, but with major regional variations. Catholics formed a notable minority in the professions, banking, the military and among skilled labourers, but as the century wore on a new Catholic middle class continued to emerge from the retail and construction sectors, along with the drinks trade. Catholic schools such as the elite Blackrock and Terenure colleges, and educational orders such as the Christian Brothers and Sisters of Charity, were intended to bridge an educational deficit. By the time of Cullen's death in 1878, Dublin was not just a more Catholic city, it was more obviously Catholic.

Dublin was also bigger, in two ways. The first was demographic. In 1800, the population was perhaps 182,000; in 1831, the total population of the city and suburbs was 265,000, and this had grown to 318,000 by 1851. The rate of growth slowed thereafter, but any growth in the second half of the nineteenth century stood at odds with the catastrophic collapse in the population of Ireland as a whole in the same period. By 1891 the population of the city and suburbs was 348,000. Dublin had continued to grow after the union, and the nineteenth century saw physical as well as demographic expansion, most especially in the ring of new townships around the city. (Changes in house styles could be seen in the proliferation of new red-brick Victorian suburbs.) In 1831, 12.4 per cent of the population lived outside the jurisdiction of the corporation. In 1891, the figure stood at 29.6 per cent, and some of the outlying townships (such as Rathmines and Pembroke) were disproportionately Protestant in composition and unionist in their political complexion, a development accelerated by the reform of the corporation in 1840, which finally broke the power of the city's traditionally Protestant oligarchy.

The Pembroke estate, beginning from Merrion Square, was built up from the 1820s, extending out towards Ballsbridge, and staking a claim to be seen as Dublin's new town. This stands in stark contrast to the rapid decline of the social make-up of the Gardiner estate from the 1850s onwards, as it was sold off piecemeal. The older patterns of the city's development played a role here, with the entrenchment of the social geography of the eighteenth century. Property prices prior to the 1840s confirmed this pattern. By the 1850s, O'Connell Street had become overwhelmingly commercial rather than residential, though Mountjoy Square remained quite exclusive and residential. By the 1840s it was a popular residential area among the members of

The new premises of the Kildare Street Club as seen from the playing fields of Trinity College, from the *Illustrated London News*, 1861. Originally established in the 1780s as a gentlemen's club, its expanding membership in the nineteenth century saw the construction of the new clubhouse in the 1850s, in a prominent location and adorned with a range of elaborate sculptures, most famously a whimsical depiction of monkeys playing billiards. In the second half of the century it was heavily associated with the landed gentry, being strongly Protestant and unionist in composition. (*Courtesy of Dublin City Library and Archive*)

6/28 Rathmines Road, Dublin.

Rathmines Road, with the spire of the Town Hall visible. Rathmines was one of the most prominent of the independent townships established outside Dublin's city limits in the Victorian era. It was formally created in 1847 and having initially been governed by commissioners, from 1898 it had its own elected council, meeting in the Town Hall; the latter building, designed by Thomas Drew, was completed in 1899. (*Courtesy of Dublin City Library and Archive, F.E. Dixon Postcard Collection*)

the legal profession, but like much of the old Gardiner estate it went into steep decline thereafter. Numerous properties were vacant by the 1850s and the profile had changed drastically by 1901. Many of the houses had been divided into multiple dwellings, and the square was occupied by a religiously diverse mix of students, domestic servants and skilled workers (many of whom were boarders), while no. 35, on the south side, was an orphanage. By 1920 it consisted of tenements, one of which was inhabited by the playwright Sean O'Casey; it may have inspired the setting for his 1923 play *The Shadow of a Gunman*.

The new townships – such as Pembroke and Rathmines on the southside, and, later, Clontarf on the northern edge of the bay – did not have the burden of an older infrastructure and charitable obligations. Consequently, they could offer attractive rates to the emerging commercial and professional middle classes, and the growth of the suburbs prompted many business premises to shift south of the river. At a time when money was needed by the corporation to tackle social problems, those who were in a position to stump up no longer had to, even if their proximity to the city ensured that they continued to operate within its commercial and social networks. Sean O'Casey's famous 'woman from Rathmines' in his play *The Plough and the Stars* (1926), lost and confused, far from home in the unfamiliar surroundings of inner-city tenements, may be a comic stereotype, but the character spoke to a deeper reality of physical, social and cultural change in Victorian and Edwardian Dublin.

There was also considerable development within the old city limits during the nineteenth century, which gives the lie to an impression of Dublin as a city in virtual stasis. The Victorian era saw a shift away from private ostentation and growth, with major infrastructural and public works developments: railways, markets and especially slum clearance by organisations such as the Dublin Artisans' Dwellings Company and the Iveagh Trust. Larger mansions were transformed for other uses. The Royal Dublin Society bought Leinster House in 1815, and some major buildings were constructed in the nineteenth century, including Trinity College's museum building, the National Library, the National Museum, the Natural History Museum, and the National Gallery, all of which were located around Leinster House, as was the imposing Royal College of Science (now Government Buildings), the construction of which began in 1904.

As for manufacturing and industry in Dublin, after the union the textile and clothing industries remained important. But even before the union, competition from the textiles industry of Ulster was taking a toll (witness the decline and eventual closure of the Linen Hall). After 1801 Dublin's market in luxury goods – such as silverware and carriage making – suffered. The mills scattered around the city's numerous waterways had facilitated the textile industry, but this suffered as the economy opened up to its British neighbour from the 1820s, as duties were finally removed and economic union followed the political one. Food production and processing became major parts of the economy; and if one adopted a flexible definition of food, certain companies stood out. The same rivers that facilitated textiles also facilitated brewing; there were perhaps forty breweries in the mid-eighteenth century, and the advent of the canals permitted their growth by bringing raw materials to the capital. In the early nineteenth century distilling was doing better than brewing, with firms such as Jameson's among the largest in the city. John Jameson, a Scot, had established a distillery on Bow Street in 1780. This area, in and around Smithfield, was traditionally characterised by light industry – metalworking and glass manufacturing. During the period from the 1780s to the 1840s, there was far greater demand for spirits in Ireland than in Britain. In the first half of the nineteenth century, whiskey was probably the most popular drink in Ireland. Demand began to decline in the second half of the century, due to various factors: the hugely successful anti-drink campaigns of Father Theobald Mathew, clerical disapproval, population decline, not to mention the difficulties of breaking into a British market that was still dominated by gin. By the 1880s Jameson's was the fourth largest distillery in Ireland, producing 900,000 gallons of pot still whiskey per annum. Its five-acre site was described by one visitor in the 1880s as a city within a city, given that all the associated crafts needed – such as coopers – were amalgamated under one roof.

The drinks industry was a major component of the local economy, and alongside distilling was brewing. Arthur Guinness had established his brewery near St James's Gate in 1759. Originally one brewer among many, as the nineteenth century wore on Guinness made use of the emerging rail network to sell its beer further away from its own doorstep. Its eventual dominance left an enduring physical imprint on Dublin. By the turn of the twentieth century, it was the world's largest brewery (it had been the largest in Ireland since the 1830s). It also swallowed up the competition: fifty breweries were reduced to a handful over the course of the century, all of which were clustered, like Guinness, in and around the Liberties. This entire area was one of Dublin's few industrial quarters in the nineteenth century. Such industry as there was within the city limits was primarily geared towards food and drink – evidence of Ireland's economic subordination to British interests – so the breweries and distilleries of the area employed thousands. Guinness remains the most famous (and the only) survivor of the trade in this district, but Watkins on Ardee Street (which claimed to have been founded in 1700) and the large Anchor Brewery on Usher Street were notable Victorian competitors. With regard to distilling, Roe's distillery, south of Thomas Street, went out of business

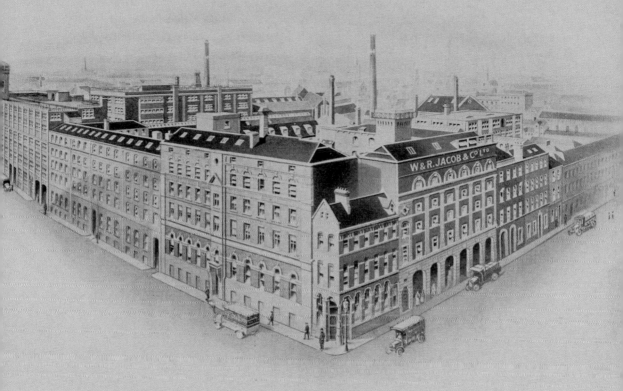

The enormous Jacob's biscuit factory on Peter Street. (*Courtesy of Dublin City Library and Archive*)

in 1890 and its premises was amalgamated into those of Guinness. The Roe family had paid for the renovation of Christ Church, completed in 1878, possibly in an effort to match the Guinness munificence that had facilitated the earlier renovation of St Patrick's Cathedral in the 1860s; this may have contributed to Roe's eventual bankruptcy.

With regard to food production, Jacob's was originally a Waterford firm making ships' biscuits. But the consumption of biscuits changed dramatically in the early nineteenth century. The ending of the East India Company monopoly on tea made it more readily available, while the growth of rail transport and wider middle-class consumption patterns added newer, less utilitarian markets. W.B. Jacob was impressed by London's Great Exhibition of 1851, and the firm established premises in Dublin, on Peter Street, a good location that gave an employment boost to the nearby Liberties. By 1858 its success saw the entire firm locate to Dublin and by 1865 the quality of its produce had become a byword. The factory gradually expanded (subsuming, in the process, a Huguenot cemetery), and was rebuilt after a devastating fire in 1880, in time to launch the ubiquitous cream cracker in 1885.

III

Major firms like Jacob's and Guinness were in a position to compete with British firms, and the growth of Dublin's infrastructure shaped its nineteenth-century economy in many ways. From the 1820s, steam-powered cross-channel shipping linked Dublin to a wider British economy, while railways converged in Dublin to ensure that it became a crucial transit point for goods moving back and forth across the Irish Sea and for agricultural exports (from 1863 there was a huge new cattle market on the North Circular Road that offered relatively straightforward access to the docks). The other side of the equation was British consumer goods being imported via Dublin. The port and docklands expanded, as the completion of the Bull Walls paved the way in and out of the port. Commercial expansion ensured that the north quays gradually grew eastwards away from the Custom House to facilitate shipping, while south of the River Liffey, chemical works and glassmaking became based in and around Ringsend. Dublin port expanded from the 1860s onwards, though vested local interests favoured the cross-channel trade and Dublin never developed a major deep-sea trade network. While there was major investment in the port, there was no comparable development in Dublin to the great dock developments of nineteenth century Britain.

For most of the inhabitants, the most visible form of new infrastructure in mid-nineteenth-century Dublin was the railways; one of the great success stories of

The Dublin cattle market near Stoneybatter in the late nineteenth century. Note the three-storey lodging houses in the distance, on the North Circular Road. (*National Library of Ireland*)

The Custom House, with a ship moored on the quays outside, at some point prior to the opening of the cast-iron Liffey Viaduct or 'Loop Line' Bridge adjacent to the western edge of the building in 1891. The rail bridge notoriously cut off views of the Custom House from further upstream. (*Trevor Ferris*)

Carlisle Bridge, originally designed by James Gandon, linking Sackville Street with Westmoreland Street and D'Olier Street. The bridge was rebuilt into its current form in 1877–91, to a design by Bindon Blood Stoney, and was renamed after Daniel O'Connell. (*Courtesy of Dublin City Library and Archive*)

Victorian Ireland. While Dublin did not have the heavy industries that characterised its urban counterparts such as Belfast or the great British industrial cities, railways offered a major business opportunity for ironworks, but the requirements for large tracts of land and the fact that rail lines could and did bisect the districts through which they ran meant that the railway companies built on the peripheries of the city. The Dublin and Kingstown Railway, running from Kingstown to Westland Row and developed by William Dargan, was the first railway in Ireland when it opened in the 1830s, and it was soon followed by the termini for the Great Northern Railway at Amiens Street; the Great Southern and Western Railway at Kingsbridge; the Midland Great Western (MGWR) at Broadstone; and the Dublin, Wicklow and Wexford terminal at Harcourt Court on Westland Row.

Broadstone was arguably the most impressive of the lot, built between 1842 and 1850 to house the terminus and workshops of the MGWR, which operated the lines that ran to the west of Ireland. The area in which it was located was quite impoverished and overcrowded, not least due to the location of a workhouse (the North Dublin Union) beside the terminus. The social problems this reflected were compounded by the coming of the railways, for Broadstone became the first port of call for emigrants from the impoverished rural west of Ireland as they arrived in Dublin. Broadstone was, along with Kingsbridge (now Heuston) Station, one of the largest industrial buildings in the city; its dramatic colonnades resembled those of a classical temple, and it was built on an equally dramatic elevated location. The final spur of the Royal Canal terminated in front of the station, which was accessed via bridges and an aqueduct (indeed, the MGWR had bought up the Royal Canal Company in order to build a line alongside it). While there were no physical connections across the city centre between the various rail companies in the first phase of their growth, though in 1891 the Belfast and Wexford lines were linked by a new cast-iron bridge (the so-called 'Loop Line') beside the Custom House, generally the city was well served by rail.

From the 1870s much the same could be said of the new tram network. The first tram lines were laid down in 1872 from Rathgar to College Green and the network expanded rapidly thereafter, most notably under the stewardship of William Martin Murphy's Dublin United Tramway Company. By the first decade of the twentieth century Dublin was the first city to possess a fully electrified tram network, and the routes extended as far as Howth and Dalkey, though the poorer west of the city was less well served. Nelson's Pillar was the major focal point, with a normal service running from 7 a.m. or 8 a.m. to 11 p.m. or 11.40 p.m. The electricity that powered the trams

TERMINUS OF THE MIDLAND GREAT WESTERN RAILWAY.

Broadstone Station, designed by John Skipton Mulvany. This was the Dublin terminus of the Midland Great Western Railway, near Constitution Hill. One reason for the choice of location was that a spur of the Royal Canal passed alongside the station; this was filled in in 1956 and the station was closed to rail traffic in 1961. (*National Library of Ireland*)

replaced oil in street lamps from the 1880s, with a new generating station at the Pigeon House in Ringsend in operation by 1903.

With regards to public infrastructure, public health and sanitation were the final pieces in this Victorian jigsaw. Calls for decent sanitation in the inner city had intensified in the nineteenth century, and figures such as the city medical officer, Charles Cameron, and John Grey, the owner of *The Freeman's Journal*, who chaired the corporation's waterworks committee, were instrumental in identifying the problem and its likely solution. The antiquated water system based on the River Poddle feeding the city basin near James's Street was clearly inadequate, but after numerous possibilities were investigated, the Vartry scheme, built between 1862 and 1867, saw huge amounts of water brought down from County Wicklow and distributed via Stillorgan, which also helped get water to the new townships. Finally, the existing Liffey bridges were reworked or rebuilt in the nineteenth century, with extensive and ongoing development of the Docklands, but on the whole, Victorian Dublin largely escaped the level of set-piece building that characterised many of its peers.

Dublin's Victorian architecture is arguably not as impressive as its earlier Georgian counterpart, but this is not to say that it should be dismissed. Banking and commercial architecture constituted some of the most obvious examples of new styles, especially around College Green and Trinity College, where Deane and Woodward's Munster Bank and Trinity College's museum building seem to have been separated at birth. Banks from Ulster brought their own distinctive styles, as seen – obviously – in the Ulster Bank Building at College Green. Banking and finance came to colonise Dame Street and College Green. Their solid and reassuring architecture of College Green was meant to send a message to prospective clients of the solidity of the financial institutions that resided there.

IV

Victorian Dublin was not especially violent, though petty crime was rife. The Dublin Metropolitan Police (DMP), created in 1836, was one of two Irish police forces prior to independence; they contrasted with the armed, quasi-military Royal Irish Constabulary (RIC), who were granted the prefix 'royal' in recognition of their role in suppressing the 1867 rebellion of the separatist Irish Republican Brotherhood, or Fenians. In the eighty-nine years of the DMP's existence up to 1925, 12,500 men served in it, and much of its infrastructure has survived: the old training depot at Kevin Street, along with stations at (most notably) College Green, Fitzgibbon Street, the

College Green, with the statue of William of Orange clearly visible. The buildings on the right of the image were predominantly banks at this time. (*Library of Congress*)

Bridewell, Donnybrook, and a number of others scattered across the city. Its recruits were (in an echo of RIC recruitment policy) overwhelmingly from outside Dublin. Religion was not a criterion for the rank and file, although, like the upper echelons of business and government in Ireland up to the outbreak of the First World War, the senior officers were disproportionately composed of British or Irish Protestants who were deemed politically reliable.

'Last night the state of the streets presented a marked and gratifying contrast to their appearance on Saturday and Sunday evenings. It is true that the principal thoroughfares – Sackville Street, Westmoreland Street, College Green, Dame Street, Grafton Street and Talbot Street – were crowded, and nearly impassable, from an early hour of the evening, but there was an almost entire absence of the military patrols. The behaviour of the populace was remarkably quiet and good tempered, and the metropolitan police were quite able to preserve order and tranquility ... whenever the crowds became so numerous as to create an apprehension of any tumult or breach of the peace, they good naturedly required the people to disperse, and kept the crowd in motion. Dame Street, College Green, and Grafton Street remained thronged with people until a late hour, but beyond a little rough horse play and one or two slight assaults nothing took place worth mentioning ... A walk through the city yesterday would have shown the great extent of the destruction which had been inflicted upon private and public property during the riots of Sunday night. The equestrian statue of King William had been considerably mutilated, and the four gas lamps which lighted around it had been smashed. Those lamps the gas company repaired yesterday, and they were restored to their original state by two o'clock in the afternoon. Little crowds of citizens stood all day along in College Green looking at the mutilated statue. The bronze bridle and reins had been battered off the horse, the King's effigy, upon which it was manifest much violence had been expended, had been but slightly defaced, but the corners of the base of the monument had been shamefully marred and shattered. Few people passed through the thoroughfare during the day who did not stand to take a look at the result of the Sabbath night's work of some of the roughs. The wreckage of property around this locality was pitiable and seemed, by its unbroken continuity in some streets, to have been the deliberate work of a large mob.' – *The Freeman's Journal*, 5 September 1882.

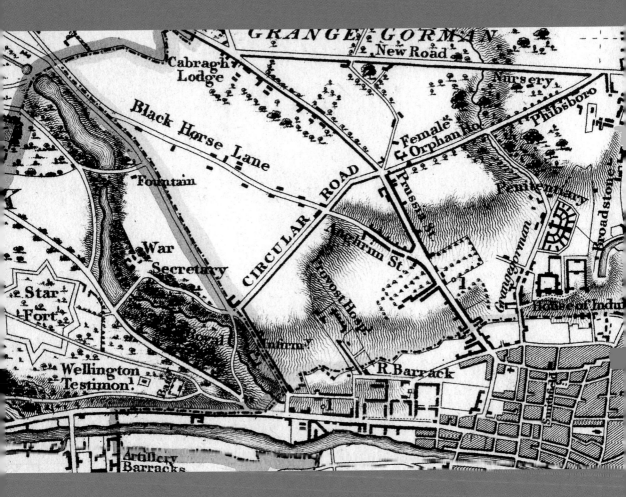

William Duncan's 1821 map of Oxmantown and the Phoenix Park. This area held a very high concentration of military installations and barracks. Note the outline of the star fort, which was never built, on the left of the picture. (*Courtesy of Dublin City Library and Archive Maps Collection*)

The early decades of the DMP's existence were marked by poor pay and conditions, and in 1882 the DMP went on strike in protest at the fact that the RIC were receiving bonuses for their service during the unrest of the Land War (a commission of inquiry later expressed its concerns about drunkenness in the ranks, a problem not helped by the inclination of publicans to stand the constables drinks in order to curry favour). The DMP became increasingly unpopular over time; a Dublin policeman was three times as likely to be attacked as his London equivalent. The distinctive conditions of Ireland were a factor here, above and beyond ordinary crime. In this regard, G Division was significant, as it was the detective unit that would investigate political crime, most famously the Phoenix Park murders of 1882. It was established in 1843 and based at Exchange Court (the HQ was later bombed by the Fenians); the 'G' arose from it being the seventh division of the DMP to be established (though unlike the other divisions, which were restricted to distinct localities, G Division operated across the entire DMP area from Drumcondra to Killiney). It dealt with all kinds of investigative crime as well as political offences, and was notorious for its use of informers to tackle both. Ironically, one of the reasons behind its foundation was to break a traditional reliance on unreliable informants.

But on the whole the DMP, as a more conventional force, were not viewed with the same animosity that was often directed at their counterparts in the RIC. They also had a new penal facility to rely upon in the Victorian era: Mountjoy Prison, located north of the city centre between two branches of the Royal Canal, which would add an extra layer of security. It was based on Pentonville Prison in London, which had been designed as a pioneering 'model' prison that emphasised reform as well as punishment. It was also built at a time when the British authorities both in Britain and Ireland were slowly moving away from the idea of transportation to Australia as a form of long-term punishment. Its construction in the late 1840s was hastened by complaints from the governor of Van Diemen's Land (Tasmania) that unreconstructed criminals were being dumped there; consequently, Mountjoy was also intended to prepare long-term prisoners for transportation. The first prisoners were detained there in 1851; women were first imprisoned there in 1858. As for the crimes in question, subversion was seen as a fringe activity, while prostitution was a far more pressing issue. Given that Dublin had a significant military presence scattered across its various barracks, soldiering could provide a career in a city that offered fewer opportunities than most.

This was not lost on the rest of the Irish population; less than 10 per cent of Irish migration ended in Dublin, and even that was from surrounding counties. In 1911, 70 per cent of the population of Dublin had been born there, but the movement of

Members of the Dublin Metropolitan Police charge Trinity College students on College Green, 12 March 1858. The occasion was the arrival into Dublin of a new lord lieutenant, the Earl of Eglinton. The charge was apparently precipitated by students throwing, among various missiles, fireworks at the horses and oranges at the constables themselves. (*National Library of Ireland*)

THE ILLUSTRATED LONDON NEWS

REGISTERED AT THE GENERAL POST-OFFICE FOR TRANSMISSION ABROAD.

No. 2245.—VOL. LXXX.　　SATURDAY, MAY 13, 1882.　　WITH TWO SUPPLEMENTS　{SIXPENCE By Post, 6½d.

1. SCENE OF THE MURDER OF LORD FREDERICK CAVENDISH AND MR. T. H. BURKE, IN PHOENIX PARK, DUBLIN.
2. CONVEYING THE DEAD TO STEEVENS'S HOSPITAL.—SEE PAGE 454.

The Phoenix Park murders, as reported by the *Illustrated London News*. On 6 May 1882 'The Invincibles', a splinter group of the Irish Republican Brotherhood (IRB), assassinated the two most senior British officials in Ireland: Chief Secretary Frederick Cavendish and Under-Secretary Thomas Burke. The two men were attacked as they walked in the Phoenix Park near the viceregal residence; their assailants hacked them to death with surgical knives and escaped in cabs (one of which was driven by one James Carey, nicknamed 'Skin the Goat'). The killings caused uproar against the backdrop of the Land War and Charles Stewart Parnell's campaign for Irish Home Rule. A number of those involved were executed (Carey was imprisoned), and a tradition survived in Dublin folklore that there was a spot on Chesterfield Avenue on which grass would not grow; this was apparently where the Invincibles had wiped the blood off their knives on the grass. (*Courtesy of Dublin City Library and Archive*)

Royal Hospital and Inmates, Kilmainham

Some of the residents of the Royal Hospital Kilmainham, originally established as a home for old soldiers in the late seventeenth century. The last veterans left the hospital in the 1920s. (*Courtesy of Dublin City Library and Archive, Postcards and Views Collection*)

skilled labourers and the presence of the British garrison meant that there was always a sizeable immigrant community, and intermarriage was common. From the 1880s a small but vibrant Jewish community was established in and around the Portobello district; a rare and eye-catching example of immigration, rather than its more familiar and common counterpart.

The Song of Zozimus

Gather round me boys, will yez
Gather round me?
And hear what I have to say,
Before ould Sally brings me
My bread and jug of tay.
I live in Faddle Alley,
Off Blackpitts near the Coombe;
With my poor wife called Sally,
In a narrow, dirty room.

Gather round me, and stop yer noise,
Gather round me till my tale is told;
Gather round me, ye girls and ye boys,
Till I tell yez stories of the days of old;
Gather round me, all ye ladies fair,
And ye gentlemen of renown;
Listen, listen, and to me repair,
Whilst I sing of beauteous Dublin town –

Memoir of the Great Original, Zozimus (Michael Moran), the Celebrated Dublin Street Rhymer and Reciter (Dublin, 1871), p. 24.

V

In many ways Victorian Dublin, while less storied, remains far more obvious now than its Georgian predecessor. A tendency to focus on the presence in Dublin of the eighteenth-century aristocracy and the architectural legacy they left behind, and also on the relative absence of the heritage of heavy industry, means that one can easily overlook an extensive architectural heritage based upon commerce and leisure. The 1830s saw the opening of the Zoo and Botanic Gardens; the latter were the subject of controversy in 1861 in relation to other forms of leisure activity, as they were open for four days of the week, but not on Sundays, which arguably denied access to huge numbers of citizens whose only leisure time was on a Sunday. Some of the arguments apparently used against opening on a Sunday were highly dubious: that members of the working class would steal the flowers; or, given that Sunday was a popular day for funerals in Glasnevin Cemetery next door, that the gardens were bound to be overrun by hordes of drunks.

New purpose-built theatres also emerged, such as the Gaiety and the Olympia, formerly Dan Lowry's Star of Erin Music Hall. Restaurants became increasingly popular from the 1860s onwards, taking over from the taverns and chophouses of an earlier era, and foreign-born cooks, especially from France or Germany, became a significant badge of status, while shop fronts or commercial façades, especially on the quays, seemed to come into their own. In the course of reshaping Dublin's streetscape, the Wide Streets Commissioners had facilitated the growth of new shopping streets such as Westmoreland Street and D'Olier Street.

'Rain was drizzling down on the cold streets and, when they reached the Ballast House, Farrington suggested the Scotch House. The bar was full of men and loud with the noise of tongues and glasses. The three men pushed past the whining match-sellers at the door and formed a little party at the corner of the counter. They began to exchange stories. Leonard introduced them to a young fellow named Weathers who was performing at the Tivoli as an acrobat and knock-about artiste. Farrington stood a drink all round.' – A fictional glimpse of pub life, from James Joyce's short story 'Counterparts', in *Dubliners* (London, 1914), p. 114.

The destruction of the Theatre Royal by fire, 9 March 1880. Dublin Fire Brigade was formally established in 1862, replacing the ad hoc services that had previously dealt with fires. (*National Library of Ireland*)

THE IRISH JAUNTING CAR.

If you want to drive 'round Dublin shure you'll find me on the stand,
I'll take you to Raheny to pick cockles on the Strand,
I'll take you to the Phœnix Park, to Nancy Hands and then
I'll take you to the strawberry beds and back to town again.

A late nineteenth-century postcard lays on the 'blarney' for prospective visitors. (*Courtesy of Dublin City Library and Archive, Postcards and Views Collection*)

An advertisement for an eye-catching entertainment in the Rotunda ('Rotundo') Gardens. (*Library of Congress*)

A turn of the century advertisement for John Kavanagh's pub, more commonly known as 'The Gravediggers'. The pub opened beside the main gate of Glasnevin Cemetery in 1833 – a year after the cemetery opened – and got its nickname from its role as a popular watering hole for both cemetery staff and mourners. (*Glasnevin Trust*)

Antient Concert Rooms.

⟶ ◆ ⟵

Mr. FREDERICK HARVEY (*Junior's*)

⟶ GRAND ✦ BALLAD ✦ CONCERT, ⟵

Thursday Evening, April 13th, 1882.

Artistes :

Miss TALLON, R.I.A.M.   Mr. BARTLE M'CARTHY.

Mrs. COLCLOUGH.   Mr. C. MACDONA.

Mrs. FREDERICK HARVEY.   Mr. J. O'FARRELL, R.I.A.M.

Mr. S. R. POYNTZ.

Solo Pianoforte :—Mr. C. K. IRWIN, R.I.A.M.

Harp Solo :—Mr. OWEN LLOYD.

Conductor :

MR. FREDERICK HARVEY.

⟶ ADMISSION ⟵

Reserved Seats, - - 3s.   Balcony, - - 2s.   Unreserved, - - 1s.

DOORS OPEN AT 7.30 O'CLOCK.   CONCERT AT 8 O'CLOCK.

Tickets to be had at Door, Mansfield Brothers, and Crutchett & Son, Grafton Street,
Pohlmann & Son, Dawson Street.

Late Victorian leisure: three very different performances. (*Courtesy of Dublin City Library and Archive*)

Gaiety Theatre, Dublin.

Sole Proprietor and Patentee ... **Mr. MICHAEL GUNN**

Business Manager .. .. MR. C. HYLAND

PROGRAMME ... ONE PENNY

MR. THOMAS E. MURRAY'S COMPANY.

General Manager .. ⎫ For THOMAS E. MURRAY ⎧ Mr. ALFRED D. ADAMS
Assistant Stage Manager .. ⎭ ⎩ Mr. KYRLEY THORNTON

This Evening (Monday), April 17th, 1899 (at 8),

THE AMERICAN FARCICAL COMEDY IN THREE ACTS, ENTITLED,

OUR IRISH VISITORS

CONSTRUCTED FOR LAUGHING PURPOSES ONLY.

180 LAUGHS IN 180 MINUTES!

Col. McMahon. an Abandoned Husband	..	**Mr. THOS. E. MURRAY**
Mr. O'Brady, a Hypocritical Friend ..	..	Mr. J. W. BRAITHWAITE
Gilly Softsolder, a Jealous Husband ..	..	Mr. HAROLD PERRY
Tom O'Brady, a Fortune-Hunter ..	..	Mr. GEORGE HUDSON
John Hyson, a Piano Tuner ..	..	Mr. W. F. GREEN
Inspector Ketcham, from Scotland Yard ..	..	Mr. E. T. JAZON
The Colonel's Wife, the Boss of the House	..	Miss HELENA COE
Janie, "The Baby" ..	⎫	Miss MAGGIE RIMMER
Katie ..	The Colonel's Daughters ⎬	Miss DOROTHY PAYN
Ellie ..	⎭	Miss FLORENCE CARLISLE
Cora Fay ..	⎫	Miss CISSY SPENCER
Daisy Dancer ..	School Friends of the Daughters ⎬	Miss MAY CARNEY
May Understudy ..	⎭	Miss MERRION BRIGHT
Mammy Diable, a Fortune Teller ..	..	Miss M. THORNTON
Mrs. Gilly Softsolder, a Superstitious Female	..	Miss FLORA HASTINGS

The LILLIE Quartette of Lady Dancers.

Act 1 - - - - **McMAHON'S HOME**

Searching for the Fortune.

Aot 2 - - - - **BEACH AT ATLANTIC CITY**

My Beauty will yet Cause my Death.

Act 3 - - - - **McMAHON'S PARLOUR**

McMahon concludes Life is still Worth Living.

GRAND DAY PERFORMANCE, Saturday next (April 22nd), at 2.

THE BAND,
Under the direction of Mr. R. G. Johnston, will play:—

1. FANTASIE	..	..	"Bric-a-Bric"			*Fink*
2. QUADRILLE	..	..	"The Gondoliers"	..	..	*Bucalossi*
3. GALOP	..	..	"John Peel"			
4. POLKA	..	..		..	..	

PRICES—Private Boxes, 20s.. 30s. and 40s. Balcony Stalls (Numbered and Reserved), 5s.
Balcony (Numbered and Reserved), 4s. ; Pit Stalls (Numbered and Reserved), 3s.
Second Circle, 2s ; Pit. 1s. ; Gallery. 6d.
Box Office at Cramers, 4 and 5 Westmoreland-street, open from 10 a.m. to 5.30 p.m Saturdays
10 a.m. to 3 p.m. And at Messrs. Moran & Lang's, 52 South King-street, from 5.45 p.m. to
8 p.m. ; and on Saturdays from 3.15 p.m. to 8 p.m.
Early Admission from 7 to 7.30, Second Circle, Pit and Gallery, 6d. extra.

MONDAY NEXT, APRIL 24th (for Six Nights and One Matinee), the Enormously Successful
COMEDY FARCE,

MY SOLDIER BOY

FROM THE CRITERION THEATRE, LONDON.

DOLLARD, PRINTINGHOUSE, DUBLIN.

Gaiety Theatre, Dublin.

Sole Proprietor and Manager - - - Mr. MICHAEL GUNN

CHRISTMAS PANTOMIME
1890-91.

ALI BABA
AND
THE FORTY THIEVES.

Produced Friday, Dec. 26th, 1890.

WORDS OF THE SONGS,
CONCERTED PIECES, SOLOS.

PRICE 3D.

A wide range of elaborate new edifices were built in Dublin in the latter decades of the Victorian era: department stores like Arnotts and Todd Byrne's on Henry Street, or Brown Thomas on Grafton Street; offices such as Lever Brothers' Sunlight Chambers on Wood Quay; and the dramatic market building on George's Street. The new department stores were to some degree middle-class institutions. These so-called 'monster houses' were a radical departure from local traditions, though, oddly, many evolved from drapery stores. McSwiney, Delaney and Co. in Sackville Street, which opened in 1853, was one of the first of its kind in the world, and the international Great Exhibition held in Dublin that same year proved crucial to the development of a new style of shopping and display. Living-in arrangements for workers might be condemned for their allegedly immoral influence on workers, but the new firms, as both employers and facilitators of consumer culture, pointed towards greater social mobility, for some at least. Yet in the shadow of this new commercial and professional city lay a parallel, and very different, city of the poor.

'It seems likely that we never walked on the quays – certain districts of Dublin being ruled out as "noisy" – and that we did not venture to cross the Liffey. So the north side remained *terra incognita*. Yes, I do see the Four Courts, to which my father went every morning, and from which his black brief bag with the thick red cord made its mysterious journeys home. Otherwise, painted with that one dome, the North Side was so much canvas on which had been contrived clouds and perspectives – smoke-and-slate grey, brick-brown and distance-blue. This canvas was pierced and entered only by the lordly perspective of Sackville St. And, till I went one day to a party in Mountjoy Square, I took it that Sackville St had something queer at the end.' – The novelist Elizabeth Bowen, writing in the 1940s, recalls her late-Victorian childhood in Dublin and articulates some assumptions occasionally shared by those unfortunate enough to live south of the Liffey, from *Bowen's Court and Seven Winters* (London, 1999, Vintage edn), p. 477. Bowen herself was from a Protestant and unionist background; her mother's family was from Kildare, and resided in Clontarf at the time of her marriage to Bowen's father, who came from gentry in Cork, but broke with family tradition to become a barrister. They lived, at this stage in her life, in Herbert Place, near Baggot Street.

Four views of Sackville Street, illustrating its development from the 1850s to the turn of the twentieth century. Much of the street had to be rebuilt in the aftermath of the Easter Rising of 1916 and the outbreak of the Civil War in 1922.

(Trevor Ferris)

(Library of Congress)

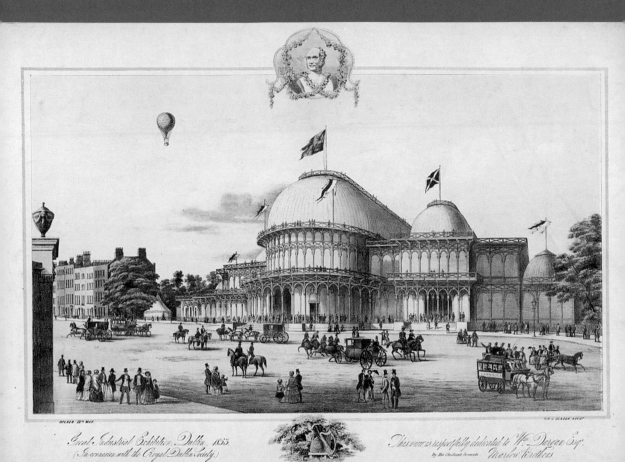

A view of the vast temporary structure erected to house the Great Exhibition of 1853. Organised by the industrialist and railway magnate William Dargan, and held on the grounds of Leinster House, it was consciously modelled on London's Great Exhibition of 1851 as a showcase for Irish manufacturing in its broadest sense. It was visited by enormous crowds, not to mention Queen Victoria and her husband, Prince Albert. Its success ultimately prompted the foundation of the National Gallery, on a site adjacent to where the exhibition pavilion had stood. (*Library of Congress*)

The success of the 1853 exhibition prompted a sequel, this time in 1865, on the site of the Iveagh Gardens: this is an interior view of the 'Winter Garden'. (*National Library of Ireland*)

An interior view of the 1907 exhibition, held on 52-acre site near Ballsbridge, again with the express purpose of highlighting Irish industry. (*Courtesy of Dublin City Library and Archive, Postcards and Views Collection*)

'A fat brown goose lay at one end of the table and at the other end, on a bed of creased paper, strewn with sprigs of parsley, lay a great ham, stripped of its outer skin and peppered over with crust crumbs, a neat paper frill round its shin and beside this was a round of spiced beef. Between these rival ends ran parallel lines of side-dishes: two little minsters of jelly, red and yellow; a shallow dish full of blocks of blancmange and red jam, a large green leaf-shaped dish with a stalk-shaped handle, on which lay bunches of purple raisins and peeled almonds, a companion dish on which lay a solid rectangle of Smyrna figs, a dish of custard topped with grated nutmeg, a small bowl full of chocolates and sweets wrapped in gold and silver papers and a glass vase in which stood some tall celery stalks. In the centre of the table there stood, as sentries to a fruit-stand which upheld a pyramid of oranges and American apples, two squat old-fashioned decanters of cut glass, one containing port and the other dark sherry. On the closed square piano a pudding in a huge yellow dish lay in waiting and behind it were three squads of bottles of stouts and ale and minerals, drawn up according to the colours of their uniforms, the first two black, with brown and red labels, the third and smallest squad white, with transverse green sashes.' – The elaborate dinner presented by the Morkan sisters on the admittedly exceptional occasion of the Catholic feast of the Epiphany (6 January), in James Joyce's story 'The Dead', the concluding story of *Dubliners* (London, 1914), pp. 243–4. High-end consumer goods, often akin to those described here, were supplied by a range of firms to Dublin's middle classes in the late nineteenth and early twentieth centuries (Findlater's, for example, offered delivery services throughout the suburbs from its enormous premises on Sackville Street), though in Joyce's story the Morkan sisters are, to some degree, keeping up appearances. Ironically, the 'dark gaunt house' on Usher's Island in which the story is set was, in reality, located beside the Mendicity Institution, which had been established as a charity for Dublin's poor; the humbler fare it offered was very, very different.

VI

In 1845 Thomas Willis, a Dublin apothecary involved in various charitable activities throughout his life, such as the foundation of the Society of St Vincent de Paul in Ireland, conducted a survey of the parish of St Michan's, where he was based. His

'There are no gentry within the district, and the few professional men or mercantile traders whom interest may still compel to keep their offices here, have their residences in some more favoured localities, This parish, that within the last thirty years might boast of as large a proportion of professional and mercantile wealth as any in the metropolis, is now the refuge of reduced persons from other districts, and very many of the houses then occupied by respectable traders, are now in the possession of a class of men called 'housejobbers', who re-let them to poor tenants. These jobbers have no interest in the houses save their weekly rents; the houses, therefore, undergo no repair; the staircase, passages, &c, are all in a state of filth; the yards in the rear are so many depots of putrid animal and vegetable matter; and if a necessary be in any of them, it frequently is a source of further nuisance. The courts and back places are, if possible, still worse, and are quite unfit for the residence of human beings. They are almost all closed up at each end, and communicating with the street by a long narrow passage, usually the hall of the front house, and not more than three or three and a half feet wide. Pipewater, lime washing, dust bin, privy – these are things almost unknown. The stench and disgusting filth of these places are inconceivable, unless to those whose harrowing duty obliges them to witness such scenes of wretchedness.

'In some rooms in these situations it is not an infrequent occurrence to see above a dozen human beings crowded into a space not fifteen feet square. Within this space the food of these wretched beings, such as it is, must be prepared; within this space they must eat and drink; men, women and children must strip, dress, sleep. In cases of illness the calls of nature must be relieved, and when death releases one of the inmates the corpse must of necessity remain for days within the room. Let it not be supposed I have selected some solitary spot for this description: no, I am speaking of an entire district, and state facts incontrovertible. I indulge in no theories as to the causes which produce this state of things, but I may state the results. They are – that every cause that can contribute to general contagion exists here in full vigour, and that disease, in every aggravated form, with all its train of desolating misery, is rarely absent.' – Thomas Willis's account of the parish of St Michan's, quoted in David Dickson (ed.), *The Hidden Dublin: The Social and Sanitary Condition of Dublin's Working Classes in 1845 Described by Thomas Willis* (Dublin, 2002), pp. 77–8.

occupation gave him an intimate knowledge of the parish, which according to the 1841 census contained 22,800 inhabitants, making it one of the five most congested of Dublin's twenty-one parishes. But in the 1830s and 1840s it had declined markedly; it was one of the areas most badly affected by the 1832 cholera epidemic (accounting for a quarter of over 6,000 cases in the city). The use of statistics was intended to bolster Willis's case (he bemoaned the absence of civil registration with which to confirm his own calculations). But from a close reading of the 1841 census, he concluded that in the parish 'the enormous number of 23,197, or very near one half of the entire number of families, have the wretched and perstiferous accommodation of a single room'. St Michan's also received many rural immigrants, perhaps due to its proximity to traditional routes into the city from County Meath. Apart from the Jameson distillery, three breweries and three foundries, the market-based nature of the area meant that most employment within it was of a casual nature: arguably a microcosm of the city as a whole. St Michan's registered an infant mortality rate of 22.15 per cent in first year, rising to 73.61 per cent by age twenty-six. In other words, seven out of ten people born in the parish of St Michan's were dead by the age of twenty-five.

'Tenement' was something of a catch-all term for housing slum. The collapse in property prices after the union had gradually seen many of the extensive eighteenth-century estates decline into slums, and become subdivided into tenements; the old Gardiner estate, located around Sackville (later O'Connell) Street, was an area that had undergone a notable and precipitous decline, having been broken up by the Famine-era Encumbered Estates court. Landlords were more often than not negligent of their properties as they gradually declined. Dublin's acidic smog and rain seeped in, and burning coal created smog that was trapped in the honeycomb pattern of the streets, corroding fixtures and fittings that would not be replaced. Wood from fittings was scavenged for fuel. And this process continued over generations, exacting its toll on the housing stock as it did so. The lack of sanitation, as noted by Willis (and Whitelaw before him), with open cesspits as de facto public toilets, and the constant presence of livestock, offal, excrement (human and other), not to mention a lack of water for washing, bred diseases such as diphtheria and typhoid. Vermin such as rats and cockroaches were rife. Endemic malnutrition was widely observed, the consequence of a diet based on poor-quality bread, tea, oatmeal, cheap meat and fish, potatoes, cabbage and margarine. On that note, it should be said Dublin got off relatively lightly during the Great Famine, being one of the few places in Ireland to register a population increase. Migration into the city during the Famine increased population pressure and the incidence of disease, though the presence of bread in the urban diet may have mitigated the death toll from starvation. Potatoes were significantly less important to the diet in Dublin than elsewhere in the country, though the supply of them in the city was by no means unaffected. Disease was probably a bigger killer in Dublin during the Famine, but, exacerbated by poor hygiene and malnutrition (which took a particular toll on infants), diseases such as typhoid, tuberculosis and even cholera were recurring killers in a city where a cut on the sole of an unshod foot could prove fatal.

The introduction of the Poor Law in 1838 had seen the creation of the North and South Dublin Unions in North Brunswick Street and James's Street respectively. The growth in Dublin's population, combined with the collapse of artisan activity that came after the Act of Union, almost certainly paved the way for the growth of

'About nine o'clock in the morning, a body of men, apparently railway labourers, tolerably well-clad, assembled at the foot of Summer Hill, adjoining Lower Gardiner Street, Dublin, and they were not long there when two bread carts approached. A portion of the party, armed with large sticks, drew out towards the carts, addressed threatening terms to the men in charge, while the rest of the mob deliberately rifled all the contents of the crates. Some three or four policemen were attracted to the spot by the commotions, but, from the attitude assumed by the fighting section of the plunderers, they did not consider themselves warranted in attempting the arrest of any of the party; all, in consequence, escaped.

'About two hours afterwards, a party, supposed to be the same gang, attacked the shop of Mr Campbell of Marlborough Street, and carried off all of the bread in his shop. They proceeded down Marlborough Street to Eden Quay, and again stopped before the door of Mr Coyne, the bread and biscuit maker residing there, and repeated their demand for bread; but, on seeing the police approaching, they retired and passed over Carlisle Bridge in the direction of Westmoreland Street. A mob surrounded the shop of Mr Jeffers, baker, of Church Street; but, the police being in the vicinity, they were called on, and succeeded in dispersing the mob. Several bread carts were stopped in the outlets of the city, and their contents taken.' – *The Illustrated London News*, 16 January 1847, quoted in Noel Kissane, *The Irish Famine: A Documentary History* (Dublin, 1995), p. 57.

further slums and tenements and ensured that public health in Dublin would be far worse than in the countryside, though descriptions of working-class poverty were not restricted to the era of the Famine. The increasing clamour that something be done about the squalor of the inner city saw the establishment of the Dublin Artisans' Dwellings Company (DADC), in today's parlance, a public–private partnership (the shift in Dublin's social geography with the flight of the middle classes had robbed the city itself of essential revenue). The DADC developed across the city, but its first development was in the Coombe; the red-brick terraces to be found there are their legacy. While the Coombe had been the hub of the textile trade in the area, by 1878 there was no commercial activity on the street. So the corporation bought up the area and leased it back to the DADC, which began construction in 1880. The web of indiscriminate holdings was cleared and replaced with a more uniform network of streets around the current Marian shrine: cottages, two-storey houses, and three-storey houses for use as shops, all clustered together. This was quite unlike the DADC's later Oxmantown development, which is characterised by long, uniform streets. The process of urban renewal continued throughout the area, through Francis Street, and culminating in the large Iveagh Trust development on Patrick Street. But, crucially, such institutions were not charities, and while they had a philanthropic purpose they expected to turn a profit; they served the skilled elite among the working class. The vast ranks of Dublin's casual labour force remained outside their remit, and inside the tenements that they continued to occupy.

Dublin's slum dwellers had little opportunity to pull themselves out of poverty. The absence of major industries in Dublin meant that such work as was available to men was casual and uncertain. The squalor these tenements contained was staggering: poverty, malnutrition, rampant disease, cramped quarters, a lack of hygiene and an infant mortality rate that far outstripped that of London. The poor of Dublin were visibly malnourished to observers, and alongside physical poverty were shocking indications of the psychological problems it engendered. Women were often forced to work in order to augment their families' uncertain incomes, or to avoid abject poverty themselves, hence the development of street trading, and also the horrific reality of prostitution, which reached its pinnacle in Monto. This area was once part of the old Gardiner estate (the name was abbreviated from Montgomery Street), but by the 1870s it had declined into tenements and had become notorious for the scale of prostitution in the area; it seems that attempts to clear prostitutes out of other parts of the city had forced the sex trade into a district that was becoming impoverished, and thus a cheaper place to rent property. Located near Aldborough House (one of the

Tenement Dublin: Engine Alley. (*Courtesy of Dublin City Library and Archive*)

Magennis's Court, near Townshend Street. (*Courtesy of Dublin City Library and Archive*)

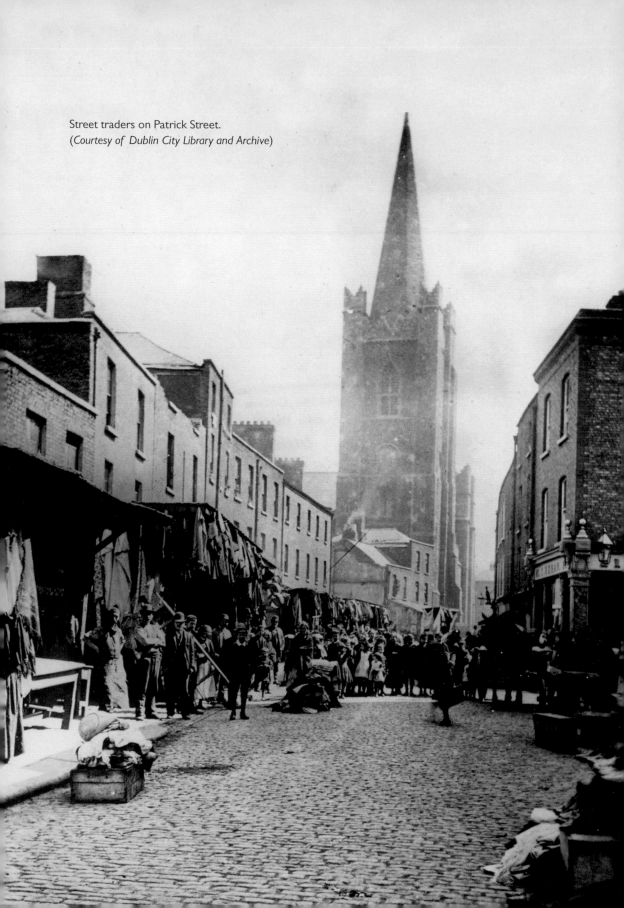

Street traders on Patrick Street.
(*Courtesy of Dublin City Library and Archive*)

Blackpitts, near the Coombe. (*Courtesy of Dublin City Library and Archive*)

Revolutions

1860-1923

I

Members of Dublin's new white-collar classes had other roles to play outside the workplace: this was exactly the class from which groups such as the Irish Republican Brotherhood (IRB) would draw their manpower and inspiration. The IRB, or 'Fenians', founded in both Ireland and North America in the aftermath of the Great Famine, resolved to stage a rebellion to secure Irish independence from Britain. It was to take place in 1867, and the securing of Dublin was seen as crucial to its success. There seems to have been a plan that the Fenians would assemble in the Dublin Mountains, then launch a guerrilla war with some limited activity within the city centre itself. There were supposedly 4,000 members of the Fenians with 3,000 weapons in Dublin. But fears of attacks within the city saw guards being placed at the Four Courts, City Hall,

Dublin who became involved in in the cultural revival at the turn of the twentieth century viewed Dublin as a hub of activism and radicalism, and a hotbed of ideas, some of which, at least, fed into the revolution that led to independence in the 1920s.

Yet in the 1880s this represented the radical fringe rather than the political mainstream. From that decade onwards, Dublin Corporation, which had become increasingly nationalist in outlook, abandoned the policy, dating back to the 1840s, of permitting the office of lord mayor to pass between various factions and, implicitly, to Protestant candidates, a non-sectarian gesture that dated back to the days of Daniel O'Connell. The change in policy arose when the incumbent mayor, George Moyers, blocked the Home Rule leader Charles Stewart Parnell from receiving the freedom of the city. Soon afterwards, by way of riposte, the renaming of streets in a more overtly nationalist manner began: Lord Edward Street was laid out and named after the eponymous United Irishman. Objections could be made to this type of renaming, often due to commercial considerations – the obvious problem of trying to find an address on what seemed to be a brand-new street – as well as political; attempts to rename Sackville Street were particularly acrimonious. In 1911, Great Britain Street became Parnell Street, but this attempt to rename Dublin's streetscape in a more nationalistic manner only began to pick up pace from the 1920s onwards, after independence.

On the other hand, Dublin also had a substantial Protestant and unionist population, not only in its outlying townships such as Rathmines; perhaps 10 per cent of Dublin city councillors could be classed thus in the early twentieth century. Alongside a more respectable form of upper-class unionism, Dublin retained a more militant loyalist and Orange constituency. Dublin's loyalism was quite diverse. Yet the public, if not the official, culture of the city was still, for the most part, broadly nationalistic, as evinced by major public events such as the massive funeral of Charles Stewart Parnell, deployed as a form of political theatre.

The turn of the twentieth century saw nationalist protests against the visits of Queen Victoria in 1900 and Edward VII in 1903. Prominent welcomes were sponsored by the authorities, but there was also widespread public support for the visits, especially that of Edward VII. That said, the protests against such events by a small but committed core of activists (such as the founder of Sinn Féin, Arthur Griffith, and W.B. Yeats's future muse, Maud Gonne) laid the basis for events that would erupt in the second decade of the twentieth century.

OBEDIENTIA·CIVIUM·URBIS·FELICITAS

To All and Singular *to whom these Presents shall come*

I Sir Arthur Edward Vicars, SSA.

Ulster King of Arms and Principal Herald of All Ireland, Registrar and Knight Attendant on the Most Illustrious Order of Saint Patrick, do hereby Certify and Declare that the Armorial Bearings above depicted, that is to say:— Azure, three Castles argent, flammant proper, for Supporters, on the Dexter, a female figure proper, representing "Law", vested gules doubled or, holding in the dexter hand a sword erect and in the Sinister an olive branch all proper, on the Sinister, a female figure proper, representing "Justice", vested gules doubled or, holding in the dexter hand an olive branch proper And in the Sinister a pair of scales or, and for Motto *Obedientia Civium Urbis Felicitas* do of right belong and appertain unto the Right Honourable the Lord Mayor, Aldermen, and Citizens of the City of Dublin and to their successors forever according to the Laws of Arms, as appears by the Records of my Office and more especially by the Visitation of the City of Dublin by Daniel M.c Lysaght, Esquire, Ulster King of Arms and Principal Herald of All Ireland in the year of Our Lord One thousand six hundred and seven.

As Witness my hand and Seal this Twenty Fifth day of May in the year of Our Lord One thousand eight hundred and ninety nine.

Arthur E. Vicars Ulster

II

Dublin may have lacked heavy industry, but the politics of labour found a foothold in the capital towards the end of the nineteenth century. In 1896 the Irish Republican Socialist Party was established in Dublin, an organisation notable not so much for its activities but for its founder, James Connolly, a former British soldier, born in Edinburgh to Irish parents. Yet such groupings were also fringe organisations; traditional trade unionism would prove far more powerful, and prominent. Strikes were common in Dublin in the later nineteenth century, but such gains as they made were usually confined to skilled workers, and the existence of unions for skilled labourers was, to some degree, tolerated by some employers in Dublin.

The question of organising a union that could represent the vast ranks of the unskilled labouring poor was another matter entirely. This is what Dublin employers

'The funeral cortege proper started from St Stephens Green to the City Hall, and it contained a notable historic figure in the person of Mr James Stephen's, once the head organiser of the "Irish Republic". The contingent from Cork bore placards, which they distributed among the crowd, containing the words "murdered to satisfy Englishmen". The historic side of the event was emphasised by a halt at the spot where Lord Edward Fitzgerald received his death blow. College Green was one dense mass of men and women, and the most striking scene of all was, perhaps, the passage by the famous old Parliament House, whose glories Mr Parnell had come so near to reviving. The crowds seemed to swell and swell as it reached beautiful Glasnevin Cemetery, where O'Connell's tomb is, but not his heart which rests at Rome. A correspondent calculates that there were 200,000 persons in all in the procession and in the streets, but it was not swollen by a single anti-Parnellite member or by a priest of the Catholic Church. The sun had set and the moon was up when the coffin reached the turf-lined grave. As it was lowered, tears and sobs burst from the strong men, attached followers of the dead leader, who stood round, and there was bitter weeping while the parting words were said. There was no disturbance of any kind, nor any outward sign of the bitter feeling which Mr Parnell's death has evoked' – Parnell's funeral, as reported in the *Illustrated London News*, 17 October 1891, cited in Noel Kissane, *Parnell: A Documentary History* (Dublin, 1991), p. 107.

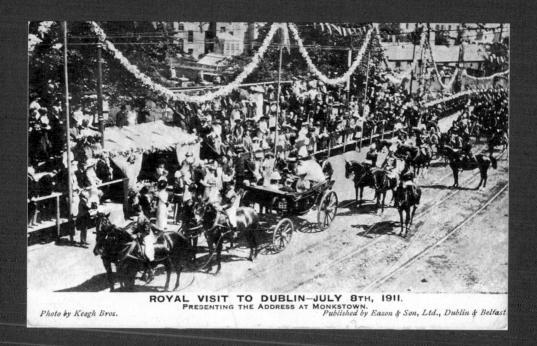

ROYAL VISIT TO DUBLIN—JULY 8TH, 1911.
PRESENTING THE ADDRESS AT MONKSTOWN.

Photo by Keogh Bros.   *Published by Eason & Son, Ltd., Dublin & Belfast.*

A postcard marking the visit to Dublin in 1911 of King George V, during which a loyal address was made to the monarch in Monkstown and other localities. Monkstown, and other southern suburbs, would have had a substantial unionist and loyalist community, though the welcome given to monarchs in this period extended beyond those areas. (*Courtesy of Dublin City Library and Archive, Postcards and Views Collection*)

A 1908 poster for a Labour Day demonstration in Dublin. Among the speakers are Jim Larkin, Arthur Griffith, the founder of Sinn Féin, and future British Labour Party leader Keir Hardie. (*Courtesy of Dublin City Library and Archive, Birth of the Republic Collection*)

were faced with in 1909, when the Liverpool-born trade unionist James Larkin founded the Irish Transport and General Workers' Union (ITGWU) with precisely that purpose in mind. Over the next four years the ITGWU flexed its muscle and won a number of wage increases for unskilled labour in the city. Larkin's message was quite radical in a city whose large unskilled labour force had traditionally acted as a buffer against strike action, on the grounds that union members could easily be replaced. Larkin, however, impressed the idea of solidarity in his followers, and by mid-1913 was coming into conflict with the Dublin United Tramways Company. Its owner, William Martin Murphy, was one of the more successful and prominent Irish businessmen of his era; he was a principal target of W.B. Yeats' famous poem 'September 1913', given that he had opposed the idea of using public funds for a gallery to house the collection of the wealthy Cork-born art collector Hugh Lane. Murphy was also hostile to the idea of Larkin's union acquiring a foothold on the Dublin tram network, and in the summer of 1913 approximately a hundred employees were sacked for membership of the ITGWU. Larkin's retaliation came at 9.40 a.m. on Tuesday 26 August 1913, when tram drivers and conductors put on ITGWU badges and walked off the job. The walkout was designed to extract maximum publicity by being timed to disrupt the annual Dublin horse show, one of the most prominent events in the city's social calendar.

Two days after the tram workers downed tools, Larkin and a number of others were arrested and charged with seditious activities, though they were released. A large public meeting was scheduled to take place on Sackville Street, but this had been banned and a warrant issued for Larkin's arrest after he publicly burned a copy of the proclamation banning it in front of a crowd the previous night. On 31 August he addressed a large crowd from the balcony of Murphy's Imperial Hotel on Sackville Street, having entered the building in disguise. He was arrested after making his speech, and the crowd assembled on the street were then baton-charged by the DMP; between 400 and 600 people were injured, an action that caused outrage among English unions, which assumed that the DMP was controlled by the corporation and, by proxy, employers (this was the norm in England, whereas in Ireland the police were actually controlled by the British authorities). The DMP behaved with great brutality over the weekend of 30–31 August, beating one man, James Nolan, to death on Eden Quay, and their actions served to galvanise the strikers. Fights between strikers and police were reported across the north inner city, and the police's heavy-handedness prompted the corporation to demand an inquiry. The dispute escalated when Jacob's was shut down by an ITGWU strike, and events progressed rapidly. The following

THIS IS NOT A STRIKERS' RIOT IN ST. PETERSBURG; IT IS A FEW DUBLIN
CHILDREN TRYING TO EARN A LIVING.

A 1913 cartoon from the satirical magazine *The Leprechaun* criticising the DMP's brutal treatment of striking workers. (*Courtesy of Dublin City Library and Archive*)

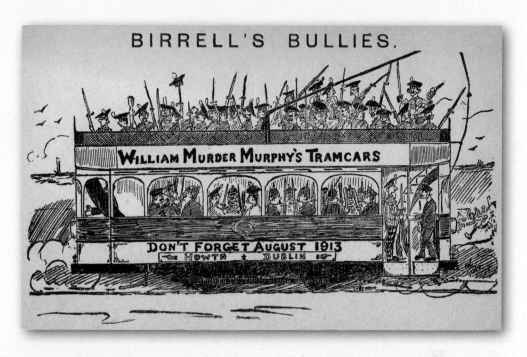

Another satirical cartoon on the 1913 lockout, this time from the ITGWU paper *The Worker's Republic*. (*Courtesy of Dublin City Library and Archive, Birth of the Republic Collection*)

day, 2 September – the same day as the catastrophic collapse of tenement houses on Church Street – the Dublin Coal Merchants' Association locked out ITGWU members. On 3 September Murphy persuaded around 400 employers to do likewise, and to sack those who refused to comply. Workers were to sign a pledge renouncing the ITGWU; refusal to sign meant dismissal.

This set the pattern. Sympathetic strikes, directed at those employers involved in the dispute, began to take place; Eason's was boycotted by dockers after ignoring a call not to stock Murphy's *Irish Independent*. There was also sporadic unrest and rioting. By the end of September, English trade unions had attempted to get involved in order to resolve the dispute, troops were being drafted in to protect property and to guarantee supplies to government agencies, and shipments of food, organised by English unions, began to arrive in Dublin. (The British Trades Union Congress raised £106,000, in contrast to the £6,400 raised by the lord mayor's relief fund, two thirds of which was pledged by the Catholic bishops of Dublin and Derry.)

The unions' bottom line was recognition of the ITGWU; a demand flatly rejected by the employers due to their profound mistrust of Larkin. But they softened their stance by mid-October, demanding extensive changes to the ITGWU and the right not to reinstate all workers. The fact that so many labourers were now out of work caused appalling privation to families, which in turn prompted a desperate attempt to send children from the tenements to England until the strike was over, but this met with a ferocious response from William J. Walsh, the archbishop of Dublin, who went as far as to state that a mother who went along with such a scheme would 'no longer be worthy of the name Catholic'. Unseemly scuffles were witnessed at the quays, and the scheme was soon abandoned. By December, workers had been starved

'In one sense Dublin is a rich city; in another sense it is a highly religious city; it is also a charitable city. Nevertheless, with all her religion, wealth, and charity, Dublin remains, in many essential respects, shockingly low in the scale of modern civilization. Our poor are housed worse than those of any other great city in Europe. Our death rate is still very high; the slums take an awful toll of infant life. A ghastly proportion of our citizens is born and dies in public institutions. The standard of cleanliness among our large class of casual workers is, and, in existing conditions, must continue to be, very low.' – *The Irish Times*, 24 December 1913.

into submission, and the strike and lockout petered out in the early months of 1914. The employers insisted that those returning to work sign their pledge, and claimed to have broken the strike, but in reality they discreetly ignored their own demand lest they face a second, disastrous period without a workforce.

During the period of the lockout, a number of paramilitary forces were formed in Dublin. James Connolly's Irish Citizen Army was set up as a militia to protect strikers from attacks, and was directly linked to the events of the lockout. But it was dwarfed in size by the Irish Volunteers, a nationalist paramilitary force founded in Dublin's Rotunda in November 1913 for a very different purpose. This arose from the ongoing stand-off over the question of Home Rule, as the Liberal government of Herbert Asquith had promised to grant it. This had met with a ferocious response from unionists, most especially in Ulster, where the paramilitary Ulster Volunteer Force (UVF) had been founded in opposition to what Protestant unionists who feared possible domination by a Catholic majority saw as the threat of Home Rule.

The Irish Volunteers were formed as a direct response. They were conceived of as a citizen army, whose purpose was 'to secure and maintain the rights and liberties common to all the people of Ireland'. Like their unionist counterparts, the Irish Volunteers deemed it necessary to back up their stance with the realistic prospect of action, and to that end bought arms in Germany and landed them in locations near Dublin and Wicklow in the summer of 1914. The largest and most prominent landing of weapons was at the fishing village of Howth on 26 July. Troops sent to intercept the weapons opened fire on civilians on Bachelor's Walk, near O'Connell Street, as they returned to the Royal Barracks; three were killed, including the mother of a serving soldier. But the outrage prompted by this British heavy-handedness was overshadowed within a week by the start of the First World War.

III

The outbreak of war in August 1914 saw one surprising manifestation of anti-German sentiment, as German pork butchers across the city were attacked by hostile mobs. For the next four years Dublin would be at war, though it would a war whose impact was felt from a distance. Food processing, engineering and even the manufacture of weapons were all elements of the city's new wartime economy. Of more significance, however, was the human cost. Dublin fell within the catchment areas of a number of units in the British Army, most obviously the Royal Dublin Fusiliers, originally created from the amalgamation of a number of British units in India (a trace of this heritage survived on its cap badge, which incorporated an elephant and a tiger). There was a long tradition of Irish units in the British Army, but the outbreak of the war saw the creation of three explicitly Irish divisions: the 36th Ulster Division, drawn largely from the ranks of the UVF; and the 10th (Irish) and 16th (Irish) Divisions, into which units that drew their manpower from Dublin and its hinterland, such as the Royal Dublin Fusiliers and the Leinster Regiment, were incorporated.

Over 25,000 Dubliners enlisted in the British Army during the war. Dublin had always had strong patterns of recruitment, due in part to the high numbers of unskilled labourers in the city; the British Army offered a job, and remaining in the reserves guaranteed a stipend. Between 'separation' money (the stipend paid to families of serving troops), the opportunity to learn new skills, and even the idea that unionist employers favoured those who had served in the British military, soldiering was a fact of life in a city that had a substantial British military presence. A range of additional factors accounted for the wartime enlistment. There was perhaps a certain degree of idealism, driven by a sense that Germany was the enemy and the enthusiastic support for the war effort of Home Rule leaders such as John Redmond. There was also a feeling that service in the war might be rewarded with Home Rule, so the level of Irish recruitment is perhaps not as strange as it might now seem.

Many of the issues ordinary Dubliners faced during the war were quite literally of the bread-and-butter kind, as demand intensified and supplies ran short. The war affected virtually every walk of life. On the other hand, it had opened doors into employment for many, including many women, in institutions such as the shell factory on Parkgate Street that was established later in the war. Soldiers had a visible presence on the streets of Dublin in the early years of the war (in early 1916 most of the crimes faced by the DMP apparently related to deserters). The British war effort had been vociferously supported by the Home Rule leader John Redmond, but as the human cost mounted (especially during the abortive Gallipoli campaign of 1915), the war had become increasingly unpopular even before conflict came to the streets of Dublin in April 1916. Of those 25,000 men from Dublin who enlisted in the British Army during the First World War, approximately one in five were killed, even aside from the wounded. The 16th Division, for example, was involved in the Gallipoli campaign, landing at Suvla Bay in August 1915 (it made up approximately half of all troops in the original landing), and experienced heavy losses that were keenly felt in Dublin (ironically, some of those who served in the campaign compared the landscape of Suvla Bay to that of Dublin beaches such as Portmarnock, Dollymount and Killiney). As the death toll mounted and those wounded in the various theatres of war needed

Richmond Barracks, near Inchicore, in the early twentieth century. Dublin possessed a significant number of military installations, and service in the British armed forces offered regular employment and was thus extremely common. Late Victorian and Edwardian Dublin was, in many ways, a garrison town. (*National Library of Ireland*)

Soldiers on Abbey Street at the 'Soldiers' rendezvous', set up at the Methodist church in Abbey Street to provide non-alcoholic refreshments and facilities for troops. (*Courtesy of Dublin City Library and Archives, Postcards and Views Collection*)

PROGRAMME

Concert

IN AID OF

Temple Hill Convalescent Home
for Wounded Soldiers,
Blackrock, County Dublin,

WILL BE HELD IN THE

Town Hall, Kingstown,

ON

Wednesday, 28th October,

At Eight o'clock.

———

Floral Decorations by Messrs. E. Browett & Sons.
Piano kindly lent by Messrs. Cramer & Co.

F. DIXON, Printer, KINGSTOWN.

The impact of the war had reverberations on the Irish 'home front', in terms of those killed and wounded. Events such as this charity concert for the wounded were a common occurrence in Dublin and its suburbs during the war. (*Courtesy of Dublin City Library and Archive*)

COOPERAGE DEPARTMENT (*continued*).

NAME.	RANK.	REGIMENT.	DECORATION.
*Leahy, John ...	... Guardsman ...	1st Irish Guards...	—
Lynch, Thomas ...	... Sapper ...	Royal Engineers...	Military Medal.
Moore, Thomas ...	... Private ...	Royal Army Medical Corps ...	—
Morgan, Joseph...	... Lance-Corporal ...	34th Machine Gun Battery	—
*Mulligan, Alexander	... Private ...	2nd Royal Inniskilling Fusiliers	—
Mullins, Fergus ...	... Private ...	8th Royal Dublin Fusiliers	—
*Murphy, Thomas ...	... Driver ...	Royal Field Artillery ...	—
Murray, Robert...	... Corporal ...	Royal Army Medical Corps ...	—
McDonald, William	... Private ...	2nd Connaught Rangers	—
McEnnally, James	... Corporal ...	2nd Royal Munster Fusiliers	—
McFarlane, William	... Sapper ...	Royal Engineers... ...	—
McGuire, John ...	... Guardsman ...	1st Irish Guards... ...	—
*McIvor, James ...	... Rifleman ...	12th King's Royal Rifles	—
*Nelson, William R.	... Sapper ...	Royal Engineers... ...	—
*Niland, Joseph ...	... Sapper ...	Royal Engineers... ...	—
Nolan, Arthur ...	... Sergeant ...	1st Royal Dublin Fusiliers	—
O'Connor, James	... Private ...	5th Battn. Royal Irish Regiment	—
O'Connor, John P.	... Private ...	Royal Army Medical Corps ...	—
O'Dea, Michael ...	... Private ...	Royal Army Service Corps	—
*O'Rourke, Peter	... Corporal ...	2nd Irish Guards ...	—
*O'Toole, James ...	... Private ...	8th Royal Dublin Fusiliers	—
Ormonde, Philip	... Gunner ...	112th Heavy Battery Royal Field Artillery	—
Pinkerton, David	... Sapper ...	Royal Engineers... ...	—
Powell, James ...	... Private ...	8th Royal Dublin Fusiliers	—
Powell, Joseph ...	... Private ...	43rd Royal Dublin Fusiliers	—
Price, Patrick ...	... Corporal ...	Royal Army Medical Corps ...	—
Quinn, Bernard J.	... Sapper ...	Royal Engineers... ...	—
Redmond, William	... Guardsman ...	2nd Irish Guards ...	—
Russell, Dominick	... Private ...	Labour Corps	—
*Ryan, Patrick ...	... Guardsman ...	2nd Irish Guards	—
*Sheehan, William	... Rifleman ...	1st Battalion Rifle Brigade ...	—
Simpson, Michael	... Lance-Sergeant ...	2nd Irish Guards ...	—

* Killed in action or died of wounds.

14

COOPERAGE DEPARTMENT (*continued*).

NAME.	RANK.	REGIMENT.	DECORATION.
Smyth, Philip ...	... Gunner ...	Royal Garrison Artillery	—
Stokes, John ...	... Gunner ...	Royal Field Artillery ...	Croix de Guerre.
Stynes, Joseph ...	... Sergeant ...	Royal Garrison Artillery	—
Tait, Thomas ...	... Company Sgt.-Major	8th Royal Dublin Fusiliers	Distinguished Conduct Medal. Military Medal.
Traynor, George ...	... Corporal ...	Royal Army Medical Corps ...	—
Trimble, R. S. ...	... Lieutenant ...	6th Royal Irish Fusiliers	—
*Waters, Alexander	... Sapper ...	Royal Engineers... ...	—
*Whelan, Patrick ...	... Private ...	2nd Royal Dublin Fusiliers	—
*White, John ...	... Private ...	2nd Royal Irish Regiment	—
Woodhead, Charles	... Sergeant ...	1st Irish Guards	—

ENGINEERS' DEPARTMENT.

NAME.	RANK.	REGIMENT.	DECORATION.
Amor, A. H. ...	... Lieutenant ...	Royal Engineers... ...	—
Bluett, Sidney ...	... Sergeant ...	Royal Army Medical Corps ...	—
*Boland, Patrick...	... Rifleman ...	1st Royal Irish Rifles ...	—
Bray, Digby T. ...	... Sgt. Armourer, Staff	Royal Army Ordnance Corps ...	—
Breen, James ...	... Private ...	Royal Army Medical Corps ...	—
Broderick, James	... Stoker ...	Royal Navy	—
Byrne, James ...	... Private ...	Royal West Kents ...	—
Byrne, Patrick J.	... Attendant ...	Royal Naval Sick Berth Reserve	—
Bonny, John ...	... Corporal ...	Royal Army Medical Corps ...	—
Burke, William ...	... Sergeant ...	Leinsters	—
Carroll, William ...	... Corporal ...	7th Leinsters	Distinguished Conduct Medal. Military Medal.
Cashell, Robert ...	... Private ...	Royal Army Medical Corps ...	—
Cawthra, H. ...	... Captain ...	Royal Engineers... ...	Military Cross.
Christian, Patrick	... Gunner ...	Royal Garrison Artillery	—
Coleman, Patrick	... Rifleman ...	2nd Royal Irish Rifles ...	—
Coole, William J.	... Corporal ...	Royal Engineers... ...	—
Cooney, Thomas W.	... Lance-Corporal ...	Bedford's 13th Battalion	Distinguished Service Medal.
Corrin, Henry ...	... Guardsman ...	Irish Guards	—
Costello, Martin	... Corporal ...	Royal Garrison Artillery	—
Costello, Joseph	... Sergeant ...	Royal Field Artillery ...	—

* Killed in action or died of wounds.

15

A page from the roll of honour of the Guinness brewery, detailing those employees who fought, whether they were killed or wounded, and any decorations they had received. The management of Guinness were, in political terms, unionist, and like many firms they encouraged employees to enlist during the war, often offering bonuses to do so; it was widely and accurately recognised that veterans would be guaranteed re-employment. (*Courtesy of Dublin City Library and Archive*)

to convalesce, the wounded and maimed returned to Dublin; indeed, Dublin Castle itself housed a Red Cross Hospital for wounded troops from 1915 onwards.

Yet the war also acted as an opportunity and a rallying point for 'advanced' nationalists who opposed it; and war came to the streets of Dublin in April 1916, in the course of a rebellion planned and orchestrated by a cabal within the revived IRB spearheaded by Thomas J. Clarke and Seán Mac Diarmada. The foot soldiers were to be members of the Irish Volunteers, though some smaller groups such as the women's nationalist group Cumann na mBan and the Irish Citizen Army also became involved. The rebellion known to history as the Easter Rising was originally meant to begin on Easter Sunday, 23 April 1916. On that day the Irish Volunteers were to assemble for regular weekend manoeuvres, where they would then be informed of the rebellion that they were expected to participate in. Clarke's obsession with secrecy meant that the rank and file were kept in the dark until the last minute, though many suspected that something was being planned. The leaders of the Rising had worked on the time-honoured basis that, as the saying went, England's difficulty was Ireland's opportunity, but the failure of an abortive attempt to obtain weapons from Germany precipitated attempts to call off the Rising, and so the putative leaders of the rebellion – Clarke, Mac Diarmada, James Connolly, Éamonn Ceannt, Thomas MacDonagh, Joseph Mary Plunkett and Patrick Pearse – were deprived of both weapons and the numbers they had hoped to mobilise. They were also faced with the possibility that the attempt to import weapons might trigger a British crackdown that would deprive them of even a limited opportunity for insurrection. From their point of view, it was better to act rather than lose that opportunity.

IV

The Easter Rising was largely confined to Dublin. There seems to have been a plan for a bigger uprising outside Dublin, contingent on the arrival of weapons from Germany, but the Rising that broke out lacked both the numbers that its leaders had hoped to muster and the weapons they had hoped to equip them with. On 24 April 1916, having initially assembled at the ITGWU headquarters at Liberty Hall on Beresford Place, members of the Irish Volunteers and the Irish Citizen Army occupied a number of districts in the city, along with key buildings within them. The GPO became the headquarters and, by extension, the most famous location associated with the Easter Rising.

The GPO on Sackville Street before the Easter Rising. (*Courtesy of Dublin City Library and Archive, Birth of the Republic Collection*)

Members of the Irish Volunteers and Irish Citizen Army under Pearse and Connolly seized the GPO early on the afternoon of 24 April 1916. The rationale for seizing it remains unclear, but the GPO was a key communications hub in Dublin. It was also a very visible symbol of official authority north of the River Liffey, and its location on the wide expanse of Sackville Street ensured that its seizure, and thus the outbreak of the rebellion itself, would be widely seen and reported. It had both a practical and propaganda value. In the early days of the Rising many observers noted an almost surreal atmosphere in its vicinity, complete with looters and sightseers, but as the week wore on Sackville Street and the GPO came under heavy bombardment and fires broke out in the commercial district around the building.

Moving west along the north inner city, the area directly behind the Four Courts, extending up Church Street towards Phibsborough, was, after the GPO, the other main area of insurgent activity north of the River Liffey during the Rising. This area took in North King Street, the Linenhall Barracks (which was burned down), and the North Dublin Union. Its location gave it a strategic importance. It was adjacent to the north quays, which ensured that Volunteers in this area were in a position to hinder troop movements to and from the Royal Barracks and Kingsbridge (Heuston) train station, the terminus of the Great Southern and Western Railway. North of this area was Broadstone Station, the terminus of the Midland Great Western Railway,

'As far as I can remember, the shells started late on Wednesday. They were shrapnel shells, and the amazing thing was that instead of bullets coming in it was molten lead, actually molten, which streamed about on the ground when it fell. I was told that the shrapnel was filled with molten wax, the bullets were embedded in wax, and the velocity of the shell through the barrel, and through the air caused the mould to melt. As the first of those shells hit the house, the volunteers rushed and told me about them. I rushed up and found an old fellow crawling about on his hands and knees gathering the stuff up as it hardened. I asked him what he was doing and what he intended to do with the stuff. He said "Souvenirs". That is all he said. From this time onwards the shelling continued.' – Irish Volunteer Oscar Traynor recalls an incongruous encounter during the Easter Rising. BMH WS 340 (Oscar Traynor), Military Archives, Ireland. Traynor later became a Fianna Fáil politician and also served as president of the Football Association of Ireland.

another venue that could facilitate the arrival of British reinforcements. In line with the manner in which fighting intensified as the week went on, the area around Church Street, Brunswick Street and North King Street saw some of the heaviest and most intense fighting in the city during the Rising. North King Street was also the location of one of the most notorious incidents of the Rising, when members of the South Staffordshire Regiment killed a number of unarmed civilians in house-to-house searches later in the week.

The remaining centres of insurgent activity were south of the River Liffey. The South Dublin Union, near Kilmainham, was Ireland's largest workhouse, housing 3,200 inmates in a sprawling fifty-acre complex roughly on the site of what is now St James's Hospital (some of the original buildings can be seen there). It was seized by Volunteers under Éamonn Ceannt. Many of the sites were chosen in order to interfere with any British reinforcements that might come into central Dublin from the various barracks around the city. The South Dublin Union was the site of intense fighting in the first half of the week, and the staff continued to look after the inmates throughout the week. The Mendicity Institution at Usher's Island, a charitable institution for the poor based in what was formerly Moira House, was seized by small number of Volunteers under Sean Heuston, in an attempt to interfere with troops who might be emerging from the Royal Barracks (Collins Barracks) across the river (Heuston and his small band held it from Monday to Wednesday). Volunteers under Thomas MacDonagh seized the enormous Jacob's factory, which was very close to both Camden Street and Patrick Street: natural routes for troops entering the city centre from Portobello Barracks in Rathmines and Wellington Barracks (now Griffith College) on the South Circular Road. As it happens, little fighting took place here, though the roughly one hundred volunteers who seized the factory were abused by local residents, many of whom were Jacob's workers themselves or were the families of soldiers serving in the British Army. Three members of the Jacob's garrison were later executed: MacDonagh himself, Major John MacBride and Michael O'Hanrahan. St Stephen's Green was also the scene of fighting: it was occupied on 24 April by members of the Irish Citizen Army led by Michael Mallin. The ICA ejected civilians from the park, and were roundly condemned when one of their members killed a man retrieving a handcart from a barricade near the Shelbourne Hotel. On Tuesday morning troops occupied the Shelbourne Hotel and were able to fire down into trenches that the ICA had dug in the park. The ICA abandoned St Stephen's Green and retreated to the Royal College of Surgeons on the west side of the park, the façade of which still bears the marks of small arms fire.

British troops organise the defence of City Hall during the revolutionary period. The building had been seized at an early stage during the Easter Rising by the Irish Citizen Army, and some of the first fatalities of the Rising occurred in its vicinity before it was captured a few hours later. (*Courtesy of Dublin City Library and Archive, Birth of the Republic Collection*)

Finally, the easternmost Volunteer outpost was around Boland's Bakery, overlooking the Grand Canal (the current Treasury Building is built on the site of the original bakery). This complex was seized by members of the Irish Volunteers led by Éamon de Valera: perhaps as few as a hundred poorly armed Volunteers were involved. The location of the area was significant, as it contained important transport links that connected Dublin to the southern ferry port of Kingstown (Dún Laoghaire): the rail terminus at Westland Row, and the roads leading into the city that crossed the Grand Canal at Mount Street. This area saw some of the heaviest fighting of the Rising on Wednesday 26 April, as British troops of the 176th and 178th Infantry Brigades (Sherwood Foresters) were ambushed as they attempted to cross the canal at the junction of Northumberland Road and Mount Street. These were relatively narrow Victorian streets that formed a natural bottleneck in which the British lost over 200 dead and wounded, as fighting continued in the area into Wednesday night. A number of the Volunteers were also killed in the fighting. One, Michael Malone, was killed in 25 Northumberland Road, and was briefly buried in the garden of the house.

There was, it seems, logic to the seizure some of these areas and buildings, but the stark reality was that the Easter Rising was doomed to failure. In the midst of a global war the British authorities could not tolerate an uprising of this nature in what was then still a substantial city in the United Kingdom that had, since August 1914, already been profoundly affected by a war being fought elsewhere. The outbreak of the Rising, less than two years after the outbreak of the First World War, took Dublin's citizens by surprise. It took the British authorities by surprise. In truth, it even took some of those who participated in it by surprise. But by the beginning of May much of Dublin's central commercial districts lay in ruins; over £2,600,000 worth of damaged was caused by both fires and fighting, while nearly 500 civilians and combatants were killed in the combat that had taken place in and around the various insurgent positions throughout the city.

The activities of looters became a notorious feature of the Rising. The DMP had been withdrawn from the streets within hours of the outbreak of the rebellion, and given that Sackville Street bordered extensive slum areas, it was probably inevitable that the urban poor would seek to get what was ordinarily out of reach for them. Much of what was taken in the initial phases of looting were not essential goods: sweets, clothes, furniture, alcoholic beverages and sporting goods, among many other items (prosecutions for larceny skyrocketed in the aftermath of the Rising). As the week wore on, however, any lighthearted aspect to the looting of Easter Week had given way to far more serious matters as the fighting brought life in the city to a halt. Shops and banks were closed, trams stopped running, the military imposed travel

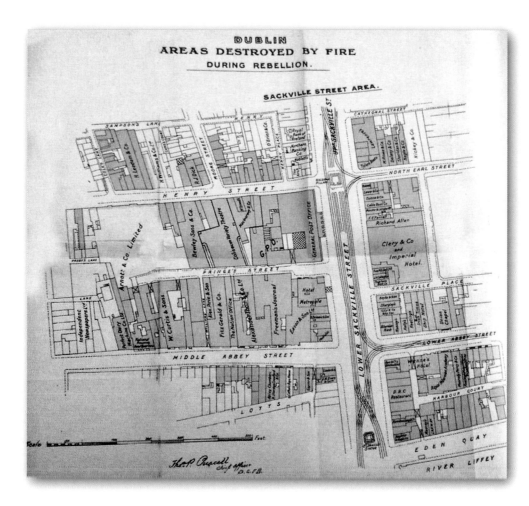

A map prepared for insurance purposes by Dublin Fire Brigade, detailing the level of destruction in the vicinity of Sackville Street during the Easter Rising: the buildings shaded in orange were destroyed. (*Courtesy of Dublin City Library and Archive*)

Postcard views of the devastation of the city centre after the Rising. Sackville Street was bombarded with artillery, which caused little damage in itself but which caused massive fires in the heart of a commercial district. Such souvenirs proved immensely popular in the aftermath. (*Courtesy of Dublin City Library and Archive, Birth of the Republic Collection*)

The ruins of Liberty Hall and other buildings on Beresford Place. They were damaged by gunfire from the Fisheries Protection vessel *Helga*. (*Courtesy of Dublin City Library and Archive, Birth of the Republic Collection*)

restrictions, gas supplies were cut off, newspapers ceased operation and food became scarce; many of the civilian casualties of the Rising may well have been killed in the crossfire as they sought food for their families in the war-torn inner city. The Limerick accountant Wesley Hanna, in what is now Dublin 4, noted that 'if it weren't so awfully tragic it would be amusing to see the swells round here carrying home bread'; a small hint that domestic servants and deliverymen may have been absent from work. In the days that followed, bereaved families began to make their way towards Glasnevin Cemetery, which became the largest single place of interment for the combatant and non-combatant dead of the Rising.

The British Army did, however, attempt to deal with food shortages in the city in the days after the Rising by distributing food to institutions from the military depot on Parkgate Street and even taking over the supplies of a Bovril warehouse on Eustace Street. They also sought to enforce order amongst the lengthy queues that were to found outside bakeries, and private charities and the local authorities stepped in to ensure a food supply to the citizens of a city that had previously been affected by war from afar, but which had now seen war come to its streets. By early May vegetables were in the shops once more, and businesses reopened as military restrictions were eased, though not lifted. As early as 6 May 1916 the Henry Street warehouse (later Roches Stores) was advertising 'costumes and coats injured by rifle fire', while Hely's Stationer of Dame Street was already advertising postcards of the ruined city centre. By mid-May most essential services had been restored in Dublin, and even cinemas were opening their doors; but the ongoing military curfews ensured that prospective moviegoers would have to settle for the matinée. Dublin's inhabitants picked up the pieces of ordinary life as best they could.

V

Separatist republicans began to reorganise themselves in the aftermath of the Easter Rising. The Irish Volunteers returned to the limelight on 30 September 1917, with the funeral of the 1916 veteran Thomas Ashe, who died after being force-fed while on hunger strike in Mountjoy Prison. Ashe was given a huge funeral in Dublin; perhaps 30,000 lined the funeral route to Glasnevin. After a gun salute by the Volunteers, a young 1916 veteran from Cork, Michael Collins, read out a brief but militant oration, thereby coming into the limelight. The funeral gave a shot in the arm to the moribund Dublin Volunteers, now increasingly known as the Irish Republican Army (IRA), who had used the funeral to host a show of strength on the streets of the capital.

At this time Dublin was still at war, and was still racked by food and fuel shortages. In early 1918, the threat of conscription provided a major platform for virtually all segments of Irish society to register a protest against British rule. In late 1918 and early 1919 came Spanish flu: in 1918, 1,500 Dubliners died in the global pandemic that followed the war, up from a yearly average of ninety-five prior to that. But at the end of 1918 the UK went to the ballot box, and with the exception of the traditionally unionist constituencies of Trinity College, Dublin and Rathmines, the newly reorganised Sinn Féin party won Dublin's Westminster seats by a comfortable margin on a platform demanding independence. On 21 January the Mansion House became the venue for the first Dáil Éireann, but the same day saw the first (official) shots of the War of Independence fired in Tipperary.

There was a definite sense among the leadership of the IRA that Dublin, as the capital, was key to the war that they would fight. The IRA in Dublin were in a good position to get weapons: they raided police barracks and even, on occasion, bought them from soldiers. Some arms remained from the Howth gunrunning and among the pre-1916 Volunteers. In 1917 grenades were being produced at 198 Parnell Street, with detonators being manufactured around the corner on Dominick Street. More significant was the strategy to be undertaken in the city: the maverick tendencies of Michael Collins took concrete form with the foundation of his assassination 'squad' in July 1919. Their targets were detectives, senior officials associated with the British

'The area of the city is approximately 8 square miles, and if the suburbs, including Kingstown, are included, the area of Greater Dublin is about 14 square miles. The population of the city is 230,000, and the inclusion of the suburbs adds about 170,000 to the above figure … the city is divided, roughly speaking, into two equal parts by the river Liffey which is also crossed by numerous bridges. It is a maze of narrow streets and alleys set in no order. There is little definite residential area, slums and tenement houses are found everywhere, and in the older part of the city there are many ramifications of underground cellars in which men, munitions, and munitions factories can be hidden. There are innumerable small shops and comparatively few large stores. It is in fact, an ideal town for guerrilla warfare.'
– The British military's perspective on fighting in Dublin, from 'Record of the rebellion in Ireland in 1920–21', cited in William Sheehan, *Fighting for Dublin: The British battle for Dublin, 1919–21* (Cork, 2007), pp. 138–9.

regime, and in late 1919 the Dublin IRA even tried to assassinate the viceroy near the Ashtown gate of the Phoenix Park.

Certainly, up to the middle of 1920, the IRA in Dublin was wary of public opinion; even some members of the organisation had reservations about what Collins was engineering. But this changed as the British regime became increasingly repressive: in August 1920 the Restoration of Order in Ireland Act effectively placed the entire country under martial law with capital powers, and militarisation continued with the formation of the paramilitary police forces (the infamous Auxiliaries and Black and Tans). The first open attack on British soldiers in Dublin came on 20 September 1920 when a number of soldiers collecting bread from a bakery on Church Street were ambushed in order to steal their weapons. But the soldiers fought back: three IRA members were killed and Kevin Barry, the eighteen-year-old son of a dairyman, and a student in University College Dublin, was captured, having been found hiding with a rifle under a lorry. He was the first member of the IRA to be captured by the British since the Easter Rising of 1916; despite his youth, on 20 October 1920 he was hanged in Mountjoy, becoming the first to be executed under the new and draconian laws directed against the IRA. His death at such a young age, despite a campaign for clemency, made him the most famous republican martyr of the war.

Later in the year on 21 November came the watershed of Bloody Sunday, when fifteen suspected British intelligence officers, including two civilians, were killed at locations across the city centre (including Baggot Street, Mount Street, Earlsfort Terrace, Morehampton Road, Upper Pembroke Street (where four were killed), and the Gresham Hotel on Sackville Street). Other deaths ensued, including the killing by British forces of two senior IRA members and a civilian who had been detained in Dublin Castle the night before, and, notoriously, a British reprisal attack on a football match being played at the GAA headquarters of Croke Park, in which thirteen spectators and one player were shot dead.

Bloody Sunday was followed by the formation of the Dublin 'Active Service Unit' of the IRA, full-time guerrillas paid £4 10s per week. This precipitated a more active policy: they aimed at three attacks per day, with Aungier Street and Camden Street being christened the 'Dardanelles' due to their popularity as a venue for attacks: the area was close to Portobello Barracks, and its side streets and street vendors provided perfect cover and assistance. The IRA fought a guerilla war in Dublin, with ambush and assassination becoming their stock in trade, often carried out with considerable ingenuity to maximise their limited resources.

In May 1921 the IRA attempted something more daring when they attacked the

'A British soldier in uniform who was walking past approached our two men who were standing on the path outside Hopkins & Hopkins (Jewellers) and asked them to direct him to the Royal Barracks (now Collins). The boys were delighted with his company as it made their position less conspicuous and afforded them a measure of protection for the job on hand. They held him in conversation while, at the same time, keeping their eyes on the scout on the Island in the centre of O'Connell Bridge. After a few minutes the scout gave the signal that the car was approaching and the boys at Hopkins & Hopkins threw the grenades into it. Hell then broke loose; the occupants of the car had apparently expected an attack and opened intense fire with automatic pistols. The car proceeded down Eden Quay and was again attacked by our men from the archway beside Mooney's public house with grenades and revolver fire. When it reached the corner of Marlborough St. and Eden Quay the Volunteers stationed there also opened fire with revolvers and threw grenades. The car went on towards Butt Bridge where it stopped. We subsequently learned that some of the occupants had been wounded. One of them was hanging from the knees out of the car, having been hit in the chest by the attacking party in Mooney's archway. Needless to mention, we did not wait to see the result of the operation, but made our getaway as quickly as possible.' – Michael O'Kelly of the IRA's Dublin Brigade describes an ambush on a party of British intelligence officers, May 1921. BMH WS 1,635 (Michael O'Kelly), Military Archives, Ireland.

Custom House, which housed a number of government departments. The IRA wanted to carry out a spectacular and public attack in Dublin, to demonstrate to International opinion that the forces of the putative Irish Republic had the means to carry out operations of this kind, and that they were far more than the murderous assassins portrayed in British propaganda. The IRA attack was planned over three months. It was obvious that the structure of the building contained little to burn, so the planning involved stealing a lorry, fuel and large quantities of scrap fabric to provide material that could burn.

The Dublin Brigade carried out the attack on 25 May 1921. They had attempted to cordon off the building, but extensive fighting broke out when regular troops and Auxiliaries arrived on the scene while the IRA were trying to burn it. This type of open warfare was in total contrast to the usual methods of the Dublin IRA, and large

The smouldering ruins of the Custom House after the IRA attack of May 1921. It was rebuilt in the 1920s, though deliberately not with the original Portland stone from Dorset; the use of 'English' stone was seen as incongruous in the reconstruction of such a major public building in the capital of a newly independent Ireland. Limestone from Kildare was used instead. An enduring and visible consequence is that rainfall causes the limestone, when wet, to discolour differently from the original Portland stone. (*National Library of Ireland*)

numbers of the Volunteers involved were arrested. The building itself smouldered for another five days and was not rebuilt until the 1920s; many of the Dublin firemen called in to deal with the blaze were themselves members of the IRA and were not inclined to put it out. This was the last major IRA action in Dublin before the truce of July 1921, but in less than a year, Dublin was the venue of the outbreak of civil war.

The period of the truce was surprisingly messy, indeed lawless on occasion, as the republican and British forces existed uneasily side by side on the streets of Dublin. Political developments took centre stage towards the end of the year, as the National University buildings on Earlsfort Terrace housed the acrimonious debates over the December 1921 treaty that established the Irish Free State. Early 1922 saw the British withdrawal begin in earnest, as the handover of power took place in Dublin Castle in January 1922, and as the network of barracks began to be transferred to the new National Army by the departing British. Yet these months also saw battle lines being drawn, as those republican forces opposed to the treaty ensconced themselves in premises in and around Sackville Street and Parnell Square and, most imposingly of all, in the Four Courts complex itself from April 1922. While venues such as the Mansion House hosted intermittent attempts to broker a compromise, the slide towards civil war was confirmed on 28 June when the new National Army of the Free State used borrowed British artillery at the nearby Liffey bridges to attack the Four Courts. The subsequent destruction of the Irish Public Record Office, which was housed in the complex, was a notable casualty. Yet the outbreak of the conflict was not confined to the Four Courts. As the anti-treaty IRA had also occupied the block of buildings on Upper O'Connell Street that housed the Gresham Hotel, it too was bombarded and destroyed by fire.

The major fighting in Dublin ended after a week, and the outbreak of the Civil War left enduring scars on the streetscape. The conflict in the capital subsequently took a very different form, and was characterised by ambushes, assassinations and extrajudicial killings up to the end of the Civil War in April 1923. By May of that year, Dublin's decade of revolution was over.

The destruction of the Four Courts following the detonation in the Public Record Office, June 1922. A vast and irreplaceable trove of documentation dating back to the Middle Ages was also destroyed; fragments of paper and parchment were carried aloft to waft down across Dublin in the hours that followed. (*National Library of Ireland*)

'It was O'Connell Street in Dublin, during the capture of the Republican headquarters by the Free State troops in June 1922. I was standing on the south side of the bridge with a comrade. We had been disbanded on the previous day and we were now watching the destruction of the hotels where headquarters were still holding out. The Free State soldiers were throwing incendiary bombs from across the street into the hotels. There was a rattle of machine-gun and rifle fire. A cordon had been drawn all round the doomed buildings, and crowds of people stood outside the barriers, watching the scene, as at a public entertainment. Then I heard an old woman in a group behind me say:

"Did ye hear that bloody murderer, Liam O'Flaherty, is killed, thanks be to god?"

"Who?" said another old woman.

"Liam O'Flaherty," said the first. "The man that locked the unemployed up in the Rotunda and shot them unless they spat on the holy crucifix. The man that tried to sell Dublin to the Bolsheviks."

"Is he dead?" said a man.

"Shot through the heart this morning on Capel Street," said the old woman. "The lord be praised for ridding the country of that cut-throat. Ho, me hearties! Give the bastards what's comin' to them."

The old woman cheered the soldiers who were now running across the street to take the headquarters by storm. A mass of flames shot up from the roofs of the buildings through a thick bank of smoke. A great cheer came from the watching people. I nudged my comrade and we walked away together.

"I'm going," I said. "There's nothing more to be done."

"Where?" he said.

"To England."

"Surely to God ye're not quitting," he said. "It's only startin' yet. We'll have flying columns in action within a couple o' days. Then the fun'll start."

"No," I said. "That old woman was right. I'm dead." ' – **The novelist and republican Liam O'Flaherty hears an exaggerated report of his demise in the opening salvos of the Civil War, from his memoir *Shame the Devil* (Dublin, 1934) pp. 35–6.**

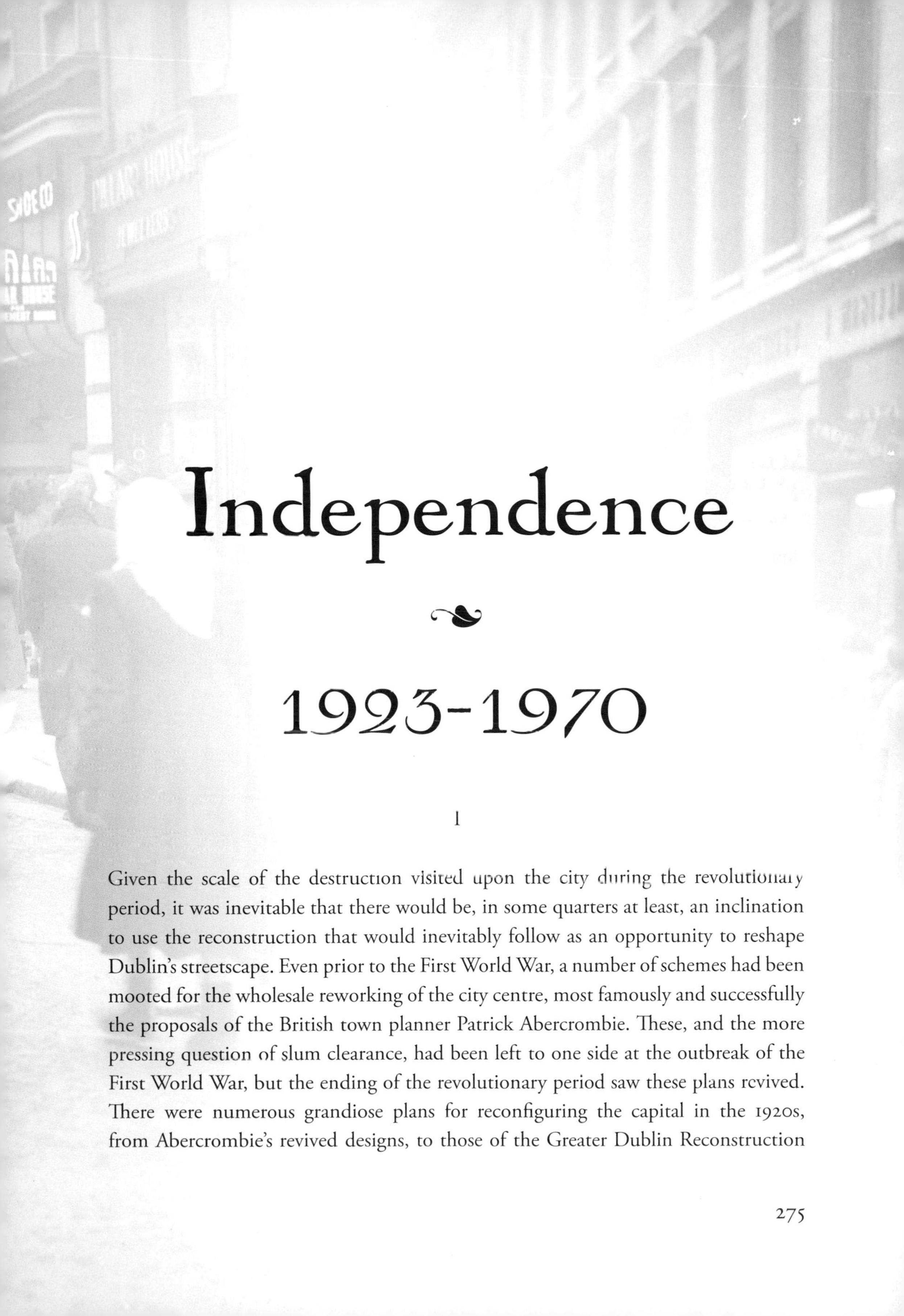

Independence

❧

1923-1970

I

Given the scale of the destruction visited upon the city during the revolutionary period, it was inevitable that there would be, in some quarters at least, an inclination to use the reconstruction that would inevitably follow as an opportunity to reshape Dublin's streetscape. Even prior to the First World War, a number of schemes had been mooted for the wholesale reworking of the city centre, most famously and successfully the proposals of the British town planner Patrick Abercrombie. These, and the more pressing question of slum clearance, had been left to one side at the outbreak of the First World War, but the ending of the revolutionary period saw these plans revived. There were numerous grandiose plans for reconfiguring the capital in the 1920s, from Abercrombie's revived designs, to those of the Greater Dublin Reconstruction

Movement, which in 1923 offered an extensive range of proposals for the wholesale redevelopment of the city: the GPO would become City Hall; the Custom House was to become a central train station and a new GPO; Dublin Castle would house the judiciary; and the Oireachtas would move out to new buildings to be constructed in Kilmainham. After all, medieval Dublin was long gone: why not continue the process of developing a modern city, unfettered by the legacy of the past?

There was an expectation that the return of an Irish parliament – and its location was the source of much debate – would naturally usher in the prosperity that was assumed to be the victim of British rule. But any hopes that such grandiose plans would become reality foundered on the rock of finance: W.T. Cosgrave's new Cumann na nGaedheal government was in no position to spend money on such schemes, even had the will been there to so – and it was not. Between 1924 and 1930, Dublin Corporation was suspended in what was a fundamentally political decision by the Free State government; instead, the city was governed by three appointed commissioners. Calls for municipal reforms led in 1930 to legislation that expanded the city limits and integrated the townships around its rim into the jurisdiction of the restored corporation: the long-cherished autonomy of Pembroke and Rathmines was a notable casualty.

But some changes did take place in Dublin in the course of the 1920s, even if these were piecemeal rather than revolutionary. Streets began to be renamed in earnest, in an assertion of the new state's official identity: Sackville Street finally became O'Connell (both renamed and reconstructed in the 1920s); Great Brunswick Street became Pearse Street; and Rutland Square became Parnell Square. The assertion of an independent identity that implied stability was of great importance to the Cosgrave government. Another manifestation of this was the vast spectacle of the Tailteann Games, a two-week festival inspired by an ancient Celtic festival and centred largely (though not exclusively) on Croke Park (swimming competitions were hosted in the pond at Dublin Zoo and chess was even hosted in Trinity College). While the Tailteann Games proved a short-lived venture (it was discreetly abandoned by Fianna Fáil governments in the 1930s), sporting events – GAA, soccer and rugby matches, and even the perennial Dublin horse show hosted by the Royal Dublin Society (RDS) – attracted vast crowds throughout the late 1920s and beyond.

Perhaps ironically, the RDS found itself providing the permanent seat of government; Leinster House was rented and then bought outright as the new seat of Dáil Éireann, rather than the iconic venue of the old parliament on College Green. For the Free State government, finances again played a role in the decision; the potential

A street trader on George's Street, early twentieth century. (*Library of Congress*)

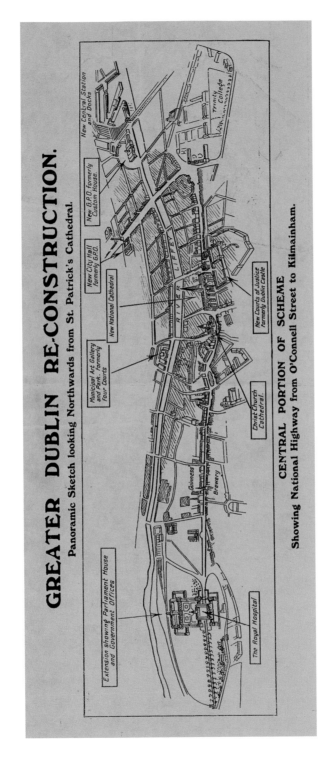

Dublin remodelled, as envisioned by the Greater Dublin Reconstruction Movement. (*Courtesy of Dublin City Library and Archive*)

cost of compensating the Bank of Ireland was prohibitive. In the absence of such an obvious marker of independence, College Green played host to other contests over identities. Armistice Day, 11 November, attracted vast crowds to College Green in the early 1920s to mark the end of the Great War, though this served as a flashpoint for scuffles, with republicans and Trinity College students being singled out as notable, if diametrically opposing, culprits. Trinity students had developed the habit of closing off College Green to commemorate the two-minute silence, which they followed by singing 'God Save the King' (which remained a fixture in Trinity long after 1922). Memorial poppies, as sold by the Royal British Legion, were a common sight in the Dublin of the 1920s, and were often denounced by republicans as imperialist symbols. It should be said that some republicans stated they had no problem with commemorating the war dead in itself; it was their posthumous recruitment into political causes such as loyalism that was deemed objectionable. Political sensitivities arising from the struggle for independence complicated the remembrance of the dead of the war, despite the fact that so many nationalists had served in the British armed forces as well.

Opposition to what Armistice Day was seen to exemplify took more destructive forms. The statue of William III on College Green, for example, was finally removed after being damaged by a bomb on the morning of 11 November 1928 (a number of other monuments were damaged on the same day). This was a deliberate action, intended as a counterpoint to the loyalism that was assumed to characterise the commemoration of Armistice Day. But if monuments were to be destroyed because of a loose association with the war, a massive memorial that was explicitly linked to the war was constructed from the later 1920s onward. The erection of a national memorial to Irish servicemen who had served in the Great War was being proposed almost as soon as the war was over; in 1919 a trust fund was established to that end. There were various suggestions as to what form such a memorial would take (such as a physical monument, or some form of practical assistance to ex-servicemen). The suggestion that Merrion Square provide the setting for a memorial gave way to the choice of Islandbridge, west of the city, and the creation of impressive (if discreetly out of the way) memorial gardens designed by no less a figure than Edwin Lutyens, the architect of the London Cenotaph.

II

Change in the capital of the newly independent Ireland was subtle rather than revolutionary, but some reconstruction was inevitable: O'Connell Street was being rebuilt from the late 1920s into a more commercialised street. The reconstruction of the GPO (little more than the original façade survives) is simply the most famous aspect of a project that saw the construction and reconstruction of iconic buildings such as Clery's and the Gresham Hotel. The new reconstruction brought a new emphasis on entertainment in the form of cinemas (such as the elaborate Savoy) and new dancehalls; the growth of the latter prompted moral panic at the notion that such institutions were corrupting the moral fibre of the youth of Dublin, and, indeed, of the Free State in general. The notorious red light district of Monto, for example, was finally closed down by the Gardaí (the post-independence police force that replaced the DMP and RIC) in a series of major raids in March 1925, following a lengthy campaign by Frank Duff and the newly formed Legion of Mary.

Physical change continued to take place at a more modest level. The arrival of the so-called International Style saw a modern trend in public and private housing throughout the 1920s and 1930s, and the creation of new flat complexes in the inner city. Alongside slum clearance and industrial development came structures associated with, for example, religion (Christ the King Church in Cabra and the Oblates' Grotto in Inchicore), retail (Clery's), the First World War (Rathfarnham War Memorial Hall and the National War Memorial Gardens), law and order (Pearse Street Garda Station) and entertainment (the Savoy cinema, and the bathing shelters at North Bull Wall and Clontarf). Elements of the city's commercial infrastructure remained largely unchanged. Grafton Street was less disrupted and retained much of its old Victorian character (not to mention its status as Dublin's premier shopping street).

What was lacking in the architecture of this period was a grand scheme or plan. Despite the hopes of some in the 1920s that the damage caused by the revolution could prove a blank slate on which to inscribe a capital city worthy of a newly independent state, this proved illusory. The 1920s saw the first major suburban expansion in a generation, with the creation of a new 'garden suburb' in Marino, in which houses were to be built in a spacious non-utilitarian style. With regard to the basic conditions of living, a vast increase in the number of cars on the streets of Dublin in this era was to have knock-on effects in terms of congestion, road safety and damage to the streets; the number of cars in Dublin doubled in the decade after 1914, with 11,000 on the streets by 1925. Traffic management was now added to a long list of issues that the city authorities would have to grapple with into the future.

Dublin between the wars was the hub of Irish unemployment, a problem that became worse from the 1920s onwards. Consequently, the rulers of the new Free State sought to devise legislative solutions to deal with the city's chronic poverty and

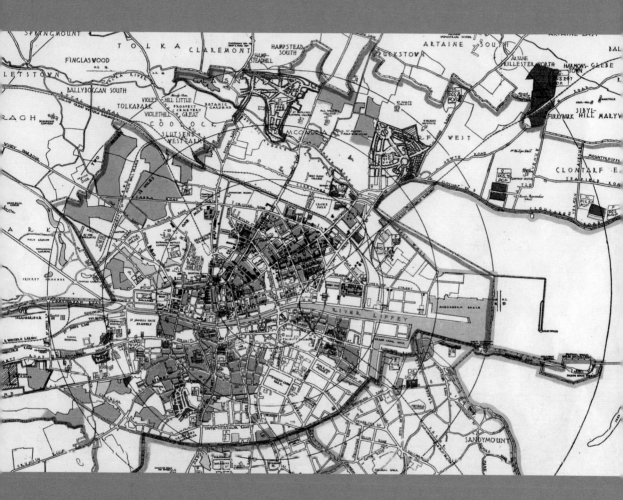

A map of Dublin from the Dublin Civic Survey, 1925; the population of the city, by 1926, stood at 468,000. (*Courtesy of Dublin City Library and Archive, Map Collection*)

A preliminary sketch by the architect Raymond Unwin for the development of Marino, 1914; constructed in the 1920s, this was a pioneering attempt to develop a garden suburb, in which open spaces and quality of life would be paramount. (*Courtesy of Dublin City Library and Archive*)

unemployment problems. The most significant building initiative after independence would be the slum clearance and housing projects initiated in the 1930s, and even they were hamstrung by lack of funds: hence the shift towards constructing flats, a strategy avoided by Cumann na nGaedheal, which favoured suburban home ownership, not least because it had less associations with 'communism'. The baselessnesss of such fears was surely highlighted in June 1932 when the 31st Eucharistic Congress met in Dublin, marking 1,500 years since the arrival of St Patrick in Ireland. This enormous Catholic festival prompted an outburst of religious fervour, with ceremonies throughout the city and crowds estimated to be in the hundreds of thousands attending masses in the vast expanses of the Phoenix Park, including a high mass, complete with a live broadcast by Pope Pius XI from the Vatican.

The change of government in 1932 brought a new impetus to resolving the seemingly intractable housing problems. Éamon de Valera's Fianna Fáil, in the 1930s, had aligned itself with social as well as political issues. There was an official awareness that Dublin had prestige, that it remained important and could be a driver of the Free State's new economic development. New industries began to be established (such as tobacco factories in Glasnevin and the South Circular Road) and Dublin became a hub for economic expansion during the 1930s. A new spate of hospital construction began to take place, generally funded by the vast sums generated by a new lottery, the Irish Sweepstakes. Some striking buildings were built under Fianna Fáil's social programme of the 1930s: the Department of Industry and Commerce on Kildare Street, begun in 1939, is perhaps the most remarkable example among many. A British style could be seen in the influence of housing in the suburbs, with a Dutch influence being evident in inner-city flats. The appointment of Herbert Simms as Dublin's chief architect was a key development. The flats were constructed in order to emphasise notions of moral as well as physical health, but they were expensive structures because they needed to be reinforced, given that they were built on a small footprint; eventually they gave way to suburban development as a means of tackling Dublin's perennial housing problems. This was to be the fresh post-independence start, with the creation of vast new suburbs in Cabra and Crumlin sparking what is easily one of the most significant developments in Dublin's history, though they were bedevilled by concerns about the lack of adequate services and infrastructure in what were, to all intents and purposes, new towns being built from scratch.

O'Connell Street at night in the 1930s, from the base of Nelson's Pillar. (*Courtesy of Dublin City Library and Archive*)

MONDAY, JUNE 17th, 1929, FOR SIX NIGHTS, at 8.0
MATINEE SATURDAY at 2.30 :: :: Doors Open at 2.0

LAST WEEK OF THE MACDONA PLAYERS

DIRECT FROM THE LITTLE AND GARRICK THEATRES, LONDON
IN PLAYS BY

BERNARD SHAW

VERNON SYLVAINE	LEAH BATEMAN	FRANK DARCH
REGINALD LONG	PATIENCE RIGNOLD	WILFRID LAWSON
GEORGE DE LARA	MARGOT LISTER	GERALD OUFF
GEORGE LARCHET	MARY TOWNLEY	WILLARD STOKER
BERTHA WOOLCOTE	DOROTHY MARLER	RAYMOND A. ROCK

TUESDAY, JUNE 18th, AND FRIDAY, JUNE 21st, at 8.0

Mrs. Warren's Profession

CHARACTERS IN THE ORDER OF THEIR APPEARANCE

Vivie...MARGOT LISTER

Praed...VERNON SYLVAINE

Mrs. Warren..LEAH BATEMAN

Sir George Crofts.......................................WILFRID LAWSON

Frank...REGINALD LONG

Rev. Samuel Gardner..............................FRANK DARCH

A 1929 programme for the Gaiety Theatre. (*Courtesy of Dublin City Library and Archive*)

WORKERS OF DUBLIN

READ THIS : "In Magee's Court there are 7 small Cottages enclosed in a court 10 ft. wide. In these Cottages live 36 families—156 people. The air is unbearable. The rooms at night walking with Sewerage Beetles. Mothers have to remain up till daylight walking to and fro to protect their children from these loathsome insects. The walls are crumbling and damp; the roofs leaking; the floors slanting.

AND THIS : In York Street some of the tenants are practically condemned to death in the basement cellars, front and back kitchens, some of which are already condemned by the Corporation Authorities."

AND THIS : A man, wife and four children occupy a closet, 8 ft. by 15 ft. in Dominick Street. No fire grate holes in the wall and no room to move when the extra bed is down for the children to sleep in."

These cases of appalling housing conditions of Dublin Workers can be multiplied a thousand times.

WHEN WILL THE SCANDALS END?

Not till the workers who build all houses and who are forced to live in pig styes assert themselves.

A PUBLIC MEETING

To protest against the foregoing housing scandals will be held in

COLLEGE GREEN,

ON

Mon., 2nd July at 7.15 p.m.

All present will march to the Corporation Meeting at the City Hall.

Support the just demands of your fellow workers for proper housing.

No Rent for Insanitary or Condemned Houses.

Rents to be fixed in relation to wages.

Real Houses for those who build all houses.

No Rent from the Unemployed.

Issued by Republican Congress Committees, 112 Marlboro' St. Dublin.

Housing remained an issue throughout the 1930s. This poster, by the Republican Congress (a small left-wing offshoot of the IRA) highlights the persistence of slum conditions after independence. (*Courtesy of Dublin City Library and Archive, Birth of the Republic Collection*)

In December 1940 Dublin corporation adopted yet another town planning scheme, again with the involvement of Patrick Abercrombie, complete with plans for new expanded estates, the creation of public parks such as St Anne's (owned by the Guinness family), and major investment in infrastructure. Yet just as one world war put paid to the plans of an earlier generation, so another war put paid to these. The outbreak of the Second World War – the 'Emergency' – prompted the authorities to address the question of how they might deal with an attack on Dublin. Indeed, there were elaborate evacuation plans in place during the early years of the Emergency, aimed at emptying the city of its inhabitants within 24 hours, with the population being decanted into the surrounding counties of Leinster in the event of a major bomb attack. In the event, Dublin was bombed twice in 1941, with the South Circular Road and the North Strand both being hit by German bombs (seemingly by mistake) in the early stages of the war; the latter attack, on 31 May 1941, was by far the more destructive, resulting in the deaths of twenty-eight people, injuries to another ninety, and the outright destruction of 300 houses. Éamon de Valera's government had put in place some precautions against air attack on the city, most obviously anti-aircraft batteries. But Dublin was not blacked out, and the air-raid shelters that had been erected in the city were often regarded as filthy venues for what might be termed anti-social behaviour, and were apparently often locked to deter such behaviour.

There was no obvious prelude to the bombing of the North Strand. Anti-aircraft batteries fired at planes on numerous occasions and the night of 30–31 May was no exception, as they opened up on a sizeable number of planes flying in an apparently uncoordinated manner around the city earlier that evening. A single bomber was reported flying over the city later that night minutes before the bombs landed; presumably this was the plane that dropped the bombs. The most damage, and most of the fatalities, was caused by a bomb that fell between tram tracks on the south side of Newcomen Bridge; the impact on the cobbled street magnified the force of the blast and the cobbles themselves served as especially destructive missiles. The explosions were heard throughout the north inner city, and witnesses reported a scene of utter devastation along the stretch of road between the iconic Five Lamps and the Royal Canal. Many of those whose homes were destroyed were housed in the new suburb then being created in Cabra.

Poverty was exacerbated during the Second World War by wage freezes and price increases and an inability to fall back upon traditional rural resources of food and fuel.

Rationing was imposed, and the 'glimmer man' – the inspector employed to check that precious gas supplies were only used within set times, and that a 'glimmer' of a gas light was not left on – became a stock image of Dublin folklore. Yet the range of goods available in Dublin during the war years compared favourably to wartime Britain. That said, shortages of timber and metal brought the building trade to a halt, with knock-on effects for casual labour. Unemployment, as always, prompted emigration, this time to the United Kingdom (wartime remittances seemed to play a role in keeping people's spending power afloat), and many from Dublin served in the British military. Dublin had the second highest rate of emigration in Ireland (after Mayo) during the war, a remarkable departure from the norm, although charitable organisations such as the Mount Street Club sought to deal with poverty and unemployment at home. Crime inevitably rose, with the theft of bicycles becoming a major issue in the privation of the war years.

Dubliners during the war had a low life expectancy relative to their rural counterparts and no economic recovery was evident until 1948. The war had seen a spike in the incidence of venereal diseases, but by the 1950s tuberculosis was one of Dublin's biggest killers. The extension of the health service in the 1950s saw better sanitation in housing and a greater use of maternity hospitals. By the 1940s Dublin's

'A fight which took place between what are thought to be rival gangs of young men at a football match played at Tolka Park, Dublin, yesterday, resulted in several people being admitted to hospital suffering from serious injury.

'It appears that while the match was in progress a number of men scaled the partition around the football grounds at the Tolka Bank. Mixing with a section of the spectators, they were soon at grips with them, and wild scenes ensued. It is stated that knives and other weapons were produced and that a number of both sides were wounded. The fight lasted for some time, and the police were called.' – *The Irish Times*, 23 March 1942. Fights between rival gangs occupied a good deal of space in newspapers in the 1930s and 1940s. Of particular interest was the so-called Animal Gang, the name of which arose from a feud between newsboys and the IRA over sales of the republican newspaper *An Phoblacht* during a printers' strike in 1931. The name was adopted by various gangs and individuals across the city, and for a while became another staple of Dublin folklore.

The aftermath of the North Strand bombings. (*Courtesy of Dublin City Library and Archive*)

'It was a beautiful day in Dublin ... the centrepiece of this picture was an American sergeant walking across O'Connell Bridge hand-in-hand with a girl in a red dress who looked like Maureen O'Sullivan. If he had looked up, no doubt he would have run for his life. Behind him were at least 50 people, seemingly unconscious that together they made a crowd, following in absorbed interest. He was apparently the first American soldier they had seen in Dublin, and the people were in a mood to be carried completely away ... Things have sobered down some, but GI's are still followed by tribes of wild, ragged, bare-footed children, whose legs and feet look as if they had been lashed with hail and rain – and, as they walk about with bare legs and feet all the year round, they probably are. Aside from that, the kids look in the pink of health.

'They are all eager to hear a genuine American accent. A favourite trick was for the leader of the gang to sidle up with a speculative look and say "what's the time, mister?" If it's your first day in Dublin you look at your watch and say, "Its half past three", or whatever it happens to be. At this the kid dashes off with screams of laughter and repeats this in an exaggerated American intonation to the rest of the gang.' – US Corporal Edward Antrobus records his impression of post-war Dublin for the US forces magazine *Yank*, 12 October 1945, quoted in Arthur Mitchell (ed.), 'Dublin, Eire', in *History Ireland*, 12.2 (2004), 45–8.

social structure – in terms of housing standards, income and rents – was firmly established. The creation of Dublin Airport in the 1930s had restricted the extent of development on the northside and ensured that official housing schemes would be dominant within this area, while the southern suburbs, extending out towards Dún Laoghaire (another new name post-independence), began to expand and evolve as relative bastions of wealth and privilege. Post-war recovery did not come until after 1948, but the provision of better housing (suburban expansion continued until 1956) and sanitation had a positive effect on public health. In 1956 Dublin was the only region of the state to register an increase in its population, but even then emigration continued to take a toll; in this case, by easing pressure on the housing lists.

Dublin in the 1950s is indelibly associated with a small coterie of writers. The most famous authors to carve out a niche in Dublin at this time were the generation of writers active after the Second World War: the American J.P. Donleavy, who

'Things suddenly took a turn for the better. I got thrown out of digs and met an acquaintance to whom I explained my problem, which was really that I could not afford ordinary digs and do my drinking at the same time. He told me he knew about a place where I might get to stay pretty cheaply and told me the name of the pub where I might find the owner. The pub was McDaid's; and the place was the since-famous Catacombs. I did not know it then, but my feet had been happily set upon the downward path, and there was to be no turning back.' – Anthony Cronin, *Dead as Doornails* (Dublin, 1999), p. 9.

studied at Trinity College, thanks to the GI Bill, and who fictionalised his experience in *The Ginger Man*; the Tyrone-born satirist Brian O'Nolan, better known as both the novelist Flann O'Brien and the columnist Myles na gCopaleen; the Monaghan poet Patrick Kavanagh; and the former IRA man Brendan Behan, author of *Borstal Boy*. This generation of writers, and their various exploits in favoured watering holes around the city (the Palace on Fleet Street, McDaid's on Harry Street, and a number of others that still survive today), copper-fastened a dubious association between drinking and literature. Kavanagh and O'Brien had regular columns in *The Irish Press* and *The Irish Times* respectively from the 1940s onwards; the acerbic observations of Kavanagh and the relentless absurdity of O'Brien's 'Cruiskeen Lawn'. The relative bohemianism of this world should, however, be contrasted with other realities of life in independent Dublin. After all, one of the most obvious features of the new suburbs around the city (and Behan himself came from Crumlin) was the creation of huge new suburban churches, as the Catholic Church sought to keep its flock well tended to. Alongside these was, however, another story of Catholic power: the abuse of children and unmarried mothers in a range of institutions run by the Church, such as reformatories and so-called Magdalene laundries. Some of the most notorious of these, such as the institutions in Artane and Goldenbridge, were to be found in Dublin and remained active in this era.

KAVANAGH'S WEEKLY

A JOURNAL OF LITERATURE AND POLITICS

Vol. 1. No. 1.   SATURDAY, APRIL 12, 1952   SIXPENCE

CONTENTS:

Victory of Mediocrity

Thirty odd years ago the southern section of this country won what was called freedom. Yet from that Independence Day there has been a decline in vitality throughout the country. It is possible that political liberty is a superficial thing and that it always produces the apotheosis of the mediocrity. For thirty years thinking has been more and more looked upon as wickedness—in a quiet way of course.

All the mouthpieces of public opinion are controlled by men whose only qualification is their inability to think.

Being stupid and illiterate is the mark of respectability and responsibility.

The basis of this point of view is a fundamental lack of belief in God. In a somewhat subtle way it is materialism. Nothing matters but the job and the salary it brings. Does anybody really believe in anything? Can any of these people who presume to be our leaders and voices be hurt in any way except through the pocket? It is very doubtful.

There is no central passion.

What is really wrong with such materialism is that it is not truly materialistic, that is the materialism which is based on realities, which brings an enthusiasm for life, expansion. This country is dead or dying of its false materialism. Where the mistake is made is in seeing life as a purely material thing. Life itself is a sort of madness, something out of a transcendent imagination.

Why are people leaving the countryside in their thousands? They go to England where conditions are extremely bad. What they are seeking is the enthusiasm for life.

In our opinion there has been an attempted upsurge of vitality in this country but which has been defeated and betrayed by mediocrity.

Throughout the country here and there have arisen young people who realised that the liberty that was being offered them was the liberty of the graveyard. They knew that the sensational vulgarity that the Irish press offered them was poison, but what could they do? They were a minority buried

in an avalanche of crossword puzzles and fashion competitions. Doped.

The reflective and thoughtful minority is always in great danger in a small nation. In England, for example, that minority is large enough to be self-sufficient. England's very advanced democracy is at heart—at least to some extent—an aristocratic tyranny.

Although our journal is small in size its readers should learn to judge by intensity rather than vaporous bulk.

Whether there are enough people with moral convictions to support such an intensity is a question which we hope will find a happy answer.

What is wanted in this volatile society which is constantly being exploded at its centre by the idle sensations of sport and entertainment is dignity and courage.

The sprinkling of intelligent, aware people whom we believe—or at least hope—exists does not believe in the glamorous idea of Ireland's achievements in the realms of the mind. On the contrary they know that

Kavanagh's Weekly, a short-lived literary and political periodical edited (and often written) by the Monaghan-born poet Patrick Kavanagh and his brother Peter. (*Courtesy of Dublin City Library and Archive*)

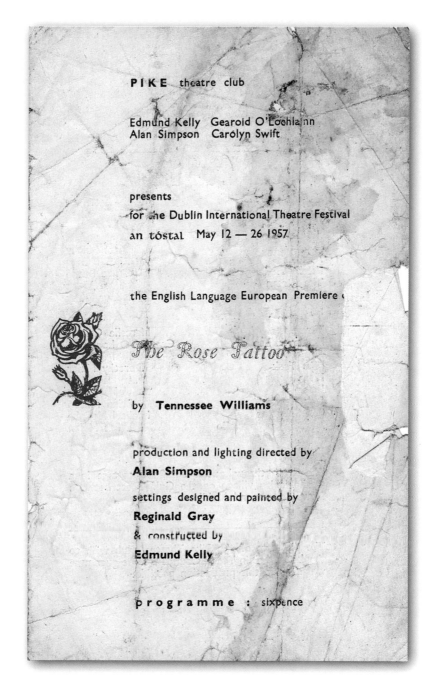

A poster for Tennessee Williams' *The Rose Tattoo* at the Pike Theatre Club on Herbert Lane in May 1957. The director of the theatre, Alan Simpson, was subsequently arrested and an abortive legal case ensued on the grounds that the play was allegedly obscene (it contained references to condoms); he was cleared, but the legal expenses dealt a fatal blow to what had been a small but well-regarded theatre. (*Courtesy of Dublin City Library and Archive*)

Gentlemen calling to the bar possibly in Mulligan's in Poolbeg Street in the 1950s. Note the conspicuous absence of women. (*Courtesy of Dublin City Library and Archive, Fáilte Ireland Tourism Photographic Collection*)

The same again, this time, it seems, in McDaid's of Harry Street. (*Courtesy of Dublin City Library and Archive, Fáilte Ireland Tourism Photographic Collection*)

An advertisement for Guinness with the iconic Guinness toucan. (*Courtesy of Dublin City Library and Archive*)

'Bring us back a parrot': according to urban myth, this was the line shouted by young wags at the Guinness barges, such as this one, that were used to transport kegs of beer from the Guinness brewery to the docks until 1961; note the retractable funnel. Guinness also operated their own fleet of freighters. (*Courtesy of Dublin City Library and Archive, Fáilte Ireland Tourism Photographic Collection*)

A night shot of Victoria Quay, alongside the Guinness brewery *circa* 1960s. (*Courtesy of Dublin City Library and Archive*)

A postcard for Dublin from the 1950s, complete with boozing theme. (*Courtesy of Dublin City Library and Archive, Postcards and Views Collection*)

Áras Mhic Dhiarmada – Busáras – under construction in 1952. Michael Scott's elegant modernist structure, first proposed in the 1930s, opened in 1953 after much wrangling among officialdom and acrimony in the press. (*Courtesy of Dublin City Library and Archive, Fáilte Ireland Tourism Photographic Collection*)

Dublin Airport in the 1950s; it was originally opened in 1940 on the site of an earlier aerodrome in north County Dublin. (*Courtesy of Dublin City Library and Archive, Postcards and Views Collection*)

Christmas shopping on Henry Street, 1952. (*Courtesy of Dublin City Library and Archive, Fáilte Ireland Tourism Photographic Collection*)

Cars parked on O'Connell Street, Christmas 1953. (*Courtesy of Dublin City Library and Archive, Fáilte Ireland Tourism Photographic Collection*)

A day in the sun: Dubliners enjoy good weather on a bank holiday weekend in Dun Laoghaire, 1953.
(Courtesy of Dublin City Library and Archive, Fáilte Ireland Tourism Photographic Collection)

The *Illustrated London News* reports on the unveiling of John Henry Foley's sculpture of Field-Marshal Hugh Gough (a native of Limerick who had commanded British forces in the first Opium War) in the Phoenix Park, 1880. It was removed after being badly damaged by a bomb in 1957. Its unveiling was apparently the earliest childhood memory of Winston Churchill, whose father, Randolph, unveiled it in his capacity as chief secretary, while its attempted destruction prompted these lines from the Dublin printer Vincent Caprani:

> 'There are strange things done from twelve to one
> In the hollow at Phaynix Park,
> There's maidens mobbed and gentlemen robbed
> In the bushes after dark;
> But the strangest of all within human recall
> Concerns the statue of Gough,
> 'Twas a terrible fact, and a most wicked act,
> For his bollix they tried to blow off!'
>
> (John Wyse Jackson and Hector McDonnell (eds),
> *Dublin's Other Poetry* (Dublin, 2009), p. 17.)

Christmas lights on Henry Street, 1960. (*Courtesy of Dublin City Library and Archive, Fáilte Ireland Tourism Photographic Collection*)

IV

During the boom of the 1960s, Dublin began to shift towards being a city of administration, but many of its old problems had not gone away. The collapse of tenements in Bolton Street and Fenian Street in 1963 and the creation of Ballymun, Coolock, Kilbarrack and other suburbs was seen as both cause and effect. The 1960s in Dublin is best known, however, for destruction. Many Dubliners of a certain age remember where they were when a republican bomb destroyed the top half of Nelson's Pillar on O'Connell Street on 8 March 1966. The bombing of Nelson's Pillar was apparently an unofficial contribution to the fiftieth anniversary commemoration of the Easter Rising later that year; the incongruous symbolism of an imperial hero such as Horatio Nelson perched outside the GPO needs no explanation. What ultimately turned out to be the fatal flaw in 1966 was the design feature that guaranteed the pillar a good deal of pragmatic affection: the 168 steps, on which the bomb was apparently placed, led to a viewing platform that has never been replaced.

Nelson's Pillar was a focal point in Dublin city centre; it was, among other things, the de facto terminus for Dublin's extensive tram network, which had vanished by the 1950s. According to one overly enthusiastic New York newspaperman, it was destroyed during the Easter Rising, but in fact the pillar survived the revolution in good shape. After independence the aesthetic qualities of the column, or the lack thereof, were highlighted by figures such as W.B. Yeats, but ideological considerations were never too far away and calls for its replacement by figures as diverse as Michael Collins or even Jesus Christ were by no means uncommon, though in 1931 the journalist P.S. O'Hegarty put a novel spin on this by suggesting that it should be retained as a trophy of victory over Britain. Yet the pillar came tumbling down in March 1966 and the remains had to removed by the Irish Army (prompting the wholly inaccurate yarn that they did more damage to the street than the original blast). The hunt for souvenirs began immediately after the bombing, culminating in the strange odyssey that Nelson's head embarked upon after it was stolen by students before briefly ending up in the window of a London antiques shop.

O'Connell Street, 1962. (Courtesy of Dublin City Library and Archive, Dublin City Council Photographic

Clery's department store in 1964. Originally opened as McSwiney, Delaney & Co. in 1853 (and thus one of the first of its kind), it had been destroyed during the Easter Rising and was rebuilt in 1919–22; the architect, Frank Atkinson, had previously worked on Selfridges in London and the new design incorporated up-to date building techniques, in the form of reinforced concrete that was seen (correctly) as less flammable than the original structure. The building also incorporated a restaurant and a ballroom. (*Courtesy of Dublin City Library and Archive, Fáilte Ireland Tourism Photographic Collection*)

A Christmas advertisement for Switzer's on Grafton Street, 1962. (*Private collection*)

Wood Quay, 1961. Christ Church can be seen in the background, with the Irish House visible on the other side of the bridge. (*Courtesy of Dublin City Library and Archive*)

The Irish House, built in 1870 on the corner of Winetavern Street and Wood Quay; it was famous for its elaborate (or garish) revivalist exterior. It was demolished to make way for the Dublin City Council offices at Wood Quay, but some of the exterior statues are retained by the Dublin Civic Trust. *(Courtesy of Dublin City Library and Archive, Fáilte Ireland Tourism Photographic Collection)*

Ringing the bell for an auction, 1960s. (*Courtesy of Dublin City Library and Archive, Fáilte Ireland Tourism Photographic Collection*)

Street life in 1950s Dublin, complete with Swastika laundry van in the background. The Swastika laundry, located in Ballsbridge, opened in 1912, long before the advent of the German Nazi Party. (*Courtesy of Dublin City Library and Archive, Fáilte Ireland Tourism Photographic Collection*)

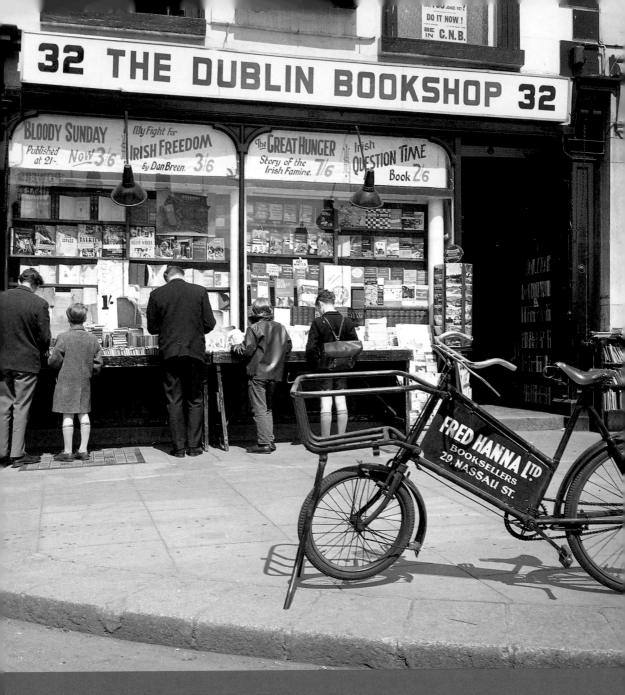

The Dublin Bookshop on Bachelor's Walk in the early 1960s. The Liffey quays were a favoured location for book stalls and book shops, though most were gone by the 1990s. (*Courtesy of Dublin City Library and Archive, Fáilte Ireland Tourism Photographic Collection*)

The River Liffey from the top of Liberty Hall, designed by Desmond Rea O'Kelly, who claimed to have drawn inspiration from the work of Frank Lloyd Wright. It opened in 1965 on the site of the original Liberty Hall, and like its predecessor it was the headquarters of the ITGWU. The long-departed industrial heritage of the inner docklands is plain to see here. (*Courtesy of Dublin City Library and Archive, Fáilte Ireland Tourism Photographic Collection*)

A Liffey ferry in 1962: one of the boats that brought passengers across the river before any bridges were constructed east of the Custom House. (*Courtesy of Dublin City Library and Archive*)

(Top): St George's Church on Hardwicke Place. Designed by Francis Johnston and completed in 1813, it was intended to be the central feature of the crescent on which it was located, and to act as a focal point. The 200-foot (60-metre) spire was modelled on that of St Martin-in-the-Fields, near Trafalgar Square in London. In the 1870s the crypt was used as a bonded warehouse for spirits, and the church itself became a nightclub for a time in the 1990s and 2000s. (Below): Two young boys on waste ground at nearby Temple Street, 1963. (*Courtesy of Dublin City Library and Archive*)

Ballymun was built in the 1960s on the northern fringes of the city, in order to rehouse tenement dwellers from the inner city in more modern housing with better facilities. By the 1980s it had acquired a reputation for social problems such as unemployment and drug abuse. The seven towers, named after the signatories of the 1916 proclamation, were demolished in the twenty-first century, as the area was redeveloped. (*Courtesy of Dublin City Library and Archive*)

'Poor aul Admiral Nelson is no longer in the air', according to a ballad sung by the folk group The Dubliners, who themselves came to prominence in the 1960s: the stump of the pillar after the explosion that demolished the upper half. The well-worn allegation that the Irish Army's demolition of the stump caused more damage than the original explosion is not borne out by the insurance claims made in the aftermath. (*Courtesy of Dublin City Library and Archive, Dublin City Council Photographic Collection*)

Travellers' caravans near Charlemont Street, 1969. (*Courtesy of Dublin City Library and Archive*)

Winetavern Street and Christ Church Cathedral, 1968. (*Courtesy of Dublin City Library and Archive*)

There was a more serious and systematic form of destruction manifest in the city throughout the 1960s and beyond: the demolition and redevelopment of much of its Georgian fabric, a phenomenon that was as much economic as ideological. The lack of legislation to protect Dublin's historic core saw the creation of groups, such as the Irish Georgian Society, who were determined to protect it; though the composition and motivations of the groups and individuals who took an interest in such conservation could, and did, differ dramatically.

There was no overall plan, however, to the development of the 1960s. These were piecemeal developments, of which the Electricity Supply Board's demolition of a terrace of houses on Fitzwilliam Street was the single most notorious example of what was seen in hindsight as a drive towards modernity but also one that came with certain cultural associations and which carried an appalling aesthetic cost. Even aside from aesthetic or political considerations, groups such as the Dublin Housing Action Committee and various student radical groups continued to lobby for the renovation and reconstruction of the inner city on behalf of its residents rather than business. The stance that many of them took could have been taken in relation to broadly similar issues that had arisen in Dublin's history at any time in the previous 300 years.

'In 1912, the watcher at the window saw the north-east end of a street that takes various names as it runs north from Fitzwilliam Place to Merrion Square, east: it breaks twice, on the west side, to give access to the south city's principal squares, Fitzwilliam and Merrion; it consisted of four unbroken terraces on the east side and of three on the west side. In the sixties, the four eastern blocks were still as they had been since the beginning of the nineteenth century and the street must have been the longest intact street of such character in Europe. On the east side, any new building would have been sufficient to destroy the street's uniformity, its proportions, its texture, its detailing. The ESB demolished almost a whole block to make way for its offices.

'It is no criticism of that building or of its accomplished architects to say that, whatever the ESB's problem was, it should not have been permitted to solve it in that way.' – Niall Montgomery, 'After reading my "Dublin Year"', *Studies* (Autumn–Winter 1971), 260.

An epilogue

If a curious traveller were to take John Rocque's famous 1756 map of Dublin and compare it to the Ordnance Survey maps of later eras, the size of the city would seem remarkably static. Apart from outliers like Rathmines and Ballsbridge (the fringe of the old Pembroke estate), Dublin was largely confined within the limits set by the circular roads and the Grand and Royal canals until the 1930s. But continue this paper journey into the twenty-first century, and it will become obvious that the surface area of the city has grown dramatically in the intervening decades. The vast expanse of suburbs that now ring the old urban core are a twentieth-century phenomenon; these may not register as the most obvious facet of Dublin when compared with the well-trodden and much-publicised fabric of the 'Georgian' or 'medieval' city (such as it is). It is ironic that the two most famous eras of Dublin's past – the Viking and Georgian periods – were precisely those elements most endangered by the growth of the city in the twentieth century.

O'Connell Street at night, 1973. (*Courtesy of Dublin City Library and Archive, Fáilte Ireland Tourism Photographic Collection*)

The aftermath of the 1974 Dublin bombings on Parnell Street. The outbreak of conflict in Northern Ireland in 1969 made itself felt on the streets of the Republic's capital, with some loyalist bombings of memorials (such as the O'Connell Tower in Glasnevin Cemetery), the burning of the British Embassy by a hostile mob in the aftermath of the Bloody Sunday killings in 1972, and the unprecedented no-warning car bomb attacks of 1974. On the late afternoon of 17 May 1974, ten people were killed on Parnell Street when a bomb exploded without warning in a car that had been stolen in Belfast and driven south for the purpose. Within minutes twelve more were killed by another bomb on Talbot Street (two more later died of their injuries), and two more were killed on South Leinster Street, beside Trinity College. The bombings were the work of loyalist paramilitaries; collusion with British security forces has been long suspected. Another series of car bombings took place in Monaghan on the same day, killing five people, with two more dying later. This day, 17 May 1974, was the bloodiest single day of the 'Troubles'; and none of the victims died in Northern Ireland. (*Courtesy of Dublin City Library and Archive*)

Street traders on Moore Street, 1974. (*Courtesy of Dublin City Library and Archive, Fáilte Ireland Tourism Photographic Collection*)

A spot of lunch on Dawson Street in the 1970s. (*Courtesy of Dublin City Library and Archive Fáilte Ireland Tourism Photographic Collection*)

The interior of John Kavanagh's (the Gravediggers) in Glasnevin in the 1970s. As of 2017, the decor remains unchanged. (Courtesy of Dublin City Library and Archive)

A playful elephant in Dublin Zoo in the 1970s. (*Courtesy of Dublin City Library and Archive Fáilte Ireland Tourism Photographic Collection*)

Playing football in Pearse Square in the 1970s. (*Courtesy of Dublin City Library and Archive*)

The Dubs. Dublin had long been one of the homes of Irish soccer, with teams such as St Patrick's Athletic, Shelbourne, Shamrock Rovers and Bohemians, and iconic grounds in such as Milltown and Dalymount Park. Gaelic games, however, occupied a particular niche: often they catered to rural migrants to the city, and could be viewed with condescension on that basis. A cramped urban environment was not ideal for games such as football and hurling that required large open spaces and involved balls flying through the air (and potentially through windows), but the expansion of the twentieth-century suburbs was tailor-made for the GAA to grow in the capital. The development of the GAA in Dublin's emerging suburbs bore fruit in the 1970s, with a string of provincial and All-Ireland successes for the Dublin senior football team managed by Kevin Heffernan, and they captured the imagination of new generation of fans as they did so.

'Heffo's army' of newly minted supporters enlist a teddy bear to celebrate in 1975; Dublin beat Kildare to win the Leinster championship but lost the All-Ireland to Kerry.

In 1976 a sombrero takes pride of place after Dublin defeat Kerry in the All-Ireland; the names of the winning team are entered in the guestbook of the Mansion House. (*Courtesy of Dublin City Library and Archive*)

DATE	NAME	ADDRESS	DATE	NAME	ADDRESS
Dublin G.A.A. Team. 1976. All Ireland Winners.					
27.9.76	_Tony Hanahan_	Mrs Anne Hanahan 143 Drimnagh Rd Dublin		Kevin Moran	
	Bernard Brogan			Billy Dpe..	
	Gwin Brogan			Kevin Synnott	
	Bruce McGill			James Keaveney	
	Gay O'Driscoll			Sean Doherty	
	Norman Bennod			Jimmy Keaveney	
	Fran Ryder			Paddy O'Neill	
	Anton O'Toole			Tom Hanahy	
	Kevin Duffy			Mrs A Relli	201 Bilkfield Rd
	Sean MacCarthaigh			Mrs O'Gorman	
	Paddy Reilly			Mrs M. Nichola	126 Claddagh Rd
	Robbie Allen			Helena Heffernan	484 Bally fermot Dublin 1
	Mick Hickey			Mrs Whelan	41 claddagh Rd Ballyfermot
	Dave Foley			Mrs B Kearney	2 Cleggan Park
	John Colcott			Mrs N Thompson	41 Ring in D4 D10
				Mrs F Swan	43 Ring in Rd D.10

Cleaning up the Liffey, 1976. (*Courtesy of Dublin City Library and Archive*)

The demolition of the Corporation Buildings on Sean McDermott Street, 1970s. They were originally built in the early 1900s as replacements for tenements. (*Courtesy of Dublin City Library and Archive, Dublin City Council Photographic Collection*)

Sam Stephenson's controversial Central Bank building takes shape in the late 1970s. The twelve floors of the building were constructed on the ground and then raised into place. (*Courtesy of Dublin City Library and Archive*)

Wacker's Pet Shop, Parnell Street, 1980s. (*Courtesy of Dublin City Library and Archive*)

The preservation of the city had emerged as a live issue in the 1960s, but the 1970s saw it revived again in relation to an earlier era. For centuries there had been a strong awareness that Dublin was a city of Viking origins, yet much of that heritage lay out of sight (and thus out of mind). Since the 1930s the idea of consolidating Dublin Corporation's various offices on a single site had been mooted, and from the 1950s onwards lands were being bought up around Wood Quay to precisely that end. Excavations began in earnest in the early 1970s, and in the process of stripping away layer after layer of buildings, the Viking city that lay beneath was revealed, on a scale that few could have anticipated. The Dublin excavation was the most important Viking find outside Scandinavia, and the excavation began in the expectation that sooner or later the archaeologists would be finished and the offices could be built. Yet it captured the imagination, and in September 1978 a massive protest march took place around the site, ultimately to no avail.

But the desire to preserve the old should not blind one to the shock of the new. If there are indeed multiple versions of a city, then suburban Dublin is by far the largest and most well-populated version of Dublin. Dublin's inner city has long been explored and catalogued in extensive detail, in terms of both its Georgian splendour and Victorian decline. The two go hand in hand, and the clearing of many of the inner-city slums after independence helped to populate the new, or newly remoulded, 'towns' on the rim of an expanding city. Suburban Dublin is fragmented and comes in many forms; the leafy Victorian roads of Donnybrook or Clontarf are worlds apart from many of the late twentieth-century suburbs, in more ways than one. The influential US urban theorist Lewis Mumford, for example, was highly unimpressed with the planning decisions that had led to creation of the suburbs since the war, and their implementation. In January 1970 the parking meter made its debut on

'Dublin's medieval city is now nothing more than a wasteland. The Vikings, who knew a thing or two about how to build cities – and how to destroy them – would be horrified by the shambles we have made of their settlement on the River Liffey. The old walled city is in ruins. Only a fraction of the wall itself is left and from Wood Quay to St Patrick, from Bridge Street to the Castle, every street, lane and alleyway is scarred by the most appalling dereliction. And most of the damage has been done in the past 25 years.' – Frank McDonald, 'The laying waste of our Viking heritage', *The Irish Times*, 4 March 1982.

the streets of Dublin, and in 1971 yet another plan for an urban development was proposed: a traffic management scheme that would involve, among other measures, the construction of an orbital motorway around the city. Unlike many such schemes suggested in the course of the twentieth century, this did come to pass: the M50, begun in the late 1980s, was the eventual result. It pointed to two things: traffic congestion in a city that was never built to handle it, and the massive growth, since independence, of the suburbs.

From the 1970s onwards, the instinctive urban history pioneered by authors such as Eamonn Mac Thomáis remained firmly focused on the inner city, perhaps in response to the perceived erosion of the inner city by 'progress'. It was only in the 1980s that novelists such as Dermot Bolger and Roddy Doyle made their names by opening a window, albeit in fiction, onto swathes of Dublin life that had slipped under quite a few radars over the years. Bolger set his early novels in and around Finglas and Doyle set his Barrytown trilogy in a fictional suburb with a suspicious resemblance to Kilbarrack. But the simmering reality of inner-city deprivation never went away, and was highlighted in the early 1980s by the appalling human cost of heroin use in the inner city, and the so-called Gregory deal. Tony Gregory was a young independent TD representing Dublin Central and, amidst the upheaval of multiple elections in 1982, struck a deal with then Fianna Fáil Taoiseach Charles Haughey to obtain a significant injection of resources into his historically deprived constituency in exchange for his support in crucial votes. Such was the system in which Irish politics operated; if an indictment were to be offered, it is that this is what it took for the problems of the north inner city to be taken seriously. Again, it points to continuities in the history of Dublin that exist along with the changes.

Dublin has its fair share of clichés, such as the nostalgic recourse to eccentric 'characters' as emblematic of twentieth-century urban life; the very existence of such notions hints at a desire to locate and participate in some kind of essentialist Dublin identity. Yet to go down this path, and to contemplate what it might mean to be a 'Dubliner', is to engage in navel-gazing. A Dubliner is surely just someone who lives, works and makes their life in Dublin, as broadly defined as the old city and its suburban hinterland, a region that by 2011 had a population of 1,273,000: half the population of the province of Leinster. Within that figure are other realities. By this time, thanks to the unprecedented immigration that characterised the late twentieth-century boom and the potent realities of early twenty-first century globalisation, Dublin had a far more multicultural complexion than ever before, a change that was particularly evident within the inner city. Much of the city was also physically altered by a series of

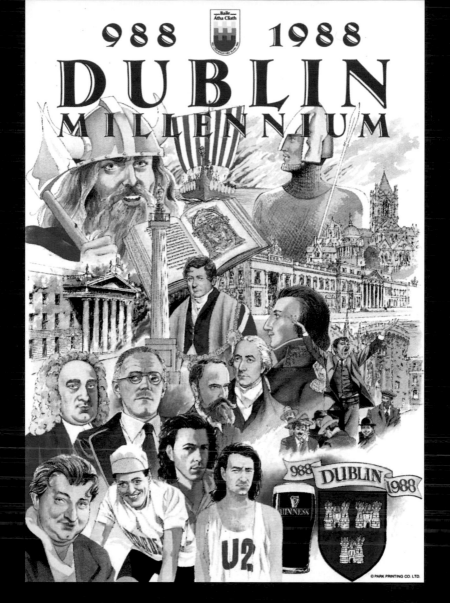

A poster marking the alleged millennium of Dublin's foundation (more properly, its capture by Mael Seachnaill in 988), highlighted as a civic initiative despite the misgivings of historians over the actual date on the grounds that a thousand-year anniversary was a good idea and the city needed a boost. In terms of those depicted on the poster in order to represent the city and its history, to some extent the usual suspects have been rounded up. (*Courtesy of Dublin City Library and Archive*)

Yes, this is a large inflatable depiction of Jonathan Swift's most famous creation, Lemuel Gulliver, outside St Patrick's Cathedral in 1988. Swift is interred inside the cathedral but the fictional Gulliver never set foot in Dublin. (*Courtesy of Dublin City Library and Archive, Dublin City Council Photographic Collection*)

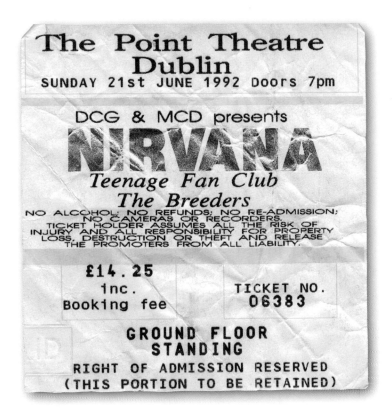

The Point Theatre
Dublin
SUNDAY 21st JUNE 1992 Doors 7pm

DCG & MCD presents

NIRVANA

Teenage Fan Club
The Breeders
NO ALCOHOL; NO REFUNDS; NO RE-ADMISSION;
NO CAMERAS OR RECORDERS.
TICKET HOLDER ASSUMES ALL THE RISK OF
INJURY AND ALL RESPONSIBILITY FOR PROPERTY
LOSS, DESTRUCTION OR THEFT AND RELEASE
THE PROMOTERS FROM ALL LIABILITY.

£14.25
inc.
Booking fee

TICKET NO.
06383

GROUND FLOOR
STANDING
RIGHT OF ADMISSION RESERVED
(THIS PORTION TO BE RETAINED)

Kurt Cobain's Nirvana play the Point Theatre, 1992. The redevelopment of a railway depot into a concert venue by the developer Harry Crosbie was a pioneering venture that foreshadowed the ongoing transformation of Dublin's docklands. (*Private collection*)

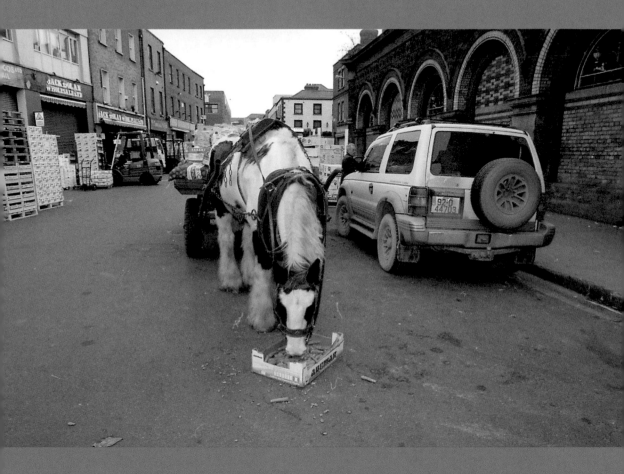

Taking a break at the Dublin Corporation Wholesale Market on Mary's Lane, which was opened in 1892 and visible on the right. (*Courtesy of Dublin City Library and Archive, Dublin City Council Photographic Collection*)

The first issue of the successful (and free) satirical magazine *The Slate* (2000), which reassured readers who felt that they lived in a miserable and pretentious city at the turn of the millennium that 'the only hope to be found is in this great magazine, where you can laugh at all the stupid people and pretend that you aren't one of them'. (*Private collection*)

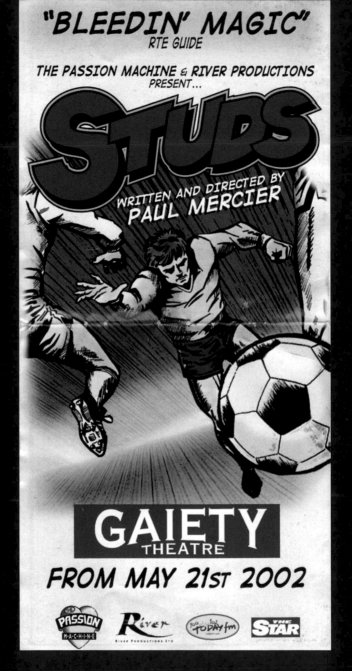

A flyer for Paul Mercier's play *Studs*, 2002. Passion Machine was founded by Mercier, a teacher; and *Studs*, the tragi-comic story of a particularly hopeless amateur soccer team given a boost by their new manager, was originally performed in 1986. Passion Machine also helped launch the careers of two of Mercier's fellow-teachers, author Roddy Doyle and actor Brendan Gleeson; the Dublin settings of many of their productions was distinctive in Irish theatre in the 1980s. (*Private collection*)

A glimpse of Dublin's clubbing scene from 2001. (*Private collection*)

'The Liffey cuts the city like a meandering blue vein': Dublin graffiti artist Maser uses the lyrics of Dublin songwriter Damien Dempsey as part of a collaboration entitled They Are Us, North Wall, 2014. On the right of the picture is the unfinished headquarters of the now-defunct Anglo-Irish Bank. (*Image by author*)

major redevelopments: notably the Irish Financial Services Centre, which spearheaded the transformation of the post-industrial docklands; and Temple Bar, which avoided its anticipated fate of being demolished to make way for a bus station to become an exceptionally lucrative combination of cultural quarter and tourist destination. The so-called 'Celtic Tiger' era saw the city transformed, with a major economic injection from new industries such as IT and financial services that easily slotted into Dublin's traditional profile as a city of administration; in that respect, change was intertwined with continuity. Much the same, however, could be said of the post-2008 bust, with the added complications of a property bubble leading to a financial crisis. Many of the issues facing Dublin and its inhabitants are perhaps universal to cities everywhere: infrastructure, housing and quality of life, to name but three headings under which much of what has been explored in the preceding pages could be filed. And this is as good a point as any with which to bring this exploration of Dublin's history to a halt.

Dublin has been here for over a thousand years and, for better or worse, is not going anywhere in the foreseeable future. It can be hard to choose a point in time, symbolic or otherwise, that can serve as a full stop to an account of its history such as this. So rather than end with a forced flourish, here is a glance back in the form of a selection of images of ordinary Dubliners across the past few decades, from the 1950s to the twenty-first century. A picture, as the saying goes, may yet tell a thousand words.

The Ha'penny Bridge, 1966.
(*Courtesy of Dublin City Library and Archive,
Fáilte Ireland Tourism Photographic Collection*)

Two young Dubliners, 1970s. *(Courtesy of Dublin City Library and Archive, Fáilte Ireland Tourism Photographic Collection)*

Crowds throng O'Connell St to welcome the Irish international soccer team home after Euro '88; their first appearance at an international tournament. (*Courtesy of Dublin City Library and Archive, Dublin City Council Photographic Collection*)

Waiting for the Liffey Swim on Arran Quay, 1999 (Courtesy of Dublin City Library and Archive Postcards and Views Collection)